Little Pasture on the Prairie

Little Pasture on the Prairie:

A Decade of Tales from a Western South Dakota Ranch

By Eliza Blue

SOUTH DAKOTA
HISTORICAL
SOCIETY

PRESS

Pierre

The paper in this book meets the guidelines for permanence and durability of the Committee on Production Guidelines for Book Longevity of the Council on Library Resources.

Printed in the United States of America
Please visit our website at sdhspress.com

27 26 25 24 23 1 2 3 4 5 6

Cover and book design by Kodi Odean-Carlin

Image credits: All images included in this book are property of Eliza Blue except for those on the following pages: 54, Bre Holt; 270, Max Loughlin.

This book is dedicated to my brilliant, tender-hearted son and my wise, wonderful, and strong daughter. I will never stop thanking my lucky stars that I get to be your mother.

To all the readers of my columns—this book was made possible by YOU!

CONTENTS

FOREWORD

When I met Eliza Blue, I was a few weeks into my first job as a journalist, and she had invited me to her ranch outside Bison, South Dakota, where a dust-coated dog met me at the sliding door. The rain had not fallen in Perkins County in weeks. Her husband was out fixing fences. I was there to ask her questions about the drought impacting her ranch town, and her son sat in overalls on the piano bench, while Eliza told stories, holding her baby.

"The collection plate is smaller at church," she said. "I can tell you that."

I did not know it at the time, but three years later, in 2020, in the midst of that anguishing year, I would be transported to Eliza's ranch again, reading about the woolly-faced sheep, the frozen chicken coop, and the ride home from church, as she gazes over the grasslands considering her pastor's words.

Known to many South Dakotans from her street dances and public television show, *Wish You Were Here*, Eliza is a folk musician, shepherdess, and writer. It was her first book, *Accidental Rancher*, that first welcomed us into the home she had nurtured as a transplant from the east. She had written companionable dispatches about coming to Bison, outlasting winter, falling in love, caring for bottle lambs and a ram named Bjorn and a "tanker truck" of a dairy cow, and ultimately meeting the "Man of the Ranch," who coaxes the chickens out of Eliza's Subaru and into his trailer, where she learns the curve of the High Plains swells.

In many ways, Eliza's first book was a testimonial for the happy wanderer finding wholeness in rural South Dakota. This is a tradition worth noting. Before Eliza Blue, there was Dan O'Brien, an Ohioan who landed west, ranched, raised bison, and fell in love, intoxicated by the land. Before O'Brien, there was Kathleen Norris, the essayist and spiritualist from the East Coast with a degree from Bennington College, whose book *Dakota*, about her life on her grandparents' farm in Lemmon, put the state back on the literary map in 1993. Far before Norris, there was Frederick Manfred, or even Badger Clark (both born in Iowa), or, shoot, Ole Rölvaag (born in Norway), whose tales of frontiersmen, prayerful cowboys, and wary pioneers literarily firmed up the backbreaking beauty of South Dakota.

In all these writers, a spirit of wild openness captivates the newcomer and converts the shy interloper to this rectangular, sparsely populated state in the nation's bosom. Certainly, for those raised in South Dakota, there's rightly a tendency to check a writer's credentials. I myself, born and raised in Minnesota, have heard this before. "You would think differently about Armour if you ever spent a disappointing fifth grade science fair there," a friend from Plankinton once told me, as I waxed on about Douglas County.

But, frankly, even the multigenerational homesteader is but a newcomer to the Lakotas and other Indigenous peoples who have stewarded the land throughout the centuries. Often enough, the best writing in South Dakota comes as exasperation from someone first coming under the massive blue dome of the sky or spying the grand green bluffs rolling up from the Missouri River for the first time.

Maybe that is what initially compelled me about Eliza's story. While my mother's family was from Beresford, I first experienced the rest of the state for myself on a solo western drive in the weeks after I graduated from college in Vermillion. In a '98 Chevy Cavalier, I chased the sun west on I-90, as far west as I could go in the Black Hills, before I noticed I had crossed the state line into Wyoming. I got out of my car and stared up. The orange sun kept sinking over the impossibly distant horizon, and with it my heart plummeted into almost grievous beauty.

When you hit a place at an impressionable age, it is hard not to feel both fear and hope for the future. It is hard not to feel both larger and infinitely smaller than the world you stand on. And that is the paradox I lovingly find in Eliza's essays.

When Eliza, who had worked as a cook on an island off the coast of Maine and grown tomatoes on a fire escape in New York City, first crossed the Missouri in her early thirties, heading west, she said she cried, acknowledging the fear and wonder for a place she did not yet know.

If Eliza works herself into and out of this introspective bivouac in *Accidental Rancher*, in *Little Pasture on the Prairie*, a selection of Eliza's journalistic epistles from her ranch, we see the full arc of a woman coming to live on and know not only the ranch and the rolling hills and the creeks, but also the colors of life in West River. And it counterintuitively often begins in smallness.

Early in Eliza's collection, which celebrates ten years of her "Little Pasture on the Prairie" columns in the *Bison Courier*, she writes of the tomatoes she plants, almost with a prescience needing to be shared. "Once those little sprouts start their engines, there is no turning back." It is the same for Eliza. And it is the same for those readers she has invited along.

Eliza carries the quick smile of Will Rogers and the turning-of-the-screw ranch life episodes of Linda Hasselstrom. There is mischief and magic in her Bison days, which begin at the "borrowed strip of land at the end of a street." After miracle rains, she nearly loses a milking cow eating up too much grass. In the spring, the flowers and chokecherry and plumb and crabapple trees are "like a choir full of converts bursting into song." Toward the book's end, she grieves after the death of friend Kevin Locke, a Lakota storyteller.

At the center of her columns, though, is the ranch. The ranch is her desktop and worldview. It is a citadel and a far-flung place, where she mourns "sushi and really good Thai food." But it is also a home, where any dip toward aestheticism is met with sharp-eyed questions.

"Is anything the whole world round," Eliza asks, at one point, after cleaning the chicken coop, "more beautiful than winter dusk in western South Dakota?" Later in the collection, Eliza asks, "If humans were influenced by the music of the birds, why wouldn't the birds be influenced by the music of the humans?"

My father-in-law, a lifelong South Dakotan, attended a grassland conservation meeting recently and told me that what he noticed about so many ranchers is, frankly, the love they share for the lifestyle. During my days covering the legislature in Pierre, it was telling how many politicians—even those who work as attorneys but moonlight out on the family spread—will put some variation of "ranch hand" in their official biographies on the state website. The rancher, after all, with the campfire-tending, guitar-strumming, hat-dipping, horse-riding cowboy ethos, holds a mystic allure for the average American—likely even more so than the ballcap-wearing farmer.

And as a nation, we are consistently losing ranks of farmers and ranchers. I have seen this in my day job as agriculture reporter for the *Star Tribune*. In the latest U.S. Department of Agriculture census, released in February 2024, South Dakota reported losing over one in ten ranches between 2017 and 2022. Plots expand to stay competitive. Bigger landowners swoop in to grow. Prime farmland is gobbled up by the expansion of suburbia's Starbucks and outlet malls. It makes you wonder what is happening to quietude, to life alongside animals, to families in the country.

Eliza's words, in this context, come to us with greater vitality and need. Ireland has her writers sitting in a Dublin bar. Russia, the clutch of dissident journalists. America has our ranchland poets.

What would it be if we start seeing flyover country not as a remote land latticed by dirt roads and tough politics, but, rather, as the breeding ground of artists and philosophers? Eliza lives not far from Thunder Hawk, South Dakota, birthplace of cowboy poetry grand dame Elizabeth Ebert, who wrote in secret until she was in her sixties, when her husband encouraged her to step up to the microphone at a reading in Bismarck, North Dakota. Just west of Eliza's ranch lived Archer Gilfillan, the Ivy-League-educated, Europe-traveling shepherd who wrote in *Sheep: Life on the South Dakota Range*, "It is necessary . . . to differentiate between the sheep herder of fact and the shepherd of romance."[1]

Eliza sews the two together. By book's end, the Man of the Ranch, who we now know simply as her husband, is texting Eliza, who is pulled over on the side of a road socked in with fog, as she works to make it to a women-in-agriculture conference in Montana. She is overwhelmed, lost in the pea-soup-thick fog. But she keeps driving, nudged by her husband's cell phone radar, onward to Miles City.

The scene illustrates both a faith and a fragility in the American West. Other writers have offered us visions of the West beyond the silhouette of the stoic ranch man against the tall-grass prairie. But when Eliza comes out of the fog, the blue sky unfolding, she writes, "This is what hope feels like."

There is a line from Eliza's collection that sticks with me. She exhorts readers, in those early, bewildering days of the Covid pandemic, to consider "stripping back [our] armor." It is a small, if profound plea to embrace vulnerability, a humility that clashes with popular ideas of the West as a stubborn, defiant place. But the statement also marks a distinct change in tone for the writer.

Eliza, no longer fresh to town and condemned by the rules of decorum to stay mum in city meetings lest feathers be ruffled and her newness be indicted, now writes from within the fold. She speaks with a constituent's power, a neighbor's grace. She is no longer the accidental rancher. She is Eliza from out north of town. She is the mother, wife, and writer with a well of love in her words. And so many of us have traveled a long way to be at her door.

Christopher Vondracek
Sioux Falls, S.Dak.
March 2024

PREFACE

My "Little Pasture on the Prairie" started out as a borrowed slip of land at the end of a street in Bison, South Dakota, and eventually evolved into a full-fledged pasture with a windbreak of elms and fruit trees, a sturdy woven wire fence, and an odd assortment of orphans and vagabonds, most of them wearing woolly suits. After three decades of life spent in cities and suburbs, I had come to the prairie for an adventure, never guessing what life had in store for me here.

As the months became years, I fell more in love with the prairie and the man who would become my husband, and I realized I was going to stay. I mourned only one thing (besides sushi and really good Thai food): being able to share my songs. I spent the first part of my adulthood as a touring musician, and sharing stories and songs onstage was my livelihood and my calling. Once there weren't many stages or audience members for a few hundred miles in any given direction, I wasn't sure what to do with all my creative energy.

I had written in journals and diaries all my life, but almost none of that writing was seen by anyone other than me. Deciding to start writing this column a decade ago was only possible because I was desperate for a creative outlet. Also, I didn't expect anyone to take much notice of it, for which I am glad. Had I suspected that this column would end up being read by folks all around the world, I doubt I would have had the courage to begin. But I am unbelievably thankful that my stories have found readers and that this book has found YOU. Sharing my life with my readers has been a joy that continues to buoy me through this crazy, unfurling journey.

Reading through ten years of columns in advance of putting together this compilation has been an interesting experience. I imagine not many people have had the opportunity to review a weekly snapshot of their lives from an entire decade. The folks at the South Dakota Historical Society Press suggested I arrange the columns in chronological order, confident that a story would emerge through the process. And, boy, were they right. I was amazed to re-meet the tender but surprisingly wise younger version of myself.

Eliza Blue is me—but she also now exists as a character outside of me. She is the best version of who I was, who I am, and who I hope to become, because writing these columns is a weekly endeavor in finding the beauty even when it is hard to see. I want to give my readers comfort, joy, and maybe a good laugh, and in doing so, I have found wellsprings of all three within the mundane details of my own life. What a gift.

So, thank you! These stories of my adventures—and misadventures—in the little pasture on the prairie, and the joy of waking up every day to the majesty of life on the northern plains, are my heart, my soul, the last of my youth, the beginning of my older age, and my offering at the altar of what it means to be human and to lead a life of service. I hope reading these columns brings you some measure of the peace and connection I received in writing them.

Much Love,
Eliza Blue
Bison, S.Dak.
March 2024

2014

JUNE 15, 2014
GARDENING

It's my third year with a big garden and once again I've overdone it. You see, I love to garden. I started out with potted tomatoes on a fire escape in New York City, then tubs of herbs and flowers and coffee cans teeming with chamomile blossoms on a rooftop in Minneapolis, and now the western range where sunshine and space are never in short supply. Even when I should have been economical about space, I wasn't. Marigolds look just as festive in milk jugs with the tops cut off as they look in fancy pots, so why not have them covering every conceivable surface? Well, I'm sure there are reasons, but I couldn't think of any at the time, so overdoing became a habit.

These days, it isn't a lack of garden space, but the long winters that get me in trouble. Around here, March is still very much winter. In fact, it's often the snowiest month of the year. But there is something about that month that makes me think it should be spring. Maybe it's stories from other parts of the country shared via the internet. Maybe it's that after February, I have to allow myself a little bit of delusion. Either way, when spring fever hit this March, I went a little crazier than usual when I got out the paper pots and the soil and the carefully sorted seed packs and started planting. And planting. And planting.

Some years I keep track of my gardening endeavors in dime store notebooks, some years I don't, and most years I lose the notebooks before summer is over anyway, so the same questions always remain. How many tomato plants do I need? How many peppers? And it's always better to have too many than too few, right? The winter wind whistling through the eaves makes it impossible to imagine ever having too many sun-ripened tomatoes. This March was worse than usual. Winter started at the beginning of October, so it somehow seemed like an early spring was guaranteed. We wouldn't be punished by the weather gods on both sides of the season—that would just be too much! This was my logic anyway, and the end result was by mid-March I had forty tomato seedlings an inch high. Oh, and as many peppers. Plus some cucumbers already trying to vine. Wow, and sunflowers really do shoot up, don't they? Anyway, I won't bore you with the list of all the other seeds I started, but I think you get the picture. It was clear I'd overdone it. And it turned out the weather gods didn't think it was unreasonable, even with the early onset of winter, to have spring start late; so, my seedlings and I watched many April, and then May, snowstorms through the big picture window. Lucky for us, we don't have guests often, so no one was denied a seat when the pots began to overtake the countertops, the table, and finally the chairs.

See, that's the thing about planting seeds too early. Once those little sprouts start their engines, there is no turning back. A few weeks in, almost everyone was experiencing claustrophobia. In desperation, most of the seedlings sent out threads of white root to see if there were roomier digs to be had. The answer, of course, was no, so I set to work repotting. And repotting again. And again. Thus, the eventual evolution of my first floor into a greenhouse.

Now, it appears summer is upon us. The plants got moved to the garden, and most of them are in the ground. There were a few casualties of the drastic shift in temperature. Mostly though, everyone is taking it in stride. These are South Dakota plants after all, so they are tough—you have to be on these windy plains. And if you don't like it, you can always find a fire escape or rooftop somewhere more temperate. But I have to say, it's better to go a little crazy in the garden when you don't have to worry about neighbors watching through their windows, and even now, as the garden greens, I'm still pretty sure you can never have enough sun-ripened tomatoes.

JUNE 18, 2014

LEARNING TO FLY

It's morning, and misty, the windows filmed with a kind of fog. Outside the birds, wakeful, are calling. The little fledgling we brought home last night is calling too, sitting on the window sill. He's calling to what he cannot see, but he knows it's more his home than the inside of this house.

What to do with the poor fellow? He's too young to be on his own. But he was plucked from the grass by exuberant boys, sure that they were rescuing him, and he's now an orphan of circumstance.

He's black and has a noble, arched beak, like a crow, and the tiny, wrinkled eyelids of a very old man. He is strangely tame. He sits on my finger and looks intently at me as though he's trying to make out what I'm about, and he makes an incredible amount of racket when he's hungry. As he perches on my arm in a sunbeam, his little wings beat the air. He speaks so urgently I feel compelled to answer, but neither of us really understands the other's language. I feed him and leave the room. He waits on the windowsill.

When I return later in the day, there's a blackbird feeding its baby in the lilac bushes on the other side of the glass, only a few feet away. My little bird cries and tries to fly against the windowpane. His wings are getting stronger. I can't keep him inside much longer—he's a wild animal, and he knows he doesn't belong here.

It reminds me of my youngest brother and my mother's tears when he got his driver's license. The world is a thrilling and dangerous place for those old enough to know what they want but not what they need.

So, I set the little bird out in the garden, which has a pretty high fence, hoping he'll stay in the boundaries where it's safe. Like my brother, he's over the fence in an instant, flying and falling his way up the leaves of an old drooping elm. I work in the garden for the rest of the afternoon hoping he'll come down and let me feed him, but he doesn't. He stays high and hidden, calling to the birds he sees passing over my head.

The next day, there are more storms, more heavy rain. By midmorning the clouds lift a little, so I go hang laundry on the line. I listen for his voice, but I don't hear it. Instead, I find a fledgling corpse—the same size and coloring as my blackbird. The cats, no doubt. "Sometimes the circle of life isn't very wide," I think, crestfallen.

Hours later, I pass the old shop on my way to the chicken coop, and I hear a familiar voice, loud and demanding. It's my fledgling calling me from the shop's roof.

I'm not scared of heights, but I am scared of ladders, especially old ones that are not tall enough to reach the desired destination. Unfortunately, that's the only kind we have, so I lean it against the tin of the shop's walls and start climbing. My baby bird hops toward me and lets me feed him a few bits. Two blackbirds fly over and land in the pine trees beside us. They call to him. He calls back. They inch closer, still calling. He's eating food from my hands, fluttering wildly. I'm leaning, top-heavy and nervous, trying to play mama bird. He gets his fill and hops away. I climb back down the ladder. Everyone is relieved. The two adult blackbirds fly away.

Later, I hear him through the kitchen window, calling out, the hungry baby cry again. I climb the ladder, thinking it's more than twice as stupid to do this a second time. He leaps toward me, then away. I reach out to him, and he hops onto the sharp branches of the pine, then back to the roof. He is attracted, he is repelled. I stand wobbling. It is hot now, past midday, and the clouds are high, the sun is bright. The melting tar of the shingles sticks to my hands as I lean against the roof for support. I wait awhile. He hops to the eastern edge of the roof, the farthest point from me, and waits too. When I finally crawl down, he comes back and watches me over the ledge, head cocked, one bright eye turned toward me, one turned away.

Evening descends misty again. I am digging in the front garden, and the rocks hold the heat of the day, but the soil is dark and cool. I am planting coral bells and bleeding hearts while thinking of my grandmother's garden, wondering if the tender leaves will get burnt by the high desert sun. The Man of the Ranch comes home dusty from fencing, and we talk, my hands on my hips, dirty to the wrists. He's tired, and so am I. I tell him of the baby bird. I'm weaving the whole story, pointing to the ladder that still stands leaning against the shop, trying to make him laugh, my arms reaching out as I wobble, and pretending to feed a baby bird that doesn't know I can't fly. That's when we hear a familiar sound in the chokecherry branches arched over our heads. The little bird has followed my voice across the yard. Down he flies, landing on a low branch just beside me.

This time he lets me lift him to my hand and feed him, his feet clutching my finger, his wings beating like a hummingbird's. He eats wildly, nearly choking as he chirps, his voice muffled by food. I can't fill his mouth fast enough. I joke with my sweetheart, "He avoids starvation only to die of suffocation!" But on the inside, I think, "Thank you. Thank you for letting me feed you." I'm not the mama he wants, but I am the one he gets, at least for a little while longer, and it feels like grace to be a part of this small gesture.

I think of my brother again, and of the high school kids I used to teach, all of them in such a hurry to be grown. We all leave the nest eventually, and the soft hands that long to cradle us. That is as it should be. I've learned so much about love through caring for animals, but perhaps the greatest lesson is this: it is as much a gift to give care as it is to receive it, but it must have limits, or it isn't love. I'm guessing this little bird will find a new flock to fly with soon, and he won't need me anymore. It's bittersweet to know you've done your job well by getting left behind. So it is with any little fledgling once it's released into the big world. Teenagers, artistic endeavors, friends or family members who struggle with addiction—all these things need a chance to grow beyond our grasp eventually, though it can be unbearably painful to let them go.

"Let go and let God" is a phrase that means different things to different people. To me it means watching a baby bird perched high in the treetops, a silhouette against a glowing, rose-colored dusk, and knowing he is not safe, that I cannot protect him any longer, but that all the safety I could provide would not give him what he needs—the chance to hold the breeze with his own wings and to see the world from an angle only tall trees can provide.

JUNE 27, 2014

CLEANING HOUSE

Living in a hundred-year-old ranch house, with outbuildings that are nearly as old, means there's always something that needs to be fixed, and almost everything used to look better. I don't mind this. In fact, I kind of like it. It takes the pressure off. I am an accidental housekeeper, meaning I usually start a job, such as making tea, and then the water boils out of the teapot because I've forgotten it, and suddenly I am washing the kitchen floor. As long as I can continue to cultivate my own absentmindedness, the house should stay relatively clean.

Really though, most days it would be very embarrassing if someone dropped in unexpectedly. I like to think there's a threshold that I don't drop below, but that's pure fantasy. On more than one occasion I've realized it was a completely different season the last time I scrubbed the bathroom floor. (I don't make tea in there, you see.) I'm fortunate to live with a man who says his mother taught him to scrub the floor the same as mine did, so if it's not scrubbed it's his fault too. And the other day when I was lamenting how helpless I sometimes feel in the face of all the ranch work I'm too weak or too inexperienced to do, he noted that I'm not a hired hand. Still, I like to contribute, and when I look down and realize the white tile is now a shade more similar to brown, I feel I'm not pulling my weight. (As a side note: Who ever thought white tile was a good idea? For those young people getting ready to decorate their first homes, be warned, it is not, unless you enjoy the feeling of failure.)

All this is a strange way to start a column that is actually about the exact opposite idea. The epiphany I am about to describe came as I prepared to host nearly every member of my immediate family, at overlapping intervals extending over a several-week period. Now, my family members, as a group, are neither hardcore neat freaks nor particularly judgmental, but my mom is a self-proclaimed germaphobe and there are several others who suffer from allergies. Since most ranches would essentially be an excellent place to send an allergy sufferer or a germaphobe if you wanted to torture them, I set about preparing to host my family by first seeing if there wasn't someone else who could do it.

Just kidding. I let myself have that little fantasy for only about a day. But it's true that as the arrival date of the first batch of visitors approached, I began to worry we were all going to regret the venture.

Then, yesterday morning, I was in the barn trying to feed an orphaned calf who can't decide if he belongs in this world or the next. He is skin and bones, stinks of scours, and has crusty, dirty blisters on his nose and lips, and when I feed him, the milk and saliva that run out of his mouth combine into a sticky, muddy paste. It's gross and it's frustrating. So, there I stood, covered in muddy milk paste, wrestling with a calf who wanted nothing to do with the whole affair. "Half a bottle, most of it on me, will have to be good enough for now," I thought and took myself inside. I'll admit I also thought, and it wasn't the first time, "If you are going to die, just get it over with already!"

Believe it or not, I wanted this. To me, this is the real deal: it is the messiness of corporeal life, and it is also the heady window between heaven and earth. On a ranch we watch babies being birthed, we watch them grow, and we watch them die, sometimes even when we've worked hard to heal them. Ironically, many of these little ones are born to be food. All our care and labor ends in their slaughter, and then people we never meet eat them. It's a heavy thought. And it is, of course, a reminder that everything born will become food eventually. It's why I also think that this labor is beautiful, important, and humbling work.

My family, like me, is full of city folk. I'd be surprised if any of them have ever been closer to a cow than the ones they might drive by while zipping down the interstate. They know where hamburger comes from . . . the grocery store. So, the adults may not want to feed the baby calf, but I hope that my nieces and nephew will. A lot of modern human life tries to look cleaner than it really is, and I think that's dangerous. It's good to remember that our roots are in the soil and the muck. Some people say God is in the details, but I believe you can find God in the dirt, where all things begin and end.

When the guests arrive, the bathroom floor will be freshly mopped, but I am guessing that the white tile won't stay white for long. We'll go to the barn and see the baby broiler chicks, the roly-poly mama-cat-to-be, the bum calves and lambs. Then we'll track all that back to the house, the kids running in to tell their mom and dad and grandma what they saw, the old dogs following them through the screen door, nobody bothering to wipe their feet. And I am okay with that. It's all part of the messy glory of life beside a Little Pasture on the Prairie.

2015

JANUARY 19, 2015

MISS PEPPY AND WILBUR, OR, DONKEY COURTSHIP

Almost exactly a year ago I met my first donkey, Miss Peppy. I had a bucket of sweet feed, so she liked me right from the start and even let me scratch her scruffy head. Like most donkeys, she is the introspective sort, and she makes her moods known with the gentle twitches of her long ears. Her mood is set to unflappable; it takes a lot to get a rise out of Miss Peppy.

Since that first brief introduction a year ago, I have acquired two donkeys of my own: the tiny brothers Orville and Wilbur. Before the deep cold hit, they were in a corral with the colts, and I went out daily to see if they wanted to be my friends. They didn't.

Eventually the more outgoing of the brothers, Orville, softened up enough to let me pat his rough, shaggy face if, and only if, I had grain. Wilbur wouldn't come near me, no matter what treats I offered. But both have one expression, and one expression only: a long-suffering gaze blended with a vast melancholy, which has led me to believe that, if required to put pen to paper, donkeys would be the most likely of all the barnyard animals to write poetry.

Once it got colder, we moved the brothers to the little pasture with the sheep, and now I usually see them only at a distance, where they watch me watch them. They almost always stand shoulder to shoulder, the winter grass nearly as tall as they are, their dark brown hair silhouetted against the white and gold and gray of January.

Perhaps it should not have come as a surprise that when Miss Peppy arrived for a short stay with us, she was not met with more fanfare. Miss Peppy is a "real" donkey, unlike the brothers, who are miniatures, so she's twice as tall, but they're twice as wide. She has light brown locks, to their dark ones. She's serene. In other words, she's a lithe, leggy blonde with a charming personality. We thought the brothers would be delighted with such a guest. They weren't. At least not at first.

Upon her arrival, we led Miss Peppy into the little pasture. She simply stood and stared, and the brothers stared back from the other side of the open field. She flicked her ears forward. So did they. She took a few steps to the side. They did too. More staring ensued. We waited awhile, but donkey time is considerably different than human time—donkeys will not be rushed, ever, into anything. Finally, the Man of the Ranch tried leading Miss Peppy over to the brothers, but they just ran away and watched her from behind a stand of cottonwoods. We humans walked back to the corral, and Miss Peppy followed.

Now, the corral that's connected to the little pasture is where the hay bale feeder resides, and it shares a fence with the colts' corral, so Miss Peppy greeted the colts with nose nuzzles and even gave Ellie the sheepdog a few sniffs before settling in for a small snack. The brothers remained on the far side of the pasture.

An hour or so passed, and no progress was made. Since we couldn't stand the suspense, we trailed the brothers into the corral and therefore got to be present for the first real contact. Once they were close, Wilbur approached Miss Peppy right away. To our surprise, Orville hung back. Almost immediately, Wilbur's whole demeanor changed. Always the more reserved of the two, Wilbur's wee legs suddenly seemed to lengthen, his back straightened, and his big donkey head lifted up from his narrow shoulders. Ears at attention, lips pointed forward, Wilbur made his intentions known. A few gentle kisses were exchanged, and then Miss Peppy was ready to head back to the hay. Wilbur followed close behind—close enough that Miss Peppy gave a small kick to let him know she wasn't that kind of girl.

Wilbur was undeterred. He came around again, wiggling his rubbery lips and showing off his fine long teeth. When he was sure Miss Peppy was watching, he gave a few hop kicks with a little twist in the air, to demonstrate his physical prowess. With his fat, squat body and short legs, the display was perhaps more comical than he intended it to be, but Miss Peppy looked on demurely, her eyes mild and soft, then went back to the hay. Wilbur shuffled forward to stand beside her, plotting his next move.

When I came out to shut the chickens in at dusk, Wilbur was still standing beside a placid Miss Peppy, and Orville was just a few paces away. When he saw me, Wilbur wheeled around, opened his large mouth, and began blaring a love song at the top of his little lungs, right in Miss Peppy's face. Miss Peppy's expression did not reveal whether she enjoyed the performance, but she didn't step back until he was finished.

We've been hearing some version of this song echo across the barnyard ever since. Like a loud, rusty hinge, Wilbur declares his love often and unreservedly. I should add here that Wilbur and Orville are both geldings, so this affair is purely platonic, but that is not affecting the breadth or depth of Wilbur's passion for Miss Peppy. Apparently, even a donkey, the most stoic of creatures—and an infertile one at that—is unabashed when it comes to courtship. And no, it's not beautiful music, but it is the music of affection and admiration, and who can help but smile upon that.

JANUARY 26, 2015

LITTLE MERI

Two springs ago, when I still lived in town, I took in a batch of bum lambs, one of whom was unable to walk. A few neighborhood girls came over daily to help with the bottles, and they named the little ewe Cutie Marigold, but I just called her Meri. She was fine when she was first born, but, weakened by scours, she lay down on the barn floor when she was a few days old and didn't get up again. She was put in the orphan pen because she couldn't get up to nurse, and that's how she found her way to me.

Unable to move herself, she was at the mercy of the other orphans. If another lamb wanted to stand on her, which they did from time to time, she had to make her peace with that. When feeding time came along, she would get lifted out and held, and thanks to lots of little girl love, she spent a good amount of time being carried. She got a little stronger, and after a week or so with us, she started to stand again when someone helped her up; however, her legs were so weak she was unable to lower herself back to the ground. The only way to lie down was to let herself fall, and wherever she landed, there she stayed until I or one of the girls moved her again.

All things considered, she seemed relatively happy. The other lambs would clamor for their bottles, shoving and jostling to get to us. They would trample Meri if she happened to have fallen near the exit, and she wouldn't make a sound. I would rescue her—she always got fed first—and she was one of the best eaters.

Of course, everyone else was growing and getting stronger, and it wasn't long before the flock needed more space to practice their little lamb antics. So, the dogs and I started taking them out of the barn for supervised walks around the pasture.

The lambs loved it, following us in a bumbling, toppling fashion. They practiced running their fastest, then changing directions at pretend danger. The older lambs would race to the gate, turn suddenly to avoid smashing into the fence, and then run fast, fast, fast away from it.

Meri couldn't do any of these things. I carried her on these jaunts, setting her down every once in a while so she could get some exercise. Eventually she began to walk, with stiff awkward half steps, but she couldn't move fast, and her balance was terrible. She cried in terror as her barn mates ran away without her, then cringed with fear when they whipped around, plunging toward her again. She stuck close to the fence line so that she could lean against the posts as they stampeded past. Still, they sometimes knocked her over, leaving her helpless as a tortoise flipped on the highway, until I came and collected her. She still couldn't stand up without help.

Spring was nearly summer, and the lambs grew big enough to be outside alone during the bright, warm days. The flock loved to romp and run in the green expanses of new grass—except for Meri, who was stranded alone by the barn while the others frolicked wherever they pleased. She was no longer improving, and at each feeding she was eating a little less. I feared my stoic little girl, left too often behind, was losing her will to live.

One evening in May, I was standing by the barn and the other babies were tossing their heads and teasing the dogs. Meri was standing alone, shivering hard. Her back was curved like an old woman's, and her hip bones jutted through the dirty wool on her back. Her head nodded heavily, oddly large on her shrinking frame. "That's it," I thought. "She's coming in for the night."

I wrapped her up and set her on the couch next to my miniature greyhound, Micah. For all his annoying qualities, he has a few good ones, namely that he is a great snuggler. I sat down too, and if it is possible for a lamb to smile, Meri was smiling. She began to nibble my shirt, his collar, the fuzzy fleece blanket. This kind of nibbling is normal for a lamb, but it's something I had never seen Meri do before. I scratched her chin, and she smiled again, this time sighing and showing her teeth like a gawky girl posing for a photo. We sat and watched a movie together, and then I tucked her in next to Micah for the night.

I had to get up at dawn to feed the other babies. Meri drank a little milk, and I took her out to pee with the dogs, then left her in the dog bed. The day passed quietly enough. Meri went out a few times for bathroom breaks, drank a little more, and ate some pellets when the dogs had their meals. Other than that, she and Micah, and eventually one of the cats, spent most of their time piled together, napping.

This went on for days that turned into weeks. She practiced walking in the kitchen. She learned to run chasing the dogs across the yard. She grew stronger, got her appetite back, and lost her starveling's boniness. When I thought she was ready, I took her back to the pasture. By the end of the summer, other than her slight limp and being a bit smaller and a bit slower than her adopted sisters, you'd never have guessed she'd had a rough start. She was my little miracle, a creature under my care who had made it through impossible odds.

Yesterday, we were out checking the flock and discovered that Meri's udders had swollen to a round, soft pink. I'd noticed one of her sides bulging as of late, and I had worried it was a rupture, thinking it unlikely that she, of all the ewes, would be the first to get pregnant this season. To be honest, I had never thought she would get pregnant at all. It seemed more likely that her health would take a turn for the worse, as she has never been as sturdy as her sisters. Well, there's no doubt about it, that little bulge (now a big bulge) is a lamb.

By the time this article goes to print, my flock might be one sheep bigger, or it might be one sheep smaller. Due to her small size and limp, I am worried giving birth won't be easy for Meri. Her "baby bump" is lopsided—favoring her bad leg—and her pelvis is unusually narrow. These are the stark realities city life doesn't prepare you for—the times when there will be a passage into life, or out of it. Certainly, beloved pets die in the city, but with so many fewer animals to care for, the odds of facing loss are lower too. I always say it is a blessing to be confronted with the true terms of the natural world, but it can be scary. All we can do now is wait, hope for the best, and pray that whatever carried Meri this far will bring her safely to the next stage of her life. In the meantime, I will be visiting her often, cherishing the gift of her for as long as I can.

MARCH 23, 2015

PEARL & THEO

Sunday morning started with the delicate rhythm of rain tapping its way into the ground. We didn't have much snow this winter, so the soil is dry, dry, dry, and the rain was a happy Sunday blessing. The clouds came in with the light and made the whole country seem gentle and soft and gray. Then, before the light was even a few hours old, the temperature began to drop. Soon our soft rain was falling as shards of ice, and all the pretty puddles were congealing into one slick pattern that covered the yard.

"I'm going to check on Pearl," I told the Man of the Ranch. Pearl and her adopted brother, Theo, were my first bum lambs. I brought them home one afternoon three springs ago in a high-walled cardboard box and took them straight inside for a bath. Because they were covered in dried afterbirth, dried milk, and the remnant of a nervous car ride, I worried about germs. They were just tiny babies, after all. Once they were all warm and white again, I made them a small pen in the corner of the garage, and on that first evening, I sat crouched in the cold of early spring, watching them sleep curled around each other and worrying that something bad would happen to them in the night. By the next day they were dirty again, but they were popping around the pen like popcorn, ready for their bottles. Cleanliness was the first standard I relaxed. Maybe lambs didn't need to be that clean to be healthy, I concluded. And, despite the never-ending cold that spring, they both thrived, so over time another worry was eliminated. As they grew, we developed little rituals—they liked to give me kisses, and they let me hold them from time to time—but they had their own lamb-y ways that, in truth, I knew nothing about. Mostly they just wanted milk, as well as space to stretch their growing legs.

I was working full-time then, so the midday bottle came during my lunch break. They always got fed; I often didn't. It was a long month, but soon enough school was out and they were down to two bottles a day, spending their days and nights out-of-doors in a borrowed pasture at the end of my street. And they weren't babies anymore. I could still pick up them up, but just barely—at the rate they were growing, it was a matter of weeks before they would outweigh me. So, there it was: my first season of parenting was complete, and it had lasted only a few months.

By the fall they were living with a goat named Franny. They were happy to see me when I dropped by, but fine with not seeing me when I didn't.

All winter I brought them hay and oats, and they seemed impervious to the ice and snow, swathed as they were in layers of thick wool. The following spring, they were taken to be sheared, and then they stayed with friends so that Pearl could be bred. When I visited, they stood on the hill with the rest of the flock. I couldn't tell if they remembered me or not. I thought they must, but they clearly preferred the company of their new friends to mine.

It was nearly a year before I saw Pearl and Theo again. I had my very own pasture by then, with a few more bum lambs, a ram, and a milk cow. (The fence around the pasture was not yet sheep-proof, however, leading to some epic battles between the Man of the Ranch and the little flock. But that is fodder for another column!)

Pearl had two babies, both long-nosed and dark-faced like her. The day the Man of the Ranch finished putting sheep fence up around the pasture, he went to pick up Pearl, Theo, and the babies. I couldn't believe my baby had her own babies and that we were all together again. Our little family was no longer little.

Since then, another winter has come and nearly gone, and now the pasture seems like the home we've always had. Contentment reigns.

This spring, when we started lamb patrol, Pearl was the one I didn't worry about. She's the veteran. At three years old, she carries a worldly air with her wherever she roams. Loud noises, naughty sheepdog puppies, even a softly shaken bucket of grain are all less likely to provoke a big reaction from Pearl than from her peers. Unlike most sheep, Pearl radiates calm.

But on Sunday, when the ice began to fall, I started to worry. Pearl was the last to lamb, and we knew we wouldn't be waiting much longer. All I could think of was her baby being born covered in ice. If the temperature was dropping, who knew how low it would go before it stopped? I had to get Pearl into the barn.

Of course, getting a single sheep into the barn requires one part luck and two parts magic. The Man of the Ranch has both luck and magic on his side—me, not so much. But I waddled out anyway, stomping my feet through the crust on the puddles so I wouldn't slip.

Against all odds, Pearl was waiting at the gate as though she knew I would be coming. So too, unfortunately, were Meri, Violet, and their two sets of twins. Bjorn, my ram, was watching from a few paces back.

A quick side note about Bjorn: Bjorn is a long-wool ram; as such, he is a bit shorter than the girls, but he also has beautiful, silky locks that hang to his knees. He is generally docile, though a bit of a dandy. However, once in a while he stomps his foot in my direction like he has a plan "to do something about it." A stern look from the human at hand and he runs for cover. Still, I like to keep him in the corner of my eye, and I have taken to carrying a stick when he is close by.

I was considering this as I watched from the other side of the gate. "Could I shuffle Pearl out without the others, especially Bjorn, escaping?" I wondered. "Or should I go back to get the Man of the Ranch?"

Of course, I chose the former, and of course, I instantly regretted it. Meri, Violet, and Meri's babies made it out with Pearl, and they immediately headed for the horses' haystack. I decided I was okay with that—they would be easy enough to gather, and the nursing mothers could probably use the grain rations that usually accompany a stay in the barn. Besides, it would give Pearl company while she waited. There was only one problem: in order to keep Bjorn from escaping, I had caught Violet's babies too, and as their mother happily munched on stolen hay, they began to cry their hearts out.

I was, at this point, mostly undaunted. I slipped through the gate, aforementioned stick in hand, and waved it commandingly at Bjorn, who stood just on the other side. He stomped his foot and backed away. Meanwhile, Violet's twins leapt and crashed together as they ran the length of the fence, their cries increasing in volume. "Come on babies!" I said in a low, soothing voice, still waving my stick as they changed directions. I cracked the gate as they approached, but they didn't understand gates yet, and they ran past the opening, stopping in a tumble at the corner closest to the haystack and their mother. Bjorn, on the other hand, understood gates perfectly, and he approached again. "No!" I said sternly, jabbing my stick forward. He backed off, but now so did the babies, who wheeled around and gathered behind him, peeking at me through his long curls, their flat brown noses and heavy brows a perfect reflection of his.

I closed the gate and appealed to Violet. "Violet," I said in a singsong, "come get your babies." Violet, normally a very attentive mother, ignored me, though she did attempt a bleat through her hay-filled lips. That sent the babies into a paroxysm of despair, but it did not move them from their station behind Bjorn.

To speed this story to its inevitable conclusion, I'll instruct you to imagine several more rounds of these shenanigans, and you'll get the picture. Don't forget to add my burgeoning belly at seven months pregnant, pants slopped with mud, and my soaking wet overcoat. It was time to recruit the Man of the Ranch.

For better or for worse, the Man of the Ranch was by now used to pulling on his boots and coat whenever I arrived breathless with some new fiasco brewing, and today was no different. I explained the situation as we walked toward the runaway sheep, who were merrily tearing into the haystack before us, accompanied by a reverberating chorus. Alerted by the forsaken twins, all the other sheep were now gathered at the gate, protesting their imprisonment while their flock mates feasted. "I think it's supposed to get near sixty degrees by this afternoon" said the Man of the Ranch as he squinted at the scene through the sleet that was still falling all around.

"Oh, really?" I said with a nervous chuckle. "Then maybe they don't need to go in the barn." The Man of the Ranch said nothing at all, though it was possible I detected a small grimace, and by the time we had everyone rounded up and herded back into the big corral, the sleet had stopped.

An hour or so passed while I puttered in the kitchen, when suddenly the Man of the Ranch arrived at the door. "Better come quick if you want to see Pearl's baby being born," he said.

We approached to find Pearl lying quietly on her side. It wasn't even two minutes before a slim, slimy bundle slipped out beside her, and she stood slowly and turned around to inspect the fruits of her labor. I took some pictures, and she began to lick the precious arrival. (Perhaps my instinct to clean them was not so far off after all!) The little fellow blinked and shook his head, surprised, I suppose, at where he had suddenly found himself.

We were heading once again to the house when I glanced back to see Pearl take a step back and begin to rub her side very slowly against a wood panel of fence. In a matter of seconds another slim bundle appeared and slid onto the ground beside the first. Above our heads the sun broke through the clouds, beaming brightly onto the brand-new babies. Instantly the ice began turning to steam, lifting like tendrils of smoke toward the suddenly blue sky. It was glorious—the kind of moment you couldn't make up because it would sound too good to be true.

So, what did I learn? It's a lesson I've learned before, but one that does not wear out upon repeating. There are some things worth worrying about—however, you usually don't know which things they are until the time to worry is over. Everything else? Well, most things take care of themselves, in ways too beautiful to believe. So, here's to enjoying the journey, and a happy spring!

MAY 11, 2015

SPRING SNOW

Friday, the weather was warm and a little windy. After last week's rain, the yard was glowing green with thick, juicy grass, and the lilac bushes by the back door were loosening their tiny purple fists, releasing their honeyed scent every time we brushed past them as we went in or out of the house. The rows of seedlings in the box garden were bursting up into the wooden frames, their tender stems unfurling into fat emerald leaves. And every tree-top held buds and bird songs aplenty. It was definitely spring.

All was not entirely blissful, however. We'd been battling the chickens all week, and we were only tentatively sure we'd won. Last summer our motley little flock never bothered the garden. We'd spy them—red, gold, black, and white—flapping and clucking all over the ranch. They'd travel east to scratch through the horses' manure, they'd travel west to sample the slim leaves of the bachelor's buttons in my flower bed, they'd even come up to the glass patio door and peck at their reflections, but they never touched the garden. Then this winter, when there really wasn't much to find, they began regularly heaving their heavy bodies over the wire fence to scratch and hunt through the mulch and snow. It wasn't doing any harm, so we let it go, and it eventually became the favorite chicken meeting spot.

The arrival of spring meant we needed to reclaim that territory as a chicken-free zone. We started small: an extra few inches of height here, another panel of sheep fence there. We added one section at a time as we attempted to isolate their entry point. But they were wilier than we had anticipated, and every morning for a week we'd find them gathered again inside the garden's growing walls. Finally, after the passage of a few chicken-less days, we thought we'd outwitted them. So, we planted two rows of potatoes, seeded the lettuce beds, and transplanted the hardy greens from indoors. The very next morning, a plump speckled hen and her even plumper speckled friend were scratching away at the newly bare ground of our carefully placed rows. "Salad seeds for breakfast!" they chuckled as they worked. "Delightful!"

A few more inches of wire were added, another panel as well, and some broken branches were shoved into holes—we did what we could—until, at long last, it seemed the garden was safe. I brought out the onion sets and seed packets. The lettuce would need to be replanted, and I might as well start some peas and carrots. Perhaps I could even transplant a few of the herbs that could tolerate a cold evening.

Then we heard the weather report: a winter storm warning with a foot of snow predicted and great gusting winds to follow. Oh, western South Dakota, you are a cruel temptress! And unlike the chickens, you're impossible to outmaneuver.

In the fading heat of a perfect gold-and-rose-colored evening, we began storm preparations. First, there were the sheep to consider. Early in the week there was a lamb born who couldn't quite figure out nursing. His mama had enough milk for ten babies, but her teats, swollen with all that delicious milk, were too big. The poor little fellow kept sucking on a strand of wool he thought seemed like a more appropriate diameter. The Man of the Ranch played sheep wrangler a few times, while my giant belly and I milked, and eventually we got mother and babe working together. After his rough start, the lamb went from woolly skeleton to plump as a pat of golden butter in just one day, but he was still far too tiny to endure a blizzard. Meanwhile, there was another mama pacing the fence line, waiting to have her baby. Fortunately, my flock is small, so finding a sheltered location to accommodate them was easy enough. Getting them there was the tricky part.

It started off well enough, but we'd get all the mamas through one gate only to have someone discover her baby was lagging behind. Her duties as mama compelled her to turn back to collect her lamb, but inevitably another sheep would worry that this change in direction meant trouble ahead and would turn to follow her friend. This would lead to another and another and another doing the same. At one point in the expedition, Twigs, one of our bum lambs from last year, became fascinated with a tree. She stopped to investigate. Everyone else was happily trotting into the corral, but when Twigs didn't follow, the group figured she'd found something they needed to see too. They wheeled around to take a look, babies and all.

And on and on. The Man of the Ranch may or may not have been contemplating a permanent change of pasture for the sheep. Thankfully, two humans are more than twice as good for this type of adventure, so we switched to Plan B. I ran ahead pretending to be a slightly panicked ewe (my background in the theater was useful here), while the Man of the Ranch followed, shooing the stragglers onward. I can't run very far or very fast these days, but I got us to the barn, and it wasn't long before the whole flock was settled in, the last gate closed behind them.

Next there were the yearlings to trail in. And then there was the radar to check, in the hopes that maybe, just maybe, the forecast had changed. It hadn't. Mulch was added to the potatoes not pre-dug by the chickens, and the cold frames were covered. Bales of hay were unfurled for Zena the nurse cow and her babies, the donkeys, the horses, Jane the colt, Rita the milk cow, and the sheep, cozy in the long tin barn.

By nightfall, we were ready—or as ready as we'd ever be. All that was left was the waiting. I woke, worried, to flakes flying outside the bedroom window. But they didn't amount to much and soon turned to rain. All day the rain fell, filling the tire tracks on the gravel path and turning the ruts into rivers. I bundled myself in rubber and flannel and wool for the evening chores, but the mud crept up my pantlegs and damp crept into my clothes anyway. When the bum calves came to the fence to get their bottles, their back flanks were shivering hard, and their long lashes and curly forelocks hung clumped and dripping wet. It was still above freezing, but the air was sharp and stinging. By the time we went to bed, the rain was snow again, or some kind of rainy-snowy mix, and fell fat and loose through the glow of the tall yard light. The storm had begun.

I awoke early again the next morning to find that the world was very wet and very white. The old elms in the western tree belt looked weary holding up the weight of all the snow that had already fallen, and the chokecherry that shades the patio was bent, its lowest branches arching down nearly to the ground. I used a broomstick to knock what snow I could off the poor thing, but the highest branches remained heaped and weighed down.

We ate pancakes for breakfast and tried not to worry. I fed the bottle babies in the whirling whiteness, then checked on the sheep, who complained loudly that everyone had been walking and sleeping on their once-pristine pile of hay all night. Everyone and no one was to blame, but one thing was clear: they needed fresh hay, and they needed it now! "You are all very spoiled," I told them. "You are the only animals on the whole ranch that get to be in a cozy barn, instead of out in the wind and snow."

They turned their backs to me and continued their loud groans. Their spiraling protestations followed me out of the barn: "We need more hay! This is soooo boring! When will there be sweet feed? We want sweet feed!"

Ellie the sheepdog walked with me back to the house. Even she shivered a little, her eyes huge and brown against the wet strands of her white mane.

"I am spoiled too," I thought as I shut the door to the house behind me, entering the warmth of the kitchen. I was wrong to tell the sheep they were the only animals snug and cozy, out of the wind and snow. We were the luckiest by far.

So I tried not to complain as the second hand on the wall clock tapped out the time. We drank coffee and tea. Ate a midday meal. Watched the weather. In the big pasture, the wind gathered itself, pulling the snow from the clouds and hurling it sideways, pushing the cows and the calves south out of the draws. The Man of the Ranch went to spread hay by the windbreaks, hoping to keep the herd from drifting farther away. Some of them came, but we could still see a long line of mamas and babies to the east, streaming south.

All afternoon, the temperature rose. Just a little, but it was enough. By evening it was raining again, and the thick mounds of fallen snow started to look a little smaller, then a little smaller still, while the muddy welts in the gravel road grew wider and wider. The blizzard was over, and, at least for now, so was the fear of drought.

Today there is still snow clinging to the junipers, but the lilacs have sprung free, their buds faded only a little, their sweet vanilla fragrance faded not at all. The sun is shining, and the wind and melting snow are singing a duet around the rooftop as I write. It is early morning, but Ellie is up and running south of the house, once again the whitest thing for miles. She is singing too, with her joyful barks: "It is spring, once again, it is spring."

MAY 19, 2015

FEAR OF DROUGHT RELIEVED

Winter was mild: just a few little snow squalls and then an eerily early spring. What's not to like about that? Well, lack of moisture, mostly. Through January, February, and March you heard people mention it over coffee and pie at the church luncheon, or while waiting in line at the feed store and the post office. Drought was never far from our minds. The beautiful, golden afternoons of warm sun. The dry, brown dust. No one wanted to complain, but by May, it was more than a small worry. There was heat, and there were bright days, but without rain, the grass stood gray and dead and could not grow.

Adding it all together, I am guessing the Man of the Ranch has spent a year's worth of hours staring at the sky, watching for clouds. And now, with the advent of the internet, he spends many more hours watching the colorful patches of clouds on the weather radar. He scrolls through the time-lapse maps looking for telltale splotches of green and yellow, hoping to see a few swaths pass over the icon of a red flag that marks the location of our place.

Early in May there were several days when rain was predicted, and he'd come in to check the radar, cheering at the sight of green. He read me the forecasts by the hour—90 percent chance by noon, 100 percent by 1:00 p.m.—only to watch the green clouds spin and scatter at 11:45, parting like the Red Sea at our property line.

One day he was in town when a steady rain began, drumming up dust on the edges of the feed store parking lot. Steering the pickup west, he watched the drops on the windshield cease their cheerful patter as he reached the turnoff to the house, just a mile up the highway. The gravel of our driveway was still as dry as when he'd left. The rain had missed us again.

Then, two weeks ago, it finally happened. Rain. A soft rain that got harder and kept up all night. We woke to glistening puddles and a sheepdog covered head to paws in mud. We could stop whispering the word drought, at least for a little while.

Then there was the Mother's Day Blizzard, a mix of rain that turned to snow that turned back to rain. It was enough moisture to carry us to summer. The Man of the Ranch teased friends on the phone, "Well, I guess you'll have to hay this year after all." The dams were full, the creeks were overflowing. One less worry to carry to breakfast after a sleepless night.

But it didn't end there. Be careful what you wish for, they always say. In the week that followed the blizzard there was a rain shower almost every day, culminating in a night of rain so mighty we found two frogs swimming in the outdoor dog dish, the deep bowl filled to the brim with water. The frogs seemed a little surprised to have arrived in the desert by deluge, with their yellow-rimmed eyes, wide and unblinking, and their long-fingered feet paddling against the sides of the bowl. Meanwhile, the pasture now featured a pond, and that pond was filled with a thousand more frogs, all singing together, deep and loud. After a few morning clouds, the day bloomed warm and postcard perfect, so I took the dogs out for a long walk. When the dogs plunged joyfully into the pond, the frogs stopped for a moment, only to resume as the dogs swept onward, shaking the droplets out of their fur coats in a second storm. They were still singing as evening fell into night. We went to bed with the windows open, the throaty frogs' songs caught and carried by the wind, along with the night birds' songs from high in the leafed-out trees.

Of course, the calendar's a mess. Brandings scheduled months ago have been moved, then moved again, and the trucks that were supposed to come pick up cattle have been canceled twice on account of mud. The driveway isn't dry anymore. Most of our outdoor shoes are caked to the ankles with the winter's manure and dirt, and trails of the stuff trickle through the house carried on pant legs and paws. But we aren't complaining. Not too much anyway.

What can we do? If it's not one thing, it's another—or so it always seems. We must take pleasure in the grass that's sprouting so lushly on our side of the fence. Glory be to the waters that are rising. Glory be to the mud tracked in after the day's work is done. In the distance there may be a dark cloud, but overhead the sky is a clear, crystalline blue, and out in the pasture the cattle graze, hooves in the mud, noses buried in the green, green grass.

AUGUST 17, 2015

RITA

I was already in love with the Man of the Ranch before he brought Rita the Jersey cow home for my birthday, but I think he knew the gift would seal the deal, and he was right. It's not every woman whose heart would be won by a milk cow, and it's not every man who can read a woman's heart well enough to know a milk cow would win it. Thus, we think ourselves very lucky to have found one another.

Plus, a pregnant cow comes with a gift of its own—Rita calved about a month later in a bawling early spring snow squall, and we named her baby Ruthie. With very little effort, we had doubled our dairy herd. A few months later we added Zena, who, like Ruthie, is a sassy Angus-Jersey cross. The plan was to use these girls, once they were grown, as nurse cows for bum calves, while Rita would be for butter, yogurt, and most importantly, ice cream.

I liked milking, and I loved Rita. She was everything you want a milk cow to be: gentle, easygoing, and, oh yes, the purveyor of thick, creamy milk that she didn't mind sharing. She was a good mama to Ruthie, who grew strong and feisty, and she almost never kicked over the bucket when I brought her in to be milked. We even put a bum calf, Baby Betty, in with Ruthie, and both calves grew chubby. Meanwhile, there was still more than enough milk left over for the table. I was in the dairy business, and I was liking it. Betty the Bum would make a tidy profit, plus we were saving money on groceries—I couldn't imagine why everyone didn't have a sweet Jersey in their barn.

Then, in August, Betty the Bum laid down and died for no reason that we could discern. And after a summer with the bulls, it turned out Rita wasn't pregnant. She spent the winter in a corral with the boys and fifteen red yearlings, getting grained and munching on ground hay. My profit margin was narrowing, but I was still in the black. In the spring, we released Rita to feast on grass with the new mamas, and after a few months, the bulls joined them all once again. Over the summer, Rita proceeded to get fatter and fatter as the clover grew taller and taller.

Nearly a year has come and gone since we got Rita, and she still hasn't displayed any signs of impending motherhood. Fortunately, Zena birthed a beautiful bull calf, who is burly and strong. She is also a part-time mother to Gus and Gracie, this year's bums, though they get bottles on the side since she doesn't have enough milk for all three yet. Ruthie, who is now a yearling herself, is a beauty and may at this very moment be carrying a calf of her own. Which is to say all hasn't been completely lost, but it has been a while since any of us humans have enjoyed fresh milk. More importantly, there's been no ice cream.

If you are a regular reader of this column, you know we recently added Caroline, a two-year-old Brown Swiss cow, and her swarthy bull calf to the mix. The Man of the Ranch sorted Rita and Zena off from the rest of the cattle when he brought in the bulls. Rita and Zena, plus Caroline, plus the calves, now hang out in one of the smaller pastures close to the house. In the evenings I walk down to give the calves their bottles, and I bring a little cake to the girls for an evening snack. Caroline hasn't been handled at all, so the cake is my way of making friends. The group is rounded out by a Black Baldy heifer we thought was blind (she kept running into fence posts when she should have been going through gates). She seems to have recovered her sight—she knows to come up for cake, anyway, and she can find me, bucket in hand, even when I don't make a sound.

With their sharp, jutting hip bones and long knobby rib cages that are the hallmark of most milking breeds, the girls don't make the best first impression. If you include a straggly bunch of mismatched calves, a half-blind yearling, and one crabby bull, the effect is even more off-putting. The Man of the Ranch briefly considered pasturing them farther south but decided against it. "People will wonder what kind of operation we've got here if they see this crew from the road," he said.

Of course, all this means they really are the perfect herd for me, except for one small wrinkle—Rita's once-docile personality has turned into something significantly less friendly. She bulldozes her way through the poor calves, headbutting with abandon. As a result, the Man of the Ranch had to construct a small, low-framed corral with a small bottle holder nailed to the slats of the wood fence so the poor calves can drink without fear of injury. After setting the bottles in the holder, I try to distract Rita, which means she gets most of the evening treats all to herself. She rears up and shakes her head at the others, and except for Zena, who isn't easily intimidated, the rest now stay away.

I fear this means Rita's days are numbered. I keep accidentally adding animals to the category of pet, but a bad-mannered dairy cow with no milk? Well, you have to draw the line somewhere. We'll be taking ultrasounds in a few weeks, and if she comes up open again, I guess we'll find out how much of a ranch girl I've become in the last year and a half. In the meantime, we'll keep buying our ice cream at the grocery store, and I'll be crossing my fingers that I don't have to find out just yet.

SEPTEMBER 8, 2015

BARN CAT POLITICS

Barn cat politics are complicated. They are full of alliances, double-crossing, and violent overthrows. My personal introduction to all this began last summer when a young beauty named Roxy arrived in our barn without fanfare. She proceeded to charm our crusty old tom, Yellow Cat, raise a litter of kittens, then slip away as unobtrusively as she had come. The litter consisted of four boys and two girls. One of the boys and one of the girls were transported via my Subaru to become house cats and are enjoying domestic bliss with my sister in Duluth. The others were left to the freedom of pack life in the wild.

We decided four outdoor and two mostly indoor cats were plenty of cats, so we spayed the remaining female, Dora. "Those toms will start disappearing though," the Man of the Ranch warned me.

"Why?" I asked. "They are all getting fed premium cat chow, there is infinite space to roam, and Dora is a no longer in a position to incite battles for her affection." As is often the case with these types of inquiries, the Man of the Ranch simply shrugged his shoulders. Some things just go the way they go.

Alfie was the first to disappear. A burnished-gray-and-white-striped cat with golden eyes, he had been the tamest of the brood. When I fed the orphan calves their bottles, he would tiptoe along the round metal fence railing and leap to my shoulders, purring. This maneuver was never once greeted with a friendly response, as his sticking the landing depended on the use of claws. He remained undeterred, and my crankiness did not lessen his affection for me. He was the cat who would emerge from the underbrush to wrap himself around my ankles, yowling for caresses, and he never missed a meal.

Then one day he did. And another day. And another. We've not seen him for two months now.

Next, Yellow Cat started appearing a little worse for the wear, a new triangle of ear missing here, a tuft of hair missing there. Fortunately for Yellow Cat, he and Ellie the guard dog are best friends, so he simply spends all his free time with her now. He visits the barn for breakfast and supper but keeps his distance from the other cats if he can help it.

That has left the remaining two toms, Francis and Thor, to vie for the position of top feline.

Francis is all gray. He is sly and sneaky, wafting like smoke through underbrush and tall grasses. He is lean and getting leaner by the day, and he has inherited Yellow Cat's slightly cross-eyed gaze, which makes him appear a wee bit sinister. If I turn to discover him staring at me, the hairs on the back of my neck begin to prickle.

Thor, on the other hand, is the biggest cat on the ranch, with muscles like a clenched fist. His coloration matches his lost brother Alfie's, but he also has a gleaming white chin and pure white socks. Thor never prowls. He strolls, struts, and sometimes stalks, but he does it out in the open, like a lion pacing across the savanna.

The cats often follow me as I proceed through my evening chores. Perhaps it is the smell of milk replacer in the calves' bottles that draws them, or maybe it is just anticipation, as they know the barn, and their bowls, will be my last stop. Tonight, Francis keeps his distance from Thor, sticking to the raggedy weeds beside the corral, while Thor saunters on the other side of the fence, unafraid even of the dairy herd's heavy hooves. Slim little Dora walks with me between the two, glancing up and around with eyes bright in her coal-black face.

When we finally make it to the barn, Yellow Cat is already waiting, hunched on the raised bin next to the empty bowls. He braces for my approach, ready to bolt if I come too close. Even after all this time, he still doesn't trust me. Thor leaps up beside him, and Yellow Cat flinches but holds his ground. Dora and Francis wait by the door. I pour out the kibble, and Yellow Cat and Thor crunch heartily into their dishes of food. Francis creeps up beside me and lunges silently onto the bin, hoping that my presence will keep violence at bay. He gobbles down only a mouthful before Thor is on top of him, hissing and spitting. I jump back—even I am startled—and Francis runs from the barn. He'll go without supper tonight. Dora stays by the door. She'll wait till the others are gone before she tries to eat.

I trudge back to the house, and I say trudge because my steps and heart feel so heavy. I wish I could keep the few animals under my care safe. I wish I could make them get along. Meanwhile, Europe is filling up with refugees fleeing crashing bombs, food shortages, and violence. I am walking back to my safe, cozy home while fathers and mothers and grandparents and small children are arriving by the thousands aboard flimsy rafts. They arrive carried by the rugged waves of the Mediterranean. Or, they arrive footsore and bruised from walking rough roads and carrying everything they own tucked into plastic bags. And when they do arrive, weary but thanking God, many of the places they arrive at tell them they cannot stay there, they are not welcome. Still, they're the lucky ones; some will not arrive at all.

I can't explain it, but every child in every photograph of these refugees looks like my baby, and every mother looks like me. A little boy's limp body is lifted from the sea, and it reminds me of my infant son, loose-limbed in his sleep, so tiny and fragile and precious. For better or for worse, motherhood has cracked my heart open and made it impossible for me not to notice that it could easily be me carrying my boy, my arms long past aching, both of us covered in a thousand miles of sadness.

I feel as powerless to influence world politics as I am to influence cat politics. I can put out more food, add an extra bowl, try standing guard while they eat, but eventually Thor will probably achieve his goal of driving Francis away. Across the Middle East and Africa, mothers and fathers will shuffle their beloved children into small boats, train cars, and the dark heat of cargo trucks to escape death and deprivation, even though they aren't sure they have anywhere to go. Bombs will keep exploding. Homes will keep being destroyed. It is so sad, it is so desperate, and it is so common. Cats aren't the only species capable of systematic cruelty and turning a blind eye to the suffering of their own kind.

So, tonight I go back to the barn, put out that extra bowl of food, and stand in the dusky shadows while the cats eat. And tomorrow I will pack a box of diapers and blankets to mail to an island in Greece that is inundated with migrants. They are small, these gestures. It is an act of faith that they mean anything at all, but they are the beginning of trying to do better.

I often think of 1 Corinthians 12:12–13, which I've quoted in this column before. To paraphrase, the verse tells us that we are many members of the same body. Myself, my baby, a mother from Syria, a father crossing the border from Mexico—we are all members of one another. Right now, it will be my hands that reach out to offer aid, and someday it will be someone else's hands that offer aid to me.

SEPTEMBER 14, 2015

ADORABLY NUTTY

"Sometimes I wonder how this happened," the Man of the Ranch says, and he sounds a bit glum. It's early morning, just a little after dawn. Work boots on, steaming cup of coffee in hand, he's standing by the sliding glass door staring out onto the patio. Staring back at him are a tiny gray kitten, a floppy-combed Leghorn hen, and a huge white sheepdog. They're lined up, waiting for him.

It's a good question. How did this happen?

Two years ago, I was living in a trailer with my two dogs, two cats, one little speckled hen, and three yearling lambs. The lambs would often sleep on my porch, as I had yet to build a fence that could keep them in, and the back seat of my car still had hay in it from the last time I'd moved them. The hen, meanwhile, was roosting on a perch I had rigged up in the bathroom.

In spite of the craziness, or perhaps because of it, I kept a tidy house. My first purchase upon moving into that trailer was a top-of-the-line vacuum, and my floors will never again be scrubbed as often as they were when I had a hen living with me. Still, I recognized that it was not the house of a "normal" person. I worried that, left to my own devices, I was beginning to veer from adorably nutty into just plain nutty.

So, when the Man of the Ranch and I began our courtship, I was up-front about my eccentricities. "You might not want to use the bathroom," I told him the first time he came over. "There is a chicken in there . . . but she is friendly!"

He offered to find a spot for her in one of his barns and even helped me acquire some chicken friends to keep her company. I jumped at the chance.

Then, when I was planning to go back east for the winter holidays, he offered to keep my lambs in one of his corrals. And when I said, "I am not sure how to get them to you—they are too big for the Subaru now," he managed to keep a straight face.

"I can come pick them up with my trailer," he said. Oh yes, a trailer. The way "normal" people transport livestock. How clever!

Eventually, the two cats and two dogs and I also moved out of the trailer and onto the ranch, and we all lived happily ever after. Sort of.

Since then, I have been able to curb my impulses most of the time, but we have had several baby lambs, a baby bird, and a few rounds of kittens spend a night or two in the house. And by a night or two, I mean no more than a week. Okay, I guess the outer limit was more like a month—but none of them ever became permanent residents, thus honoring an early agreement that was made, which capped the indoor animal count at four.

Still, when the Man of the Ranch came home one evening to discover a small animal carrier perched in the bed of the pickup, he was terrified. "Honey," he called to me as he entered the house, fear evident in his voice. "Why is there an animal carrier outside?"

"It was for two kittens that needed a home," I said, "but they will be barn kittens."

"Oh," he said, his mouth widening into a smile. "Well, that's not so bad."

"Um, they are in the bathroom right now, though," I said. "Just for tonight," I added.

They ended up staying for three nights, and I'd like to say I would have moved them after that anyway, but their dismissal was certainly aided by one of them mistaking the Man of the Ranch's leg for a tree as he was stepping into the shower. That eliminated all doubt that they were destined to live in the barn.

Unfortunately, they have no desire to be barn cats. At first, they were content with a hay-filled stall in which to play and snooze and snuggle. I went out to feed them twice a day, and they would come running to the sound of my footsteps, returning to tumble together in the cobwebs after I left. Now, however, they take matters into their own hands, or, more accurately, their own paws, and sneak out through a gap in the barn's foundation to follow us around whenever we are outside.

The chickens sometimes do this too, as does Ellie the sheepdog, and depending what pasture you're in, a small flock of sheep or a herd of dairy cows might join as well. So, while doing chores, it often feels like you are the grand marshal of a barnyard parade. I enjoy this feeling. The Man of the Ranch? Not so much.

At least the barnyard parade was mostly confined to the barnyard—until recently. You see, Ellie was the only outdoor animal that got fed on the patio. I say was the only animal, because lately she hasn't been finishing her supper. There are coyotes out almost every night, so she's busy from dusk till dawn. We've also seen her dragging around a few half-eaten rabbits, which clearly are more delicious than dry old kibble. Either way, there are often a few bites left in her bowl at daybreak. I don't know who figured it out first, but it wasn't long before the hens noticed the leftovers. At the same time, the kittens realized that if the humans couldn't be found elsewhere, they would eventually appear on the other side of the big glass door.

So, that's how it happened. Most mornings a quiet cup of coffee includes a stare-down from a weary Ellie waiting for breakfast, one or more hens wondering when the next dog food delivery will arrive, and a kitten or two mewling for attention as well. The Man of the Ranch remembers when things were different, when walking to the barn didn't include kittens snaking between your feet, when the patio wasn't decorated with chicken plops. I'm pretty sure he still finds it all adorably nutty, not just plain nutty, and he wouldn't trade us if he could.

Well, maybe just those kittens.

SEPTEMBER 21, 2015

HARVEST + TEETHING

The sky is the bright blue of a robin's egg, and the sunlight beams down in shafts that catch the lemon-yellow leaves as they shiver in the breeze. The grass is mostly brown and dry. It's fall in western South Dakota. Mornings are so chilly I put a knit cap on the baby while I do chores. By noon I've stripped him down to shirtsleeves again, though the house stays cool all day.

I wear slippers inside, even as the sun warms the patio. The cats nap curled on the porch furniture, soaking in the last of the heat.

I wonder, do they know what's coming? Ellie the sheepdog's thick, woolly undercoat is growing in again, as are the sheep's fleeces. The two ewe lambs we kept this fall aren't knob-kneed babies anymore. They have grown into their legs and are as lovely as I had hoped they would be, their lengthening locks bright and tightly curled. The other babies are growing up too—the wee chicks, balls of fluff just a week ago, are sprouting pin feathers by the second. They will be ready when the real cold hits. For now, they can still snuggle beneath their mama's pillowy breast at night, but they won't need to much longer. The other chickens cluck across the yard, dashing after grasshoppers, fattening themselves in preparation.

Evening comes and we head to the garden. The Bean sits in his stroller, bundled in a soft blue blanket, while we dig potatoes. The garden is closing down. The salad beds are full of shadowy skeletons; the lettuce and most of the herbs bolted weeks ago in the heavy heat, and the seed pods stand golden brown on reedy stems, ready to be released back to the soil.

Not everything is ready to concede to the end of the season, though. The zucchini plants soldier on, their leaves spreading like emerald canopies over the withered onion tops. The green beans are also putting in a surprise final appearance. We'd left them for dead—they were snaking up the trellis with only a few crisp leaves left—but the cool weather has revived them. The twisted brown stems are dotted with small white flowers and the tiny fingers of new beans.

The tomatoes aren't giving up yet, either. Their leaves are wilted and yellowing, and their vines are leathery, but they are full of fruit. They remind me of our oldest ewes, whose hip bones poke out of their matted wool, but who wean the biggest, fattest lambs in the flock. The pumpkin plants look about the same, as though the plants have grown old and weary raising such fine, robust children. Pretty soon we'll march those large, round babies and stack them by the entryway door—ready to be roasted for a midwinter supper.

In other news, the Bean is doing important work of his own. He has teeth coming and announces the fact with drooly groans and constant chewing on whatever is available. Sleeping on his own is temporarily a thing of the past and has been replaced by snuggle sessions that last pretty much all day. If I'm tempted to get crabby about this, the Man of the Ranch reminds me how lucky I am. "Doesn't it make you feel good that just being close to you helps him feel better?" he asks. Yes, as a matter of fact, it does make me feel good.

Our pantry and freezer may not be as full as usual this year; I'm almost certain the cupboard reserved for jars of pickles and tomatoes will remain bare. And I'd like to think next year will be different, but I'm already imagining chubby fingers "helping" Mama by pulling seedlings out by the roots. In the meantime, the Bean and I will be cozy under blankets while I type with one hand and he does the hard work of sprouting teeth. Hopefully, we'll get enough put up that when the Bean's little pearly whites finally appear, we can all three of us enjoy the fruits of the garden together as the snow falls, swirling and white.

OCTOBER 12, 2015

DIGGING POTATOES

Outside, the wind is blowing the raspy yellow leaves right off the baby trees in the windbreak. The lilacs and the elms in the yard are still green and full, and they thrash around like they're caught in a whirling riptide. It's not just warm today, it's hot. There hasn't yet been a killing frost, which is usually one of the hallmarks of an unseasonably steamy fall. Instead, we've had a few days cool enough to pull out woolen socks and sweaters for the morning, but the heat returned by midday. Now, here we are, halfway through the month of October, and it feels like the beginning of August again.

Except it doesn't, really. There is something strange in the wild heat. A note of foreboding plays beneath the dry wind and burnished, sun-soaked grass. This weather, with its bright, warm days, is only an imitation of robust health. It is, in fact, a time of death and decay.

Last week we sent a young heifer to the butcher, and soon we will sell some of our steer calves. Even with the heat, the garden isn't producing much more than a few knobby zucchinis and a smattering of mealy, half-ripe tomatoes. The weather only partially masks that this is a time of endings, that things are closing down.

The Bean and I are sitting on the couch. He's sleeping, and I'm listening to the way the wind makes this old house creak. It sounds like it has a voice—a voice that is old and maybe a little cranky. The Bean isn't bothered. His arms flop to the sides loosely. When we first brought him home, he fell asleep only in my arms. That also seemed to be the only place he could stay asleep. Now he usually does fine on his own, though not today, for some reason. I worry that I should let him cry more than I do, but I don't worry that much. Several wise friends have told me that you can spoil children by giving them too many things, but you can't hold them too much, or give them too much love. I agree with this, so it's back to typing one-handed, for today at least.

The Bean wakes up, and the Man of the Ranch comes in from working. He takes the baby, and they go into the kitchen for a cup of coffee. The Bean perches on his papa's arm like a little bird. He is alert to every movement, bending his head to peer at the fluff of ground beans as they cascade into the black funnel of the coffee maker.

I listen to them talk to each other. The Bean uses words that are full of vowels, and long passages of singing interrupted by grunts. It is hard for us to understand his language, but he often seems to understand ours perfectly. He finds us quite funny.

I am trying to write, but I keep looking up from the computer screen at my two sweet boys. The wind has died down, so now it's only their voices I hear. "Should we finish digging potatoes?" the Man of the Ranch asks from the kitchen.

The Bean yawns, but that must mean "Yes," as he would almost always rather be outside than inside. "Yes," I say for both of us, and get up.

Sometimes life happens on the page. Sometimes it just happens. Sometimes, even as things are ending all around you, you get up and walk outside. You find it is still hot—hotter than you expect. You find there is stillness, as in a calm before a storm. And you dig potatoes with your sweetheart and your small son. Why not? Tomorrow the wind will blow again, and the next day snow may fall. Tonight, there is quiet and a velvet dusk. Kittens play at your feet while you pull roots from the earth; the nighthawks call to one another over your head, long and loud, till at last it is dark.

OCTOBER 16, 2015

BJORN

What do you do when you need to get rid of an animal that is perfectly healthy, just no longer useful?

For the record, there is already blood on my hands. I've taken some wether lambs to market (more on that in a minute) and we dispatched a rooster who had started to attack people. None of that was any fun, but it's not exactly what I'm talking about. Now, after he has given us nearly two years of faithful service, I've got to get rid of my ram, Bjorn.

Let me backtrack a little. It all started with those first two bum lambs. I brought them home in a cardboard box, and I didn't think much past their cuteness. Once they were grown, I treated them like giant woolly dogs. For a while they weren't even fenced in. They would come onto the porch and peer in the windows when they wanted me to come out. I'm sure visitors found it unnerving to be greeted at their car doors by these affectionate critters, but to me they were part of the family. A few more years led to a few more bum lambs, and before I knew it, I had a very small, very friendly flock. In the meantime, I taught myself to knit, with visions of harvesting, processing, and then spinning the wool from my fluffy pets.

Since I had no intention of letting anyone eat my darlings, but the bill for winter feed came due whether I turned a profit or not, I knew I needed to figure out how to make some money from them. I must have been thinking of the old adage, “It takes money to make money,” because my solution was to purchase a fancy long-wool ram and cross him with my girls, so they could have fancy long-wool babies.

Because the Man of the Ranch likes me well enough to let me make my own mistakes, on a bitterly cold January day, we traveled a few hundred miles to pick up Bjorn, a yearling Teeswater/Cotswold cross. We turned around and drove the few hundred miles home, and almost exactly five months later, the first baby was born.

I can’t say for sure when I realized there was, in fact, no real market for a Rambouillet/Hampshire/Teeswater/Cotswold wether lamb, but it wasn’t long before I had many of them. For better or for worse, when fall came, I sold those gorgeously fleeced boys, knowing that, despite my best intentions, they’d be on someone’s dinner plate.

Now, two seasons into this grand experiment, the first of Bjorn’s beautiful ewe babies are old enough to be bred, and yet another conundrum I had been too naive to contemplate has emerged. What to do with Bjorn? His locks are still lovely, long, and shimmery, he is as fertile as they come—all the ewes have gotten bred and most have had twins—and as far as rams go, he’s got a pretty docile personality. But short of “wetherizing” him, he can’t stay here.

So, if the good news of not knowing what you are doing is that you don’t know to be embarrassed, the bad news is the heartbreak when you finally figure it out.

I guess the only question left to ask is: Anybody need a ram?

NOVEMBER 1, 2015

SELLING CALVES

Today is the noisiest day of the year. To the north the black cows are bawling; to the south it's the reds. Some of their voices are muffled, some are so loud I swear they are in the house with us, their bellowing discontent rattling across the stone tiles in the kitchen and bouncing over the sofa to where the baby sleeps. It's a sad day for them, a pensive one for us—the calves are going to market.

Yes, a whole year of work comes down to one day. You send those calves off to a sale barn, where they will be hustled onto and then off the auction floor, and at the end of it you will hold a check for an as-yet-undetermined amount, your income for the year. A friend who, like I, is new to the ranching life says, "It feels like high stakes gambling!"

Of course, so much preparation takes place first. Instead of simply laying some chips on a table, you must lay out heavy bales of hay every day of winter, no matter how tired you are, or how rotten the weather is. You must check that there is open water, and when the mechanism on the automatic waterer freezes, you must lie on your back atop the avalanche of ice that a busted hose has created and reach frostbitten fingers in to fiddle with the guts of the machine, even though your fingers are so numb you can't feel a thing.

And last summer, when one of those calves fell ill, it didn't matter what you had planned for the afternoon, or that the whole prairie simmered like an oven. You rode out through thigh-high clover while the mosquitoes landed thickly on your neck, biting behind your ears and drawing your blood. The calf you needed to doctor hid, half buried in the tall grass, until you were nearly upon him, and then he ran and ran. Every time you tried to rope him you got a lasso full of clover instead. Now it is fall, the grass is low to the ground, and that calf is being loaded on the truck.

In the corral by the barn, Rita the milk cow watches the commotion, her mouth full of hay. She's probably wondering why we aren't loading up the bum calf we want her to adopt. She's made it quite clear she has no intention of warming to him. Morning and night for nearly three weeks, she's gotten her cake in the head catch so the poor fellow can get a little milk. Still, she kicks him every chance she gets. She doesn't want another baby.

Rita wasn't like this last time around. We had popped a Black Baldy heifer named Baby Betty in with her right after she calved, and it wasn't more than a few days before Betty might as well have been Rita's blood relation. Out in the pasture Rita's bumpy brown back would lumber through the greenery, followed by two little slips of brown and black—the backs of Rita's calf, Ruthie, and Baby Betty, just behind. Once, when the Man of the Ranch trailed all the mamas out to the summer pasture, Betty got lost. Rita peeled away from the herd, calling Betty, who, stuck behind a gate, waited patiently to be rescued.

It's the same call the mama cows are using now. The mamas don't know it yet, but their calves are already gone, rumbling along the highway. They're hoping their little ones are just over the ridge, or maybe down in the draw.

Tomorrow, the Man of the Ranch will have fence line to fix from all the mothers who give up calling and break through the wires to search for their missing children. They will return bewildered. Where have all the babies gone? Meanwhile, Rita will remain placid until it is time to feed her bedraggled orphan. "Take him away!" she'll say with every kick.

"Be careful what you wish for," I'll tell her. "It will happen soon enough."

Selling calves is how we ranchers put bread in the mouths of our own babes. It's how we pay for the winter hay and the new parts to fix the waterer, and the electricity to make the waterer run. It's how we buy medicine to doctor next year's calves.

But I can't help it: I hate to hear those mamas crying, and I want to cry with them. I wish there were another way, but there is no place under heaven that can solve the sadness of a mother separated from her babe, and there is no way they can all stay.

In a few more days, the worst of the noise will be over. The mamas will return to their quiet lives of munching and milling, crossing the wide pasture slowly, eating as they walk, their heads bowed to the ground. And in only a few more months, there will be another round of babies, and the whole circle will begin again.

NOVEMBER 15, 2015

SHETLAND SHEEP

They are black with white freckles on their faces, thin peg legs, and great, fluffy coats. One is named Fifi, and she is very skittish. The other is named Elsa, and she is also shy, though she will come up to nibble a little grain from your hands, provided you remain quiet and move slowly. They are Shetland sheep—the sheep I have been waiting for since before I even knew I was waiting for sheep.

It will surprise exactly no one to learn that I hate docking lambs and usually cry over it. Since I actually have a sheep without a docked tail (I kept thinking she was going to die, so I never bothered), I can attest from personal experience it is pretty important to dock lambs. Every time I am tempted to chicken out and not band the new babies, I think of Meri at shearing time, and I shudder. Her undocked tail with a year's worth of crusty wool is not a pretty sight. Still, I just hate it. I usually hold the lambs while the Man of the Ranch does the deed, and I always say the same thing through my tears: "I don't think I want to keep breeding sheep." Shetlands, however, are naturally short-tailed, so you don't need to dock the lambs. I was ready to sign up as soon as I found that out. I mean, it's almost too good to be true.

The other thing I love about the Shetlands is that they are considered an "unimproved breed," which means they developed over time to meet the needs of their environment, rather than through selective breeding programs. So, they grow slowly, are easy keepers, and are very hardy—all handy traits for a shepherdess who still doesn't really know what she's doing. And you know what Shetlands are not good for? Meat. Their meat is supposedly quite delicious, but there isn't much of it. Meanwhile, their wool is copious and of the finest quality. As I have mentioned in this column before, selling my lambs feels a little like selling my friends' children. A sheep who doesn't cost much to run and produces a fleece more valuable than its meat is the perfect sheep for a small holder who is far too attached to her flock. In fact, many people who breed Shetlands actually keep wethers because they are said to have the best wool.

There are more qualities to love: Shetlands are small, which is nice for a small person; they are docile; they are good mothers; and they are prolific—with the right feed they almost always have twins or even triplets. The list goes on and on, but perhaps the thing that really sold me on Elsa and Fifi is that they are black sheep. As a person who spent most of junior high and high school feeling pretty out of the loop, I've always had a soft spot for black sheep of all types. Now I finally have two of my own.

But buying these ewes means I have to move from fantasy to reality. The title of a famous short story by Delmore Schwartz, "In Dreams Begin Responsibilities," comes to mind. For the past two springs we have bagged the wool shorn from the sheep I already own and piled it in a dark corner of one of the outbuildings, where it has sat, a bit forlornly, waiting for me to figure out what to do with it. Extensive internet searching turned up only befuddlement—the intricacies of processing fine wool are utterly overwhelming. Eventually I decided I couldn't do it myself, but the closest mill that would take such small quantities was hundreds of miles away, and it would have cost so much to turn the fleece to yarn that the skeins would have been worth more than yarn spun from gold.

All this should have deterred me from acquiring more fine-wool ewes. But it didn't. When Fifi and Elsa came up for sale, I jumped at the chance. Finding Shetland sheep anywhere in South Dakota is tough; I didn't know when I'd come across another opportunity. However, I promised myself that if I bought these girls, I would finally confront the pile of wool in the shed, no more putting it off.

Which brings me to the present moment. The Bean is not in the best mood. He must have more teeth coming in, as he has once again transformed from a sweet-cheeked angel baby to a young wolverine. He makes it seem that falling asleep can only be achieved by clawing one's way through a bed of brambles—a painful and time-consuming process. Meanwhile, I have this column due in a few hours. Unfortunately, I also chose today as the day to fulfill the promise I made to myself. Currently, in order to pass from one side of the house to the other, you have to weave around the hulking mass of two dirty, smelly mounds of raw wool. I lugged them in this morning during what I thought was the Bean's nap, which turned out to be a brief rest between bramble clawings. Now, as he tries to tear his way back to sleep, I try to write, but the smell of lanolin and old straw keeps interrupting my thoughts.

NOVEMBER 20, 2015

WESTERN WINTER

Outside the wind is tossing our tallest tree's branches around as if they are mere twigs. It's also picking up dirt in tiny tornadoes and hurling it against the windowpanes, so it sounds as though we're under attack by a pack of small boys armed with handfuls of gravel. I'm working in the kitchen, trying to decide if I should flick on the overhead lights. The clouds are racing across the sky at record speed, so it's dark as evening one second, then bright as midsummer the next. I clatter about as the house creaks and groans. This poor old house is so far from airtight that I can hear the glass rattling in the window frames and the pocket doors rattling in the jambs. In the next room, the Bean naps. He always sleeps best when it's windy—he must find these soaring gusts soothing.

In related news, winter is finally right around the corner. We've been waiting to say that for two months, but each new forecast has predicted yet another string of warm, gentle days. Not so this morning. This morning the Man of the Ranch says it's official—next week the temperature will be in the single digits.

I don't mind. I've claimed winter as my favorite season. Last year, when I said as much, people chalked it up to being a newlywed, half-crazy with love, but it's been true ever since moving to South Dakota nearly five years ago. Unlike in Minnesota, or the East Coast, we boast a dry cold here. Sure, the wind can cut right through a body, but it can't get in your bones the way dampness can. The creeping, wet cold of lake country is too sly a beast. I will take the bright, shouting cold of the plains every day of the week to miss even one day of the dank cold you find in a wet country.

Plus, I love the colors of winter. At dusk, the sky is layered with serene pastels that warm the gray grass to violet, lavender, and gold, and the snow to a glowing pearl white. I remember once, during the first winter I was here, watching the sun set in those glorious, delicate hues as a full moon rose on the opposite horizon. The ground around me was luminous, radiating a soft splendor that gleamed as shyly as the moon itself. I felt as though I were on a sister planet—a second moon—and no longer dwelling on the blue-green marble I'd previously inhabited.

There is also this region's winter wardrobe to consider. Last year, I wrote a column that was almost entirely devoted to my love of coveralls. You cannot imagine my excitement upon discovering that in coveralls one can reclaim her childhood—moving through the world in a bubble of warmth, undaunted by getting dirty. For example, you can slide down a snowy incline on your caboose (accidentally, or on purpose) and will be none the worse for wear. In New York City, women wear fashionable shoes and smart jackets year-round. In Minneapolis, fashionistas may sport knee-high boots and thick thigh-length coats, but there is still an eye toward what is "cool." In South Dakota, at least when it comes to daily life on the ranch, people are more sensible about dressing for the weather. What a relief!

Of course, these are the thoughts of a woman whose outdoor chores are very limited. When the Man of the Ranch is sputtering across the open pasture in a skid steer, the wind pulling the temperatures below zero, even coveralls can't keep the cold at bay. Ask him how he feels about winter, and he might tell you the luminous beauty of the moonrise is outweighed by the ache of frostbitten fingers or the worry over impending winter storms. I got a little taste of it this morning when I milked Rita, my bare hands turning stiff and icy cold instantly, despite the contact with her warm udders. After that, I was a little less excited about winter's imminent arrival. And last night, snuggled under the heaping down of our winter coverlet, I worried over the chickens, huddled in their coop. Last year, several lost bits of their combs in the first cold snap, and poor Callie the calico hen lost the tips of her scaly toes. She has to scratch for seeds with fleshy nubs now, instead of claws.

So, yes, the cold, it's real and not to be trifled with, even if it isn't of the damp-to-your-bones variety. Now we have a baby to consider as well, which also complicates my love of winter. Last night, I bundled up the Bean to drive to town for an evening event, only to discover that, in his fuzzy blue snowsuit, he was far too wide to be wedged into his car seat without the use of considerable force. He was not a fan of the procedure and made his displeasure known. I can only imagine what he would have said if he had the words at his disposal. No doubt it seemed like torture. Indeed, how strange it would be to have one's usually gentle, careful mama pulling and pushing and squeezing one's overly padded limbs between too-tight straps until no movement whatsoever was possible. The Bean tends toward the placid, but even for him it was too much. The car ride to town was punctuated by grumbles and groans from the back seat, as the poor boy tried to get free of the straitjacket that is his winter wardrobe. "We are almost there!" I kept telling him in a falsely cheerful tone . . .

Oh dear, now I am beginning to think I need to reevaluate my winter obsession. How long till spring?

DECEMBER 18, 2015

WATER FOR CHICKENS

The chickens used to have an old aluminum waterer in their coop. On winter mornings when I went to open the door, I would carry a steaming teapot to pour over the rim and loosen the ice. A few swift bangs against the side of the coop, and the ice would fly out, the waterer ready to be refilled with the rest of the cooling water from the pot. After the first winter, the waterer was no longer circular, but dented into an odd oval.

Summer was simpler, as the waterer needed only to be rinsed and refilled. Until we got Ellie the sheepdog, that is. For reasons that we cannot discern, Ellie is the thirstiest dog of all time. If she comes across open water—a muddy puddle, a small stream, or, yes, a chicken waterer—she will drink like it's going out of style. Keeping the chicken waterer full of water thus became an impossible task. Fortunately for us, the chickens are free-range, and they quickly discovered the automatic waterers in the nearby corrals. Problem solved.

Until winter came around again. If the sun is shining, the chickens will venture out, even on the most frigid of days. But if there's even a little cloud cover, they stay close to home. At dusk, when I go to close the chicken door, I might spot a few triangular tracks in the snow around the coop's perimeter, but that's it. So, water must again be packed in, or they go thirsty.

Which brings us to last week, when we had two of the foggiest days I've ever seen. The weatherman predicted a storm, and all around there seemed to be signs he was on to something. The sky was white as old bones, like it was holding the snow in its frozen fingertips, just waiting for the right moment to drop it in one giant pile. The sheep came in early from the pasture and lounged around the corral. The cats swarmed us at every chance, begging for a little extra kibble. And the chickens stayed in the coop, not leaving so much as a toe print in the thin layer of snow outside their doorstep. Our neighbor reported seeing pheasants roosting on the power lines.

"What does that mean?" I asked the Man of the Ranch.

"I don't know," he replied, "but it probably isn't good."

So, while the Bean was napping, I carried a shallow bucket of warm water out to the chickens. Though it was early afternoon, most of the flock was already roosting in the coop's roof joists, but they were happy to flap down and see what I'd brought. Kitty 2, the queen of the coop, got to the water first and, as is her custom, pecked authoritatively at the head of anyone who tried to approach. Pippa, the floppy-combed Leghorn, ran in circles making forlorn clucking sounds, but the others simply stood at a safe distance, waiting. I figured Kitty 2 would get her fill, then let her flock mates have a turn. I watched for a few minutes as Kitty 2 dipped her narrow beak into the bucket, then threw her feathered cheeks back and gurgled down the few drops she had collected, never once straying from her post.

The other hens started to lose hope. Coco and Chanel, the two Barred Rock hens, were the first to fly back up to roost. They are usually Kitty 2's interchangeable sidekicks, but not today. Red Molly, the biggest hen, gave up next. The others followed a few at a time until, finally, the only hen left was poor Pippa, still squawking and circling.

Meanwhile, the bucket remained pretty much full. Kitty 2 was no longer drinking, yet she stood vigilantly beside the bucket. The impending storm, it seemed, had turned her into a crazed water hoarder.

It all got me thinking about the sermon from last Sunday. The readings for the week included a verse in which John the Baptist exhorts the crowds who have come to hear him speak: "Anyone who has two coats should share with the one who has none. Anyone with food should do the same." This verse really struck me because it is not asking you to give away your only coat, to go without warmth in a cold season, but simply asking that you share what you have if you have more than you need.

On the drive home after church, I couldn't help but think of the closet by the front door, so jammed with coats the rod is bowed in the middle. There are fancy leather jackets, manure-spattered canvas parkas, knit coats, woolen coats, and the coats of deceased relatives that are either five sizes too big or two sizes too small. All in all, that closet probably has thirty coats in it.

Many of the coats haven't been touched in years. I've given a few away, but I can't bring myself to part with more. What if we have visitors? What if one of our coats gets ripped or ruined beyond repair? What if we need those coats someday? So, we have thirty coats for three people and Kitty 2 has a whole bucket of water to herself while her friends go thirsty. By morning that bucket would be frozen—making it impossible for anyone to drink—and my closet would still be full of coats that rarely get worn.

I went to the barn and got another plastic dish to fill with water. All across the globe, people have set out tiny replicas of a barn, open on one side. In it kneel a man and a woman, perhaps some shepherds, and three men in elaborate gowns. They are looking at a tiny naked newborn baby. A baby who grows up to tell all who will listen, "If you help one another, if you give of yourselves, and don't take more than you need, I promise, there will be enough."

Back at the coop, I set down the second dish of water. Kitty 2 was torn between her impulse to guard the first water bucket and her desire to survey the new item I had introduced. The other hens fluttered down again and, dodging between Kitty 2's divided attentions, were able to grab a few quick drinks before ascending to their roosts one final time. Kitty 2 relented at last and climbed up to join them.

Just then Ellie rushed in and lapped up the rest of the water with great gusto. I had to chuckle. All that time Kitty 2 spent guarding the water from her friends because she was worried there wouldn't be enough? In the end, she would have lost it anyway—even a hen as tough as Kitty 2 is no match for a sheepdog.

I walked back to the house, Ellie bounding beside me. The sky still held the snow. Long after dark, it will finally let go, covering the prairie in a thick blanket that will last until the next thaw, when some of the snow will sink into the earth, collecting underground, waiting for spring so it can be reborn as the grasses and the wildflowers. Some of it will linger in dams and move on to become rivers. Some of it will float back up into the air, gathered by another set of clouds and carried away. And some of it just might trickle into an automatic waterer by a little pasture on the prairie, where a naughty brown hen named Kitty 2 will drink it up, even though she doesn't deserve it.

DECEMBER 28, 2015

WINTERING

We wake up, and the bedroom is dim and gray, the light playing like a hushed lullaby. It's after seven, but the sun is only barely peeking above the horizon, and since our bedroom is on the western side of the house, the light is so soft it could still be moonlight—nothing at all like the garish morning light of midsummer. The Man of the Ranch gets up and pulls on long johns and insulated jeans, a long sleeve T-shirt, a sweatshirt, and thick woolen socks. First light means time for chores.

It is rare these days for us to set the alarm clock; dawn is the wake-up call most mornings. The winter solstice—the shortest day of the year—is past, but we don't notice the difference yet. It still feels like we get to sleep in every day. The Man of the Ranch jokes that the days are so short he has to start evening chores as soon as he finishes the morning ones, and he isn't exaggerating much. He gets up and makes coffee, while I dress the baby and make breakfast. He heads out to grain the calves, and the baby and I settle into our own little rituals; I tidy while he plays. Before long it is time for his morning nap.

The shadows are already leaning and blue, pulling against the snow, as we eat our midday meal. I wipe the dishes, put the red stock pot on the stove to simmer, and lay the Bean down for another nap. In the west, the horizon begins to glow, striking the trees in the yard with its fire. The branches turn to flames, red fingers of late afternoon light reaching out of the blue snow. Beneath the trees, the barn cats chase one another, rolling across the yard while they wait for their dinner, and the chickens fly up to roost in the coop. I can hear Rita calling from the corral. She is hoping for a pan of cake. Inside, the soup pot is gently roiling, the bread dough has risen. It won't be long and we'll be ready to eat, too.

We don't eat our supper until after dark. In June and July, when one day lasts forever, we often find our heads nodding over our plates when we finally sit down to an evening meal. In the winter, we eat our supper and still have hours before bedtime. It is an odd sensation to know the day's work is done and we still have time left to do as we please.

Five years ago, before I came to South Dakota, I lamented the shortness of the winter days. Like many people I missed the light. Leaving a windowless building midafternoon, it was a shock to discover the darkness was already chasing the sun away. City life doesn't change with the seasons, so day in and day out, in darkness or in sunlight, the work of a day progresses pretty much the same. Now, I revel in the short days as a cozy respite from the hustle of summer. It's a chance to catch up on reading and knitting and resting.

There is something else about it, too, that I can't quite put my finger on. Something soothing about the routine of seasonal living. There is a balance to my life here, and I like the sensation of being a pendulum passing back and forth between so much light and so little. It is reassuring to be carried along by such an ancient pattern.

This year we celebrated the solstice for the first time by making a bonfire and roasting marshmallows in the early evening. Some people hold these celebrations to welcome back the light, but for me, it was a celebration of the darkness and the quiet of these short, dark days. This summer, when the days are endless, we will probably do the same in reverse.

The poet Kahlil Gibran wrote, "Your joy is your sorrow unmasked. And the selfsame well from which your laughter rises was oftentimes filled with your tears. And how else can it be? The deeper that sorrow carves into your being, the more joy you can contain."[1] So it is with the seasons. How much easier it is to rise up singing with the birds in the summer, when you have lain curled and cozy through the long nights of winter, the whole prairie silent and sleeping.

5¢
FAIRY
SOAP
HAVE YOU A LITTLE FAIRY
IN YOUR HOME ?

2016

JANUARY 6, 2016

EMOTIONAL AFFAIR

When Rita, my beloved Jersey, arrived on the ranch, we didn't know anything about her history, including whether she had been previously hand-milked. I was therefore overjoyed when she let me give it a try without a problem. Rita was the only cow I had ever milked, so I had nothing to compare her to, but it didn't take any expert to see she was making it easy for me. She happily munched cake and hay while I leaned my head on her smooth brown flank and went to work. If she kicked, it was at flies, and it was half-hearted and slow—easy to avoid. I've written about this before, but it really felt like a revelation to get milk straight from the source. What a thrill!

That first spring I got quart jars full of sweet, fresh milk for our table, and Rita raised a second calf too. I made yogurt, cheese, and butter and still had cream left over for my coffee. Rita was earning her keep and then some. I couldn't imagine why everyone didn't keep a dairy cow. I milked on and off through the summer and fall, letting the calves pick up the slack if we went out in the evening, or if the fridge was too full. I hoped it was the beginning of a long and beautiful friendship.

Then we preg-checked, and Rita came up open. I was devastated.

I was thankful our story didn't have to end there. We ran her with the bulls all through the winter and spring, and in September she gave birth to an itty-bitty red bull calf. Rita's first baby, Ruthie, was stout and black like her Angus papa. Other than a certain Jersey curve to her nose, Ruthie didn't at all resemble her skinny milk cow mother. An excellent quality, the Man of the Ranch would say. Rita's new calf, however, was as scrawny as they come. His hip bones were whittled so sharp they looked dangerous, and all the rich milk Rita had to offer couldn't change that. Unlike Ruthie, who had a bright, useful future as a nurse cow, Rita's new baby had no marketable skills. It was hard not to feel sorry for the little guy even though the only thing wrong with him was his Jersey genes.

There was also the downside of Rita calving out of season. Putting another calf with Rita made a little extra money and also allowed me to be a part-time milker. But, while there are bum calves on every corner in the spring, finding one in the fall could be a challenge. Which was how we ended up with what might be the ugliest calf of all time. Born to a yearling who'd accidentally gotten pregnant, and therefore didn't have enough milk, the poor thing arrived at the ranch even skinnier than Rita's calf. His breeding was a mystery, but the little fellow sported a coat that fell somewhere between mottled brown and mustard yellow. It rose over his bony rib cage in odd, curling tufts as though some of his hair wanted to grow but the rest couldn't muster the courage. Both calves walked like their legs were recently-acquired stilts, and standing side by side, they were about as sorry a sight as I had ever seen.

The yearling's looks weren't the only problem. The first time around, it had taken no more than a few days for Rita to soften to a second baby. Her kicks at the little orphan had been as slow and half-hearted as her kicks at the flies, and before long she had let the little one nurse as if it were her own. During Rita's yearlong vacation, however, my once mild-mannered gal developed an ornery streak. All summer, she terrorized the bottle calves and bullied the other nurse cows. Finally, we had to put her in with the sheep, where she ruled with an iron hoof, the flock giving her a wide berth.

So, I guess we shouldn't have been surprised when she wasn't interested in taking on a second calf. Every morning and evening we would put her in the head catch with cake and hay, then sneak the new calf in for a drink. "Thwack!" her hoof would crack against his skull as he tried again and again to steal a few sips. I wondered if it would be possible to fit the poor guy with protective headgear, and even the Man of the Ranch, who is much tougher than I am, seemed a little worried.

Thankfully, that calf was a fighter, and after a few weeks he got wise to Rita's ways. By sneaking in just beside her baby, he discovered he could fill his belly without suffering cranial damage, and the head catch was no longer necessary. He even started to fatten up a little, though his adopted brother continued to look as starved as ever.

Meanwhile, things were going better for me. Rita still stood quietly when I milked, just as she had that first spring.

Until last week.

Two mornings in a row she was great about going into the stanchion and then a stinker once she got there. I tried to ignore her naughtiness, milking the best I could while she kicked and shuffled and mooed loudly. On the third morning, Rita was making such a fuss that the sheep figured they had better come over to investigate. They gathered on the other side of the gate, poking their woolly noses in, adding their inquisitive "baas" to Rita's angry lowing. As soon as they realized Rita had a pan of cake, their cries grew agitated, and all eleven began to shove and bicker, thrusting their whole heads through the metal piping to register their displeasure. The calves, who were also waiting on the other side of the gate, bucked and cried too. They were hungry, and they didn't see why I should be taking what was rightfully theirs. Several barn cats who usually gather at my heels while I milk turned away disgusted. "Get a handle on your herd!" they seemed to be saying as they slunk off.

Over my head the sky was aglow with rose and lavender clouds, the wind carrying them with its softly whispering breath. It was a beautiful morning. Exactly the kind of morning that usually makes milking a pleasure, not a chore. I tried to ignore the racket and focus on the beauty, but it wasn't easy.

"Hiss, sloosh, hiss, sloosh." With every pull on her udder, Rita lifted her manure-encrusted hoof to kick me away, and nearly as much milk was splashing to the ground as was ending up in the milk jar. I gritted my teeth, my head bowed down. I wasn't about to let her get the best of me. But beneath my feet the ground was slick with ice and frozen cow piles, and despite my thick-soled boots, I was having trouble keeping my footing.

Suddenly, Rita shifted her weight, no doubt to kick me more effectively. I tried to shift as well but slipped instead, sliding well within stomping range, my head just missing the metal gate. Rita turned to glare at me between the wood slats that confined her, while the sheep laughed at my misfortune. I scrambled to my feet, still holding what was left of my milk. With less than a pint, I decided to call it quits. After all, Rita outweighs me by about 1,000 percent. I walked back to the house defeated while the calves drank up my butter, yogurt, and ice cream.

Later that night I found myself looking longingly at pictures on a website called "South Dakota Livestock for Sale." On the site there was a Jersey listed, who was described as "docile" and "loves attention!" In photographs posted with the description, the cow mugged for the camera, flashing big chocolate-brown eyes. One shot featured her owner effortlessly milking her. In another, she had scaled the steps of a front porch and was peeking impishly into the house.

Of course, now I can't stop thinking about this cow. I've revisited the website more than I care to admit, just to stare at those pictures . . . I didn't know it was possible, but I think I am having an emotional affair with someone else's Jersey. Still, I hope that Rita and I can work it out—I don't want to break up.

Apparently, she doesn't feel the same way. The Man of the Ranch just came in to tell me she busted through the fence last night and took off, her two babies in tow. She is out in the big pasture with the other cows now. Perhaps she thinks we need space to sort through our issues?

For now, I guess I will be eating my toast dry and drinking my coffee black. And, I guess I now have one explanation for why not everyone keeps a Jersey around.

I hate to admit it, but the dairy section at the grocery store is looking better and better . . . .

JANUARY 18, 2016

CLEANING THE COOP

My first hatching of chickens lived in a coop built by a young friend and his father for the boy's first flock. It was built tall and sturdy, and the boy emblazoned the rough outer walls of the coop with bright blue letters, spelling out each of his chicken's names, as well as the coop's name: "Poultry Palace."

I felt very lucky to inherit a coop that was well-appointed, well-designed, and well-loved. Every morning and every night, I would open and close the coop's narrow door for my flock and think of the little hands that helped place the square hinges and by-then rusty latch. Once inside, the roosting ledge divided the back quarter of the coop from the front to form a box. I could stand upright, but I could take little more than one step in any direction. I would fill the box with fresh hay once a month or so, tossing the old hay in the compost pile. The two nesting boxes in the eaves of the coop were similarly easy to clean. It was the work of an hour at most. All in all, the coop was the perfect home to start off my adventures in chicken rearing.

These days, my chickens have a whole outbuilding all to themselves, with five spacious nesting boxes and a dozen wood rafters on which to roost. They even have a green square of fiberglass that serves as a window and the giant fiberglass garage door on the front of the building to let in light. There is also plenty of floor space to scratch, so on the coldest days we can keep the whole place buttoned up, and they still have room to range a bit. The new coop isn't as cozy as the old coop was, but on the whole it has made winter less miserable for them, and I no longer worry about them suffocating from heatstroke in the dog days of summer.

This bigger coop required some adjustments in my cleaning regimen, though. A monthly cleaning was no longer feasible, so the job became seasonal instead. I quickly discovered that a good time to clean a big chicken coop is in the spring. A warmish, breezy day is perfect, as it cuts down somewhat on the smelliness of the task. Fall is also not a bad time for the same reason, which is why most people clean their coops in the spring and fall.

When I say "most people," I mean me, at least the first year the big coop was in use. This past spring, however, we were anxiously awaiting the arrival of our little Bean, and somehow coop cleaning just didn't make the to-do list in time. The chickens had the run of the ranch from dawn till dusk, only using the coop for a few hours of shut-eye at night. Plus, the big door was open all day, giving the place plenty of time to air out. I felt a little guilty about not making the chickens' home a priority, but maybe not as guilty as I should have been. Once the baby was born, all thought of the chickens faded from my mind, until fall came along with its crisp mornings and early evenings. The chickens, by necessity, started spending more time inside, and I knew I needed to do something about the coop.

Now, I'm usually quite cavalier about germs. I think there is such a thing as being too clean, and good old-fashioned dirt makes a body stronger. But even I will admit that chickens are the bad kind of dirty, so I didn't relish the idea of cleaning a year's worth of chicken manure with my tiny newborn baby anywhere nearby. And, as fall is the Man of the Ranch's busiest time (if you want to see him during daylight you'll have to head out to the pasture or stop by the sale barn) it was either clean the coop by flashlight or bring the baby along.

I mentioned my conundrum to a friend who also keeps chickens. "We don't clean our coop in the fall," she said. "The manure keeps the coop warmer." Well, that was all I needed to hear to move coop cleaning off the to-do list once again.

That is, until last week, when I finally admitted to myself it had officially gone too far. The coop had to be cleaned.

Which is how, on the coldest day of winter so far, I found myself standing pitchfork in hand and boots deep in chicken poop.

I'll spare you the grimy details and skip straight to the plot twist: it felt awesome. After I had spent two weeks of being mostly housebound, the sharp blades of wind on my face blew a little color back into my cheeks and a little of the fog of sleep deprivation out of my brain. Bundled in coveralls, a flannel coat, two hats, and thick work gloves, I wasn't a bit cold. In fact, a few forkfuls in and I was sweating. The air was so clear I could see past the first and second pastures, past the highway, all the way to the neighbor's ridge a few miles south, the sky that lined the ridge a perfect robin's-egg blue, the lemony-yellow sun streaming down in bright beams. And the hens, skittering around my feet, were giddy at the prospect of having things freshened up.

Their gay chatter was infectious. Before long the barn cats, never wanting to miss out on a party, joined us, alternately lounging and skulking, and sniffing the new hay as I unrolled it. The half-grown kittens tumbled and pounced on the feathers gathered in the coop's corners, while the hens scratched and pecked. I had brought two pockets full of cracked corn to toss out for a treat, and every time I scattered some kernels, cats and chickens would scurry to investigate. One sniff and the chickens would begin clucking with delight, while the cats turned away in disgust.

The afternoon passed quickly. When the job was done, I stretched my arms, fingers spread wide, and let out my own cluck of delight. As I walked back to the house, the sun began to warm the sky to its evening shades of salmon and rose, the first fingers of purple appearing on the eastern horizon.

Is anything the whole world round more beautiful than winter dusk in western South Dakota? And there I was, right in the middle of the show. I stopped once more to open my arms to it, the beauty of the cold resting upon the vast, sweeping face of the prairie.

Then I stepped through the front door to a cheerful fire, a wonderful husband, and a smiling baby. I shucked off my boots, and coveralls, my two hats, and thick gloves, and hugged them both. "How was it?" asked the Man of the Ranch.

"It was wonderful!" I said. I hugged them both again.

I think the moral of the story is this—and I've written it before, but it bears repeating—we are lucky to live here, in this land where beauty is so commonplace. Even amid the dirtiest jobs, we are surrounded by splendor.

Also, it is a privilege to spend so much time with my baby, to watch him grow and learn, to be his constant companion, to witness him discover the world and all its everyday miracles. But, when cleaning a chicken coop in subzero weather feels like a mini-vacation? Well, I guess that speaks for itself in saying I might need a little more time to myself. Needless to say, it is a strange sensation to be thankful to have a big chicken coop to clean!

FEBRUARY 18, 2016

ALWAYS CLOSE THE GATE

Now that lambing is upon us, I've been going out to check the ewes a few times every day. Anyone who bears the signs of impending motherhood gets brought into the small corral that borders my little pasture, where we can watch them more closely and get them into the barn easily at night. The first to look really ready was Twigs, the ewe who came to me as a bum lamb two years ago. Even now, Twigs has the long, skinny legs of Twiggy, the famous supermodel from the '60s after whom she was named. She has never been a "people" sheep, so we also brought in Malka, her best friend, to keep her company. After nearly a week of waiting, I went into the barn one bright morning to discover a bleating, still slightly damp baby lying in the hay. But it wasn't Twigs's baby. It was Malka who had given birth to the first lamb of the season, sometime just after dawn.

I guess I shouldn't have been surprised when, despite my best efforts, the next baby wasn't born in the barn at all. I had kept an eye out for anyone who might be close and had even brought a third ewe, Meri, into the little corral. But this morning, the Man of the Ranch came in from chores to deliver the news: Violet had lambed outside during the night. The baby seemed fine, and he had moved the newest family to the barn and out of the wind but hadn't had time to do much else. With that he left in a hurry, a long day at the sale barn ahead of him.

I gave a sigh. This news was not great for morale, but I figured all's well that ends well. I finished feeding the Bean and got him bundled up to head out to the barn.

Here's a little side note about the Bean: The Bean comes from prairie stock. He's already ten times tougher than I am and he seems determined to outweigh me before his third birthday. That is because I, on the other hand, do not come from prairie stock. I'm small-framed, with no discernible upper body strength. You would not want me as your hired hand. Still, when we have things that need to get done, I strap my big baby to my back, and off we go. Slowly.

The Man of the Ranch had left Violet and her baby in the front of the barn, while Meri and Twigs, plus Malka and her lamb, remained in the back. So, our first job was to open the back door, let the girls out, then move Violet into their spot. We got that done easily enough. Next, we needed to fork up a wheelbarrow of ground hay, fill up a bucket with water, and pour out a little bit of grain for the new mama. The grain we got done easily too, but the rest of the chores proved more difficult. For starters, the wind was blowing about one million miles an hour, leaving most of the hay to be delivered to our neighbor a few miles to the east, instead of ending up in the wheelbarrow. The Bean and I persevered, and with a mostly full wheelbarrow, began our plodding, creaky return to the barn.

Another side note: There are two gates between the hay pile and the barn, and both gates are latched by long, jangly chains. As we passed though said gates, ground hay flying every which way, I decided to swing them closed, but I did not loop the chains over and into their catches. Perhaps you can guess where this is going?

If not, let's take a break for some trivia . . .

> Q: What is the first rule of ranching?
>
> A: If you open a gate, close it.
>
> Q: What is the second rule of ranching?
>
> A: If a gate is open, (insert name of animal you are trying to contain) will find it.

They make these rules for a reason, but I thought I could break them because the gates were not visible, in fact, were not even on the same side of the barn as the hay feeder, where I knew Meri, Twigs, and Malka were gathered. I waddled my way through the gates and delivered the ground hay to Violet, who gave a tired but thankful sigh as she dug right in. The Bean and I took a moment to appreciate the happy scene, the new lamb nestled under her mama enjoying a few sips of warm milk. Then we exited the barn, water bucket in hand.

This is when I really should have closed the gates, but still I didn't. I could see three hungry ewes, plus one fuzzy lamb, gathered at the feeder, heads buried neck-deep, so I walked over to the waterer with my bucket instead, only to discover it was frozen solid. Trying to crack the ice with my boot required some maneuvering, what with that baby strapped to my back, and even when I did get myself balanced, I discovered I was too short to get enough leverage to break the thick crust of ice. I tried the edge of the bucket next, which bounced helplessly, not making so much as a chip in the ice's surface. Perhaps noticing my consternation, or maybe just hoping for a drink herself, Malka tiptoed up to me, her little baby toddling behind. Malka is a smallish ewe with a dark face and soulful, sympathetic eyes. "You are doing a good job," her eyes said as she approached.

"Thanks, Malka," I said, giving her woolly forehead a scratch.

This is when I noticed Meri and Twigs were no longer standing at the feeder. "No, no, no, no, no . . ." I started muttering, walking as fast as I could to the edge of the barn. Maybe they were just on the other side.

But they weren't. The two gates stood wide open, their long chains listlessly hanging. Beyond the gates, I could see Meri and Twigs gleefully trotting through the side yard. And what were they trotting toward? The giant bag of grain sitting beside the calves' pen, of course.

"No!" I shouted as I thumped after them (finally shutting the gate behind me, to Malka's dismay). If they got their heads in the grain bag, I knew there would be no getting them away from it.

Now, these ewes and I are old, dear friends, and I visit often to pass out head pats and treats, so it probably was very surprising to see me running up, shouting and flapping my arms wildly. Meri noticed me first and stopped to regard me with concern. Twigs, on the other hand, was nearly to the grain and took no notice whatsoever. "*No no no no no no!*" I shouted again, in my best Man of the Ranch impression (they take him quite a bit more seriously). This did the trick, and both ewes ran past the grain, thoroughly startled.

At a time like this, one can't help but wish for a trusty shepherding dog, and as if by magic, Ellie, my Great Pyrenees, materialized out of nowhere barking and loping toward Meri and Twigs. For one brief, shining moment, it actually appeared she would herd them back toward me and the barn, but at the last second she veered between the two frightened ewes, splitting them up, so that one ran east and the other west.

I sometimes complain to the Man of the Ranch that since the baby came, I can't get out and about as much, and I don't get enough exercise anymore. Today, that was not an issue, as I ran up and down the curved road beside the corrals, doing my best Border Collie impression, the Bean bouncing behind me all the while. When I finally managed to round up the ewes and get them back through the gate, we were all pretty winded. They returned to their hay feeder, and I returned to the house only a little worse for wear. And, I must admit, feeling victorious as well.

If I just remember to keep the gates closed, I might not make such a bad hired hand after all.

FEBRUARY 22, 2016

FEBRUARY THAW

It's windy today, but warm. There wasn't even frost on the ground at dawn. It's not the kind of weather you'd expect for February, that's for sure, and I feel like a time traveler, confused as to where I've landed. Last night it rained and rained, turning the yard into creeks and rivers, and the little corral into a lake, so now the wind smells damp with a hint of green, like spring is right around the corner. Even the raised garden patch outside the kitchen window is confused—overnight it sprouted a few inches of bright, emerald crabgrass, and it is wearing the small thicket like a crown.

It's a weird quirk of memory that makes every September remind me of being a little kid. With the first hint of winter in the wind, I'm transported to the brick and linoleum hallways of my elementary school, the squeak of new school shoes echoing down the corridors, the smell of chalk dust and books, and the bulletin boards beaming bright patterns and teeming with construction paper leaves. Fall is excitement and apprehension, bittersweet because it also means the loss of summer's open hours, the leisure to spend whole days watching ants colonize a crust of bread.

Spring, on the other hand, reminds me of my twenties. It reminds me of eating a pastrami sandwich on a wooden park bench in New York City. It reminds me of wearing only shirtsleeves for the first time in months, dappled sunlight cascading through the shifting buds of the sweet gum trees. It reminds me of walking by the Hudson River on Sunday afternoons, everyone else out walking too. Skinny ladies speeding by with their fluffy dogs, old folks who know the virtue of taking it slower, couples too delighted with each other and the weather to notice the blossoms of the stubby crabapple trees sprouting out of cement planters. Spring means everything is possible. We are no longer weighed down by coats and mufflers, thick boots and socks. We can step freely into the day, unencumbered.

I am thinking of this feeling as the Bean and I, wearing only our sweaters, go out to check the sheep. It doesn't matter that this is just a thaw and not really spring. It is giving me that feeling of endless possibility anyway. We slog through the corral lake, my boots slurping as the mud tries to suck them off my feet. We've had five lambs born in the past three days, two sets of twins and a single, each born onto ground so sun-kissed it might be late April. Those babies don't know what deep, bitter cold feels like yet, but their mamas do. The ewes spread across the high ground in the big corral like sunbathers at the beach, while the babies leap and chase each other nearby.

Last night at midnight, the wind blew as hard as I've ever heard it, and then, when it began to rain, it blew even harder. After a few minutes the rain turned to fat plops of snow mixed with tiny pellets of ice, and the sound of it slapping against the windowpanes woke me. All I could think about were my lambs, two of which were barely twenty-four hours old, standing out in that weather—the evening had been so mild it seemed silly to lock them up in the barn. I slid out from under the warm blanket and went to stand by the window. The tree branches were lurching and circling with the gusts; the rain and snow was falling sideways. I thought of trying to move the ewes across the corral, the wind screaming around us. There was the possibility interfering might make things worse. Plus, there wasn't room for everyone in the barn, so I'd only be able to take the five youngest lambs and their mothers. The idea of leaving some, and rescuing others, made me want to quit before I had even begun.

I decided I had to try. And I succeeded. An hour later, plastered head to boot tips in splattered sleet and mud, my heart pounding like a drum, my skin prickling with adrenaline, I had successfully herded three ewes and five lambs into that barn, as cozy as it was possible for eight very wet sheep to be. I stood for a moment and watched them sort themselves out. "Are you my mama? Are you?" I thought of my own baby, sleeping soundly, as I crossed over the yard, the wind blasting its icy breath in my face, its wet fingers clawing their way inside the hood and sleeves of my slicker. I looked over the fence to the three babies, only a few days older than the ones I'd just rescued, lying beside their mothers. They closed their eyes against the beam of my flashlight, their eyelashes already heavy with ice. It would not be a cozy night for them.

Back at the house I shucked off my coveralls and raincoat and left them dripping in the hall. I crawled into bed, but I couldn't fall asleep. I lay there for more than an hour feeling exhilarated and terrified. If the storm raged on, if the temperature dropped, when morning came, I knew I'd find five happy, healthy lambs inside the barn. I didn't know what I'd find outside it, but I had done the best I could. Lying awake in the dark, I folded my hands over my chest and hoped my best was good enough.

Today, the Bean and I stop at the fence. He is riding in his back carrier as usual, and I turn to the side so that he can see everyone too. I let the littlest lambs out at first light, before the Bean was even awake. Now, all the lambs are running together like clouds racing across the sky, and the Bean is laughing at them as they skitter-skatter past us. He slaps his chubby palm against my shoulder and tugs my braid.

I wonder what I'll remember when, someday in the future, I think back to this first year of motherhood. I hope it will remind me of lambing in a February thaw: the anticipation, exhaustion, joy, a lot of hard work, some fear, the knowledge that I did the best I could, and my gratitude that it was good enough.

MAY 23, 2016

THE BEST OF BOTH WORLDS

It has been a strange spring. It seemed we had April in February, and February in May, with March sandwiched between them, simply shaking its head, unsure what to do. It's made gardening a challenge, that's for sure. Friends who followed the old advice to plant their potatoes on Good Friday complain that they rotted in the ground and are starting over. I'm always late to the garden party, which in light of a freeze just last week seems a blessing; but yesterday, when I finally set aside some time to continue transplanting (some of the plants I started indoors have gotten so leggy they look ready to walk to the garden themselves) the wind blew and blew and blew, leaving the few plants I'd put in earlier flat and bedraggled.

Then this morning, we woke up to a mist so thick you could barely see the trees rooted a few feet from our bedroom windows. By nine o'clock the sun had burned off the haze, and now the air is oozing and humid, shimmering with heat. It feels tropical, or as if there is a lake somewhere nearby, and it's all I can do not to put on a swimsuit and go hunting for it. No doubt if I did find a lake, it would be as cold as ice, seeing as less than two weeks ago there was snow on the ground.

The days are getting long. Even without the heat, that's a sure sign of the season. By 5:00 a.m. the whole prairie is bathed in full dawn, and it's after 8:00 p.m. before it begins to fade again. In only one more month, it will be the longest day of the year, the first day of summer. Today's heat makes it seem like we are already there, and I can't wait. This year I am more excited for summer's arrival than I have been since I was a kid, and here's why: before I became a parent, I thought having children of my own would mean a second chance at experiencing some of the pleasures of childhood. Chalk drawing on the sidewalk, splashing in the creek, collecting pocketsful of interesting rocks, and watching ant hills while pretending to be a giant—all things that would be quite peculiar for a childless adult to do (and honestly, really don't hold the same appeal they once did). But involve a child in these activities, and it's hard not to catch the spark of enthusiasm. Since the Bean is still a baby, I didn't expect the fun, or rather the anticipation of fun, to start so soon, but it has.

Of course, when you live in a state where winter sometimes claims more than half the year, how could you not get excited for summer? But this year it feels different.

It started a few days ago when I was putting the Bean to bed. His bedtime hasn't changed, so now when I lie down with him in the evenings, the sun is still glowing merrily above the western horizon and the birds are still chatting cozily in the windbreak. It's just exactly as I remember it from my own early years: that going to bed while it's still light feeling, the heavy sweetness of lilacs wafting in through the open window, time slowing down a bit while you lie there.

I grew up sleeping by the window, too, at least part of the year. In the winter, my parents moved my bed to an interior wall to avoid drafts, but as soon as the warm weather hit, they'd let me scoot it back to its home beneath the window. I remember listening to bird conversations as the evening deepened, their casual cadences washing over me as I drew closer to sleep.

Now I lie beside the Bean while he wiggles and sighs, trying to get comfortable, and it washes over me again, like a delicious sip of childhood. In the windbreak the trees rustle, singing their own song. Some evenings when the wind comes up, it sounds like the ocean, other nights it's just a gentle ruffling. As it gets darker, the Bean's eyes get heavier, and by the time the bedroom fills with the last of the sun's deep amber light, he's usually asleep.

I tuck him in his own little bed and sneak out. And that is the best part—I now get to enjoy both worlds. The pleasure of a quiet twilight, the company of birds and wind and your own drifting dreams, then "grown-up time," usually spent watching a television show that, just as my parents used to watch, is "not appropriate for children." The Man of the Ranch and I relax, enjoying the long slide into night, and when I go to shut the chicken coop before bed, I count the stars that poke through blackness as if each one were an old friend.

And this is just the beginning. There is so much to look forward to in the weeks ahead. Perhaps tomorrow we'll build a fort on the patio with lawn chairs and an old sheet, or maybe we'll drag the plastic baby tub outside to splash around on the grass. Who knows? It's summer vacation, after all, with hours and hours of bright day to fill with adventures big and small.

JULY 16, 2016

A HARD RAIN

Every night for weeks we've watered the garden. In just twenty-four hours the soil dries completely, even beneath the protective layers of mulch. Water from the hose pools around the twisting stems of the shell peas and green beans, but the puddles don't last long. The earth drinks the water down in seconds, leaving the surface nearly as dry as when we started. None of the seeds I laid down weeks ago will germinate. Even with a daily watering, the soil is just too dry. There are wide gaps between the potatoes and tomatoes where the carrots and summer squash ought to be. Instead, those bare spots are the site of our battle with the Creeping Jenny—it has no trouble spreading in the sultry weather. Up and down the rows we go, hoes in hand, only to find a fresh tangle of vines the following day.

Meanwhile, outside the garden fence, the dirt is thirsty. It seems like it gets a little hotter every day, and the wind won't stop blowing. We already know there won't be any hay this year. In the hayfield, the alfalfa is low to the ground and straggly, the grass dust-colored and sharp. When I go to lead the milk cow in from the north pasture, the few strands of yellow grass that are still standing above the tangle of roots and dead plants scrape my bare legs till they bleed. The wildflowers are just stems now, too tired and burnt to send up new petals. The prairie buzzes with flies, the only sound for miles. Along the highway, mule deer and antelope gather in the road ditch, the last place they can find a few bites of fresh foliage.

It's not a drought yet, but we're getting there. Every morning the Man of the Ranch checks the radar, and he doesn't stop checking it all day long. He sets up a sprinkler over one tiny patch of the yard, so the Bean has a place to play that won't be covered in the tiny daggered husks of dry grass. The rest of the yard is long dead. At the feed store they talk about the weather, and the talk is always the same. For most of the ranchers in our area, it looks like a tough road ahead. The usually quiet summer sales at the sale barn are getting busier—if there isn't grass to last the summer, the time to sell is now. A few miles south of us, there's talk of "the garden of Eden," an area where the alfalfa is waist-high and full of fist-sized purple blooms, the air still fresh and sweet. But that's the exception; every stingy storm cloud that has passed over the rest of us must have lingered over them.

Then, yesterday morning, it rained. A soft, golden rain, barely strong enough to mute the stinging blue of the sky. The night before, it rained too. In five minutes, half an inch fell, plummeting from clouds that were sinister and humped. As they traveled east those clouds dropped fat balls of hail and tore the doors off barns. Here, we heard howling in the distance and looked across the pasture and worried, but the worst of it passed us. Still, all that rain was gone before darkness even fell, not enough to get anything growing again.

So, we keep praying for rain, but not those soft rains that turn into steam heat before they even hit the ground. And not the rain that hardens to ice in the cloud, crushing the grass and tearing the leaves from trees. We pray for steadfast, even rain that falls and falls and falls, patting the dust back into the soil, seeping all the way down to nourish the deep roots of the grasses and flowers, a salve for the parched cracks that are hip deep along the canyon ridges. We pray for a rain that will transform gently, without destroying. It's a lot to ask for in this part of the country.

A few more days pass. The wind keeps blowing, and the temperature keeps rising. A dear friend has a birthday party by the lake, and everyone can go because no one is busy haying. We pull up to the celebration a little before five o'clock in the evening, and the thermometer in the pickup reads 101 degrees. We are in bathing suits, and we head to the water, sweating like we're in an oven and not on a beach. The Bean's cheeks are poppy red, and he looks a little wilted until we plop him in the water to float in his inner tube. The rest of us splash and dive while over our heads, clouds begin to pull across the lake, thin and white at first, then silver-gray, then charcoal with brushstrokes of navy blue. "Time to get out!" someone shouts. They've seen lightning high in the clouds.

Back at the cabin, people begin to gather under an awning as the first drops splash down. A minute passes, and the drops fall harder. A few more folks join the growing crowd of those who've ducked for cover. When it really starts to rain, the last holdouts scurry under, already soaked to the skin. Everyone stands shoulder to shoulder, while kids huddle down by their parents' knees. The Bean looks around wide-eyed; he can't remember when he has seen this many people so close together. We wait for it to pass. And wait. And wait. The wind picks up, splattering with water the backs of those standing at the edges of the awning. The temperature is dropping. No one feels hot anymore. "There's plenty of room inside," someone says, "and the food is ready!" Together, the crowd moves across the deck, whooping and laughing.

We pile our plates high with roasted pork, pasta salad, baked beans, coleslaw, and pickled watermelon. Grandmas bounce babies on their knees, the small fry run wild, and when we run out of chairs, folks set their plates down and eat on the floor. The rain falls and falls, while people go back for seconds and thirds.

The rain and the party show no signs of slowing as the cake is cut. Everyone is full and sighing, the babies are getting sleepy, the kids are gathered in corners to eat their cake. "Well," the birthday boy, a fellow rancher, says, "rain was what I wanted for my birthday, so I got just what I asked for."

When we get home later that night, we find the Bean's new blue kiddie pool lifted off the patio and carried a hundred feet across the yard. The ranch sign lies on the ground, broken in half, and my potted plants are tipped over, spilling dirt and blossoms on the cement. But we don't mind because the puddles last all night and through the next day, a cool drink in a dry land.

AUGUST 22, 2016

SPINNING WOOL

When we were kids, my brother always wanted to play army and I always wanted to play pioneer family. It is funny how things work out—my brother has been employed by the U.S. Army his entire adult life, and I live in a house built by a pioneer family. And though I am by no means living the life of a pioneer, I get to brush up against it with some regularity. So, several months ago, when I was asked to participate in a Women Homesteaders event, celebrating the skills of early homesteaders with hands-on demonstrations, I was all in. I knew right away what skill I wanted to share—working with wool.

It was kind of sneaky, really. You see, I've been knitting off and on for over a decade, keeping sheep for almost half that long now, and, for the past few years at least, reading about all the steps in between. I've even been gifted a beautiful spinning wheel and a set of hand carders, but since the birth of the Bean, I haven't found time to use either. Meanwhile, the storage shed has several years' worth of bagged fleece just waiting for me. I figured volunteering to demonstrate some of the homesteader skills required to turn a sheep fleece into a sweater would be the kick in the pants I needed.

Step one is pretty obvious: wash the wool. Of course, as anyone who has ever accidently put a fine-wool sweater in the washing machine knows, you have to be careful when washing wool. You must use the hottest water possible and plenty of Dawn dish soap to remove the lanolin, but water cannot be poured directly on the fleece, and you cannot agitate the wool at all.

Okay, sounds easy enough, right? Somehow in reading accounts of how to do this, however, I glossed over the part where they mentioned you may have to wash the wool dozens of times. During my first attempt, ten rinses in, the water I was washing off the fleece was still thick with grit and grime. And not agitating it was completely impossible—you'd have to have the patience of a saint to calmly and slowly wash wool for hours on end, which I can now say with assurance, I do not. By rinse eleven, I was pretty much wildly swishing the wool around, not caring if it ended up felting, just so long as it came clean. In the meantime, I'd come up against the dreaded VM.

But let me backtrack for a moment. The first step in preparing a fleece is actually skirting, not washing. Skirting is a process by which the nastiest parts of the fleece are removed before you even bring it inside. You can probably guess which parts of the fleece I'm talking about. During the skirting process, you also remove VM, or vegetable matter, from the wool. As you might imagine, a sheep out to pasture for a year will accumulate a lot of vegetable matter. Every twig and hay needle, every cocklebur and burdock bur, it all must extracted before the wool can be spun into yarn. Some of the VM will come out during carding, but most of it needs to be removed during skirting and washing. I had pulled off a lot of yucky stuff before plopping my fleece into the tub, but there was still plenty left behind. "I'll get that out in the wash," I reasoned.

This is why people who keep fine-wool sheep often put coats on their flocks. That always seemed a bit fussy to me. It certainly wasn't the way the pioneers did it. But, hunched over the bathtub, neck and back arched and aching, I began to see the wisdom of the practice. Each painstaking rinse, done as gently as I could muster, also gently wore away my desire to do things strictly the "pioneer way." In the end, I determined the first fleece was "clean enough" after fifteen washes, though it was still grayish (the sheep from which it was shorn is white) and full of small bits of hay. I've since decided it adds to the authenticity.

Fortunately, I found the other parts of the process much more pleasant. Carding, especially, has a quality of timelessness that I love, and it keeps your hands busy while your mind is free to roam—or you can watch your baby, as the case may be. However, I will still be telling the visitors who come to see my wool demonstrations, "We are so lucky!" Like garden tillers and antibiotics, factory-spun yarn is certainly one of the perks of modern life.

I am not giving up on turning my fleeces into warm, cozy garments, though. I plan to continue my pioneer experiments because I still think it's good to be reminded of our heritage, to slow down, and to see something unfold from start to finish. I will just be making a few minor adjustments—namely, the flock is going to be wearing coats come autumn, and I am not going to feel a bit guilty about it!

SEPTEMBER 12, 2016

THE WORK WE LEAVE UNDONE

When we wake up, we have to unburrow ourselves from the down comforter like moles emerging from an underground tunnel. The house is cold. It's been like this every morning for a week, and though the temperature will rise by midday, there is no doubt about it: autumn is upon us.

I can also tell summer is at an end because I'm in the middle of the seasonal chore of changing out clothes from the closets and dressers, and the house looks like a clothes tornado just swept through. The task is more daunting than usual. I need to accommodate for the Bean's changing size, as well as my own. My belly is as round as the pumpkins in the garden, ready to ripen by mid-December. Which means we also need to make room for a drawer of tiny winter clothes for a newborn. Soon, the Bean will have a set of big boy drawers all his own, and the new baby will take over the drawers of the wooden changing table.

The Bean clears the drawers as I sort. He thinks this is a lot of fun. One of his favorite jobs is pulling clothes (or Tupperware, or pots and pans) from their resting places and tossing them out onto the floor. Unfolding is also one of his favorite activities. As a result, most of the drawers get cleared many, many times before we are done, and the clothes get folded and unfolded as well.

I could wait for his nap to work on this project, but that would mean I don't get to nap, and boy do I look forward to those naps. So, we work together, and instead of taking an afternoon, it's taking days to get it all pulled back together.

It's early evening, and the Man of the Ranch comes in from fencing. He wants to know if he and the Bean should go on an "adventure." Their adventures usually consist of checking cows or driving into town to stop at the feed store and chat with whoever else happens to drop in. The Bean likes going on adventures even more than he likes emptying drawers and unfolding clothes. I also like it when he and his "Da" go on adventures. "Have fun!" I call to them as they drive away.

The clothes tornado is too daunting to confront, so I decide to take myself for a walk—a luxury I rarely get to indulge in these days. The dogs follow me north up the gravel path. In the past few weeks, we've had two good days of rain. Not enough to get the grass growing again, but enough to conjure a second wave of wildflowers. In the road ditch, prairie sunflowers wave their sunny heads as we pass. Down by their knees, the starry, feathered faces of fleabane and the mustard-colored cones of goldenrod peek above the dried grass. I pick a few of each, bending to breathe in their bright, peppery scent.

When I hit the fence line, I cut across the pasture and drop down to the dried creek bed. The cows who linger by the dam put out a call to their calves. They do not appreciate me, or the dogs, stopping by for a visit. Their voices echo against the canyon walls, guttural and urgent. More cows gather at the crown of the draw, looking down to see what the commotion is all about. Their large rectangular heads are silhouetted like dark clouds against the bright blue sky, and they open their wide mouths to respond to their herd-mates' consternation.

Back when the Man of the Ranch and I weren't much more than acquaintances, I spent an afternoon riding one of his horses in the pasture just south of this draw. I was enjoying myself immensely, and I had stopped to pick some wildflowers that day as well. That's when his herd of heifers spotted me and came over to investigate. Up to that point I had never been on the same side of a fence as a cow, let alone on the same side of the fence as a whole herd of them, so what else could I do but panic, scattering wildflowers across the prairie grass as I tried to hastily remount the horse. How was I to know if a herd of cattle was dangerous or not? There were a lot of them, and they were huge.

I was back in the saddle by the time the heifers arrived to inspect us, but that didn't make me feel much better. They swarmed around, mooing insistently, and I kicked that poor old horse in the ribs with a squeal of terror. We made it nearly to the gate before they lost interest and turned back. Meanwhile, I was left with the feeling of having only barely escaped disaster.

Standing in the draw and looking up at the cows, my hands once again full of flowers, I take a deep breath and start walking toward them and back to the house. I've learned a lot since that first ride, but I'm still a little intimidated. Honestly though, I'm more scared of the clothes tornado waiting at home, but my bravery will be rewarded by the last of the summer blossoms glowing warmly in a vase on our table—a welcome sight, even if there are a few piles of unfolded sweaters surrounding them.

OCTOBER 31, 2016

KITTY 2

After the Great Chicken Massacre of 2013, I was left with just one chicken, Periwinkle. When I moved to the ranch I brought her with me, and we acquired two companions to keep her company—Mike, the oldest hen in Perkins County, and Kitty 2, so named because she was a dead ringer for Peri's deceased best friend, Kitty. Mike has since passed on. So too, sadly, has Peri, but Kitty 2 remains.

If you are a regular reader of this column, you know more chickens have joined our flock in the ensuing years, and for a while I still named all new chickens, though it got harder to tell them apart. The two Barred Rock hens are the Cocos, the Buff Orpington is Red Molly, the Araucana is Calico (Callie for short), the Leghorn is Pippa, but the two black Australorps are just called the black Australorps. And last April—on Good Friday to be exact—I brought home three California Whites, Flopsy, Mopsy, and Cotton Tail, and I have no idea who is who.

Kitty 2, on the other hand, is and always has been quite memorable. She is a smallish hen with mud-brown feathers, but her personality belies her diminutive appearance. From the first, Kitty 2 was the queen of the flock. As the other chickens arrived, one by one, Kitty 2 put them in their place.

Until our first rooster, Fancy Pants, came of age, that is. Fancy Pants arrived in a shipment of mail order chicks, and he was so tiny and delicate I worried he wouldn't survive the rough and tumble jostling of his sisters. He was also slow to grow. He didn't lose his baby fluff until a month after everyone else. Once they stopped growing, however, he kept right on, until he towered over the rest of the flock. I never saw how it was accomplished, but Fancy Pants eventually dethroned Kitty 2 to become head honcho.

Unfortunately for us (and ultimately for Fancy Pants) he was mean. After literally scaring a visitor out of her shoes while chasing her across the yard, it was decided he had to go. We did not go rooster-less for long, though, because a small brood hatched in the last days of Fancy Pants's reign. All last winter we watched those chicks grow, wondering how many would turn out to be male.

As fate would have it, there was just one. He started out a pearly gray, just like Fancy Pants, with a smattering of the fluffy leg feathers that had inspired Fancy Pants's name. But as he matured, orange and gold hackle feathers sprouted around his neck, and his tail feathers came in a dark, iridescent green. With this new ornamentation, he took on the manners of a dandy, bowing to the ladies and preening more than seemed necessary, his bright, shiny head visible peering above the rest.

Meanwhile, once Fancy Pants was no longer in the picture, Kitty 2 reasserted her dominance with a vengeance. No hen was safe from her wrath, and she was brutal to anybody who didn't claw the line. We often spotted her wildly plucking feathers from the heads of those in the wrong place at the wrong time, just to prove a point.

She was especially tough on the new rooster-in-training. After losing her authority to his father, she was not about to let it happen again, and she was merciless in her assaults. Thus, Fancy Pants's son grew up unable to call his soul his own, and I can't say we're sorry about it. To this day, he is about the most un-roostery rooster you'll ever meet, scared of his own shadow and everything else. For example, we worried at first about the baby being around the flock, but though that rooster is still a good deal taller than the Bean, he runs away squawking whenever the Bean approaches. He has learned fierce things come in small packages. He is, however, quite prolific (his forty or so babies prove that point), so I would assert he is enjoying a pretty fulfilling existence anyway.

I am not so sure we can say the same for Kitty 2. She's currently molting, and while she was never a particularly pretty chicken, she is downright homely now. She is also getting older. All around her the chicks born this summer are sprouting up, so Kitty 2 must spend a great deal of time and energy reminding them she is the boss. All in all, she is neither an appealing figure, nor an enviable one.

In 1963, John F. Kennedy said, "When power leads man towards arrogance, poetry reminds him of his limitations. When power narrows the areas of man's concern, poetry reminds him of the richness and diversity of his existence." Chickens don't read poetry, or I would be tempted to pass that advice on to Kitty 2. But we can read poetry, and in this season of power struggles, being reminded of the richness and diversity of our existence can only aid us as we move forward. We are all in this coop together, after all. So here are a few lines of poetry for you, from the poet and farmer Wendell Berry: "When despair for the world grows in me . . . I go and lie down where the wood drake / rests in his beauty on the water, and the great heron feeds. . . . For a time / I rest in the grace of the world, and am free."[1]

DECEMBER 5, 2016

SO PREGNANT

Rita, my Jersey cow, had a beautiful calf last week. He is a long-lashed, tawny little steer, too young to be into any mischief, happy to follow his mama around the corral or lie hidden behind the bale feeder for a winter's nap. And it is definitely winter now. One day the Bean and I were outside playing in only our sweaters and jeans, and the very next it was snow boots and big coats. We enjoyed those warm, lush autumn afternoons, but it had to end eventually. The beautiful fall weather was a gift that lasted much longer than expected, so when it drew to a close abruptly with the arctic blast of our first blizzard, we couldn't complain. Well, not too much.

Meanwhile, unlike Rita, I'm still pregnant, and getting those snow boots on is a chore. The Man of the Ranch came across me crying in hormone-induced frustration the other day, my foot wedged halfway in the aforementioned footwear. What could he do but shove my foot in the rest of the way, looking as sympathetic as possible?

We also found another calf to take over my milking duties with Rita, thank goodness. The fact that putting on my own boots has become a hardship should indicate how successful I would have been at milking. The new calf is also a Jersey steer, already a month or so old, and tenacious enough to convince Rita to adopt him against her better judgment. Usually there is a steeper learning curve with a bum calf, especially one that is a little older, but this young man is as sneaky as he is deft, and after a couple days of putting Rita in the head catch so he could get a few sips, we found him stealing big drinks while Rita's calf nursed. The threesome is now well on their way to being a family.

The other happy development is that the Man of the Ranch has finally succeeded in getting the sheep flock fenced in—just in time for "date" month. Bing, our Shetland ram, is very happy. It was a tedious summer for him, watching all his lady friends thwart our best efforts at confinement, while he remained imprisoned inside the only truly sheep-proof pen on the ranch. Fifi, the fence crawler who pretty much taught everyone else how to break out, is not as pleased with the new arrangement. Her angry blatting can be heard echoing across the yard at all hours. Her noisy ruminations are a small price to pay, however, for the end of the roving. The square bales stacked by the barn are once again safe from itinerant wanderers, as is the Man of the Ranch's sanity.

Speaking of the Man of the Ranch's sanity, now that it's cold (and because there are less of them) the chickens have all begun sticking closer to the coop, so you no longer feel like you're being stalked by a horde of hungry birds every time you step foot in the yard. For a while there it was beginning to feel like outtakes from Hitchcock's movie *The Birds* around here, only instead of approaching from the sky, they swarmed you from the ground.

All this is to say we're getting our metaphorical ducks in a row, and not a moment too soon. It feels a little like the calm before the storm, though, and I keep wondering which twinge will turn into the first tremors of labor.

We never truly know what the next moments of our life hold, but uncertainty is exhausting, so our brains usually don't register that fact. In late pregnancy, however, that fact is unavoidable. Waking from a deep sleep, with the bedroom so dark I can't see my hand in front of my face, I think for a moment, "This is it!" But it's not. It's just my little girl kicking hard, testing her strength against the edge of her round, quiet world. One day soon, she will kick against blankets instead, pushing her tiny fist out from between the folds, her body unbound from the cocoon of my own.

When that day comes, whether it's tomorrow or a few weeks from now, we will begin again the rollercoaster ride of meeting a person we're madly in love with and don't know the first thing about. In the meantime, we will continue our preparations. But really, how can you ever be ready for a journey as thrilling and mystifying as that? I suppose you do the best you can, and you send up a prayer of gratitude when, at least for a little while, the cows and calves, and the chickens and sheep, seem to be helping you along.

2017

FEBRUARY 19, 2017

THE PERILS OF PRAIRIE LIFE

Last Monday was the beginning of the balmy streak up here, though no one told the wind. It roared and howled and carried on like it was heralding the storm of the century, but all across the country the snow went ahead and finally began melting. For a winter that started late, this one sure has felt long, but I think it is safe to say the spine of winter has been broken; it will get cold again no doubt, and will almost certainly snow again too, but after the warmth this past week, it is easy to believe spring is not far off.

But that's not what this column is about, or at least not directly. Monday is the day the Man of the Ranch works at the sale barn, and last Monday's sale was a long one, so he left the ranch a little after eight in the morning and wasn't expected home until after eight that night. There was no way the Bean wanted to spend the day indoors with Mama and baby sister, and after he had hurricaned his way through every room on the first floor, I didn't want that either. It was unanimously decided (with baby sister abstaining) that an outdoor mission was in order. Baby sister was bundled into her carrier and buttoned into my flannel coat, and she promptly fell into a deep slumber, while the Bean paced the floor wondering why it was taking so long to get this show on the road. Once outside, he took off running as fast as his bandy legs could carry him, Mama and baby sister trotting along behind.

The sun was glinting off the snowbanks, and the air beneath the scolding shouts of wind was warm and sweet. The Bean headed for the scraggly stand of pines beside the old tin-sided shop. Just the day before he had discovered the joys of pinecone collection and was ready to take up where he left off. I thought pinecone collection was a grand idea, hoping the trees would provide a little cover from the wind. Once we were there however, the gleaming slope of a steep snowbank suddenly beckoned. The Bean plunged forward, climbing the side of that bank with gusto.

This was when I became the tiniest bit alarmed. Though the mud puddles of melted snow were growing by the minute, the piles of still frozen stuff, especially in the tree belts, were tall—much taller than a small boy—but not nearly as sturdy as they'd been these last few months. Sure enough, the Bean had barely made it to the top of that first hill when his foot went crashing through the frosty crust. I was no more than a few steps behind, but at four times his weight, I went crashing through much sooner.

The Bean, as you might imagine, is not the type to be easily deterred. He grabbed hold of a nearby branch in the hope of pulling himself out of the hole he had created—and it worked! But though his body was freed, his boots remained ensconced in snow, his little socks tucked warmly inside as well. With the baby on my front, I couldn't lean over and scooch across the snow as the Bean had done, and I couldn't very well untie her and set her on the snow either. There we were: a young boy lying on his belly atop a snowbank, clinging to a tree branch while his chubby, bare feet waved in the wind; I stood just out of arm's reach, calmly reassuring him, though I was myself nearly thigh deep in the same bank and showing no sign that I could extract myself and rescue him. Meanwhile, the Bean's early optimism had turned to tears as he wailed "Uh-oh!" over and over, his little toes growing cold, no doubt. It was at this point that I began to imagine how we would spend the next ten hours waiting for the Man of the Ranch to come home and help us.

They occur less frequently these days, but sometimes I still have moments when I wonder if I am cut out for the prairie life. Getting stranded in a snowbank on a gorgeous, sun-soaked morning, in full view of our house, is an example of such a moment. I did eventually manage to pull myself up and out of the hole I had created, only to fall right back down into a new one. I crashed my way up the embankment like that, one hole after another, until I was able to pull the Bean toward me and retrieve his sunken footwear. And then it was a long slog back down the snowbank half-lugging, half-dragging him as we once again fell into every hole along the way.

I feel certain there is a parable in this story, but now, a full week later, I still can't say for sure what it is. One thing is certain, however: you have to be pretty tough to endure a climate where you can become stranded in deep snow in your own backyard on a warm, sunny day.

APRIL 23, 2017

BABY LAMBS

After getting home from a recent trip to Minnesota, I'll admit, I felt a little blue. I missed my family and friends, and our return coincided with the Man of the Ranch's side business as a fencer starting up again. In the winter he sticks pretty close to home, but all the other seasons he is out most daylight hours, sometimes an hour or two away.

The Bean was also sad. His favorite place in the world (along with the barn, of course) is the Dakota Feed and Seed, where he and his fellow ranchers spend their winter mornings discussing the weather and other news. The Man of the Ranch is too busy now to spend much time there, but nobody told the Bean hanging out with his friends was seasonal. Every morning since we've been back, he's stood by the sliding glass door chanting, "Ah-Bee, Ah-Bee." I finally realized yesterday he was asking for Bobby, the owner of the feed store and his best buddy.

Lest we both fall too far into despair I decided drastic measures needed to be taken. What is the antidote for sadness, my friends? If you are lucky enough to live on a ranch, and it is spring, the answer is, and always will be, baby lambs.

Ordinarily, we would have baby lambs aplenty in April, but I was extremely pregnant when it came time to put our buck in last fall. The idea of lambing with a newborn was fairly unappealing, so we waited until just before my due date. Thus, our first lambs aren't expected for a few more weeks. In our current state, we couldn't wait that long for a joy injection—we needed lambs, and we needed them fast. I packed up our little family, drove to a good friend's place (the friend who, incidentally, gave me my first two bums five years ago), and we returned home with two new members of the little pasture, Willow and Iris.

Willow is the younger of the two. She is tall and slender, hence her name, but not very strong. Her tongue curls up on itself whenever she tries to drink her bottle, and it takes her twice as long as her sister to drink half as much milk. Her woolly coat is a wee bit rumpled, and she always looks surprised and relieved to see us.

Iris, on the other hand, is not as tall, but is as sturdy as an oak tree. She'll suck the bottle right out of your hands if you aren't holding tight, and she loves to shout. Her lamby cries can be heard from the minute you step foot outside of the house until you make it to the barn with the bottles. Willow doesn't talk much at all. She doesn't have to—Iris has already said it all for her.

The Man of the Ranch recently read me this definition of little boys: noise with dirt on it. This certainly doesn't describe all boys, but it does describe my boy. And also Iris. They are kindred spirits, of that there is no doubt. Whenever I ask the Bean if he is ready to visit the lambs he simply shouts, "Baaaa!" Once we all get together, he and Iris tumble across the yard, while Willow and I follow in their wake.

Meanwhile, the days are getting longer and warmer, though still windy. After the lambs get their bottles, we all go to work in the greenhouse sorting seeds and filling peat pots with dark, rich soil. Iris and Willow snooze beneath the wooden potting table beside baby Roo's stroller until the Bean decides he has other chores to attend to outside. The baby and I stay in the greenhouse to enjoy the sunshine but avoid the gusts, while the Bean, followed by Iris and Willow, heads east toward the barn. There is a certain mud puddle he has been meaning to investigate all morning, and with the help of some sticks and his rubber boots, he goes ahead and does just that. As a general rule, lambs don't get quite as excited about mud as small boys do, so they leap and dance around the edge as he wades in. Roo laughs and I smile. It's a pretty great view.

The countertops are sticky from spilled milk powder, the sink is full of bottles and mixing cups, and sleep is lost for those early morning and late-night feedings, but my goodness if those lambs don't make the extra work worth it. So, when I caught wind yesterday that the very same friend had a tiny goat and another little lamb who wanted to join our flock, what could I say but "Yes, please!" That, however, is a story for another week and another column. Until then, I hope you are all finding as much joy in this season as we are!

APRIL 30, 2017

TINY

When I first moved to the ranch, I brought with me two old house dogs, two young house cats, three tame sheep, and one lonely bantam hen. For the Man of the Ranch, who had a single crusty barn cat and nothing else but cattle, it was a big adjustment. He was pretty cool about it though, and as he does with most things, he took the changes in stride. Sure, there was some grumbling when the sheep, who ran loose like puppies around the yard, would get into the calves' grain, or when the flock of chickens I later acquired left their smelly calling cards on the patio, but mostly, he accepted my menagerie as part of the package.

There were two things he politely requested, however: that the count for indoor animals be capped at four, and that we never get goats. The list was later added to—no pigs and no llamas. Agreeing to no pigs and no llamas was no problem. But no goats? That was a little harder. You see, a few years prior, a pretty little nanny goat named Francesca (Franny for short) had captured my heart. White as a snowflake, with long lashes and dainty golden hooves, Franny loved to dance and leap on bales of hay, farm implements, and wire chicken runs. She also loved to snuggle. A series of upheavals in my life resulted in us parting ways. Originally, I hoped the parting would be temporary, but after the Man of the Ranch's request, I accepted that though Franny and I would remain friends, we would have to continue living separate lives.

Fast forward three years. When we went to pick up our bum lambs a few weeks ago, we also happened to meet a baby goat named Tiny. I tried my hardest not to fall in love with her, but it was impossible. She was smaller than a half-grown cat and had silky black ears that hung nearly to her narrow shoulders. I held her with one arm, and the Bean, who was settled on the opposite side hip, was just as charmed. He extended a chubby finger to pet her smooth head, then looked up at me with a shy smile.

The Man of the Ranch happened to walk into the barn at that moment, and perhaps he knew then what was to come. I was resolved, however, to keep my promise of no goats. So, we left with our two lambs, and that would have been the end of the story.

Fortunately, or unfortunately, depending on how you look at it, a few days later I heard through the grapevine that my friend was selling the rest of her bums, and she wasn't sure what to do with Tiny. She too had fallen in love with the wee girl and worried the little goat's heart would be broken if she were left alone in the orphan pen. This friend has helped me out on more occasions that I can count, so I wanted to return in some small measure all the kindness I had been shown, and I wondered if this situation didn't represent a loophole in my promise to the Man of the Ranch. If we only borrowed Tiny until she could rejoin my friend's herd as a weanling, I wouldn't be violating our agreement, right?

"Remember that baby goat . . ." I began. I didn't need to say more; the Man of the Ranch simply sighed.

"Okay," he said.

"It's only temporary!" I called to his retreating back.

And that is why we have a goat. Oh, yes, and another bum lamb—he is Tiny's adopted brother, and we couldn't part them. Besides, what's one more baby?

The addition of Tiny and her adopted brother has come with both problems and pleasures, of course. When I first proposed this whole scheme, I figured it would be a fun experience for the Bean and maybe he'd help with a bottle here or there. He is only twenty-two months old, after all. When we feed with bottles, however, the most I can hold is three at a time (one in each hand, and a third wedged between my knees). Since the lambs are bigger, stronger, and pushier than her, Tiny has to wait. But the Bean really loves Tiny too, and the first time he saw me feeding the three lambs while Tiny went hungry, he picked the remaining bottle out of the bucket and, with no instruction, figured out how to feed her all by himself.

The same holds true when we let them out to run around the yard. Tiny can't keep up with the lambs, whose legs are taller than her entire body. Instead, she finds a sunny spot to curl up in, and more often than not, the Bean will hunker down right next to her, patting her soft, sun-warmed head until some other chore draws his attention away.

I worry about her, though. She isn't growing like she should. The lambs, already so fat and sassy, look like completely different creatures than when they arrived. Meanwhile, Tiny has barely grown at all, though only a few days ago she still had to be helped over the small lip of the barn door, and just yesterday she cleared it in one effortless leap.

As for the Man of the Ranch's no-goat policy? This morning he went out to move cows into a closer pasture, and what should he find running amongst them but a large yellow goat. The cows, confused, kept trying to chase it away, but, undeterred, it kept returning. Thus, the Man of the Ranch's worst fear has been realized—namely, that one goat inevitably leads to another . . .

MAY 22, 2017

WHAT A MESS

Some days I look around and think, "How did this happen?" The sink piled high with dishes, the dining table piled high with wrinkled laundry, the tracks of dirt and manure that always manage to trail in from the corrals—it sometimes seems I never stop cleaning, and yet, it often appears we've been burglarized, but instead of taking things, the burglars have simply left a mess behind.

Other days I look around at the dishes, the laundry, and the dirt, and I think, "I know exactly how this happened." Mother's Day this year was that kind of day.

It all started innocently enough. We had a big family breakfast of fluffy sourdough pancakes with extra eggs, and then we headed out to do chores together. Since chores this time of year, when done in a leisurely fashion, include snuggling lambs and kittens, they are not really a chore. We had plans to go out for brunch, but we were in no rush, so the morning unfolded warm and bright, smelling sweetly of new grass and sun. The bottle lambs and goat are as fat as pink piglets now, and they slurped down their milk in no time at all. When they finished, I opened the barn door and off they bounced, looking for green shoots to nibble, the Bean in their wake, practicing his herding techniques.

Before too long, it was time for the baby's nap, so I headed in to lay her down and get a little writing done while the Bean and the Man of the Ranch fixed some fence in the pasture. Soon enough, she awakened, the boys returned, and we left for our midday meal. In other words, everything was going as planned.

There is an old joke: "How do you make God laugh? Tell him your plans." This is doubly true when you live on a ranch, and you had better go ahead and double it again if you have small children. So, it was no surprise when a cascading series of events resulted in the afternoon getting away from us. I had planned to work in the garden, but diaper changes, toddler mishaps, an escaped nurse cow, and a birthing mama sheep occurred instead.

Which is how I found myself recklessly trying to transplant overgrown pea shoots, fussy baby strapped to my back, when I should have been starting supper. I could have waited another day perhaps, but the tendrilled limbs of the peas were already reaching out longingly, hoping to find something to cling to, and I could ignore their pleas no longer. Beside me, the Bean plucked the flowering tops off the dandelions I had also planned to weed, thus ensuring there would be more of the same coming up soon. I shook my head and shoved those poor peas in their new, hastily dug holes.

The sound of lambs and their mamas calling to each other across the pasture is a staple of our springtime soundtrack, but a lamb's distant cry slowly began to pierce the cocoon of my rushed bustling. I placed the last pea in the ground and stood up. The Bean continued his work, the picture of calm contentment, but I knew it was only a matter of time before hunger got the best of him and he entered meltdown mode. Still, something about that cry just didn't sound right. "I'll be right back, buddy," I told him, though he was too engrossed to pay me much mind.

I climbed over the garden fence bordering the pasture, baby still securely attached, and took off trotting toward the sad bleating. I found her right away, trapped in the crook of a fallen branch and the bramble of a large tumbleweed. She was dry but covered with a yellow crust—evidence that her mother had not licked her clean after giving birth. I thought of the ewe who'd lambed an hour before. Her name is Dot, and though she is one of my favorites, it was not hard to imagine her having twins and forgetting about one of them. I scooped the wee babe up and circled back, looking for the mother.

Sure enough, when Dot saw me approach, she and the lamb I had watched her deliver walked over to greet me, and she sniffed at the lamb in my arms. She murmured, the throaty cooing that mother sheep use when talking to their babies, and I congratulated myself on reuniting the family. "Silly Dot," I said as I patted her woolly head.

I wasn't even two steps away before Dot started headbutting the poor lamb into the tin windbreak. "Not mine!" she said in no uncertain terms.

I picked the baby back up, and we made another loop, checking the remaining ewes. No one else had lambed that day; the baby was definitely Dot's, which meant the baby was now definitely mine.

That was how I found myself standing at the stove, simultaneously warming frozen colostrum from when the milk cow last freshened, and leftover potato and hamburger hot dish, a windblown baby human on one hip, a crusty, crying baby lamb at my feet, and a toddler, covered in dirt from toe tip to blond curls, running around us all, shouting "Baby!" with glee and awe at the new arrival. I looked over one shoulder to the breakfast dishes still piled in the sink, then over the other shoulder to the laundry piled high on the table, and thought, "Yep, this is how it happens."

And you know what? I am okay with that.

JULY 17, 2017

GEORGE

Last Christmas, we were gifted a pony for the Bean by a neighbor whose grandchildren had outgrown the wee creature. Named George by the aforementioned children, this sturdy fellow is the perfect first horse for a small boy. He is affectionate, docile, and low to the ground—a tumble off him amounts to a bruising at most.

All winter, George lived in the corral closest to the barn with the sheep and the miniature donkey brothers, Orville and Wilbur. I had hoped he might bond with the latter, as they are all the same size, but the brothers preferred being a party of two rather than a crowd of three. Friendship with the sheep wasn't even on the table, as most equines (like most cattle ranchers) think sheep are silly and stupid.

George, though deferential with us, demonstrated a toughness that quickly made him ruler of his small roost. After a swift kick to the shins, even Rita the milk cow, no shrinking violet herself, gave him a wide berth. Most mornings, the Bean and his "Da" brought George a few handfuls of cake, stopping to scratch his smooth auburn nose. So, he may have been a bit lonely, but George's life was not without pleasure.

Winter was endless, and yet, it miraculously ended, giving way to the soft, sweet breath of spring. The sheep were let out to the little pasture, and George, Wilbur, and Orville went with them. Evenings found the ragtag crew nose-deep in green grass. George would lift his head, his gold mane glowing in the lavender dusk, and watch as we passed by on our nightly walk. Sometimes he would jog over to the fence to say hello, lifting his dainty hooves in a jaunty trot, shaking his forelock with stately grace. He carried himself with the majesty of a much larger animal, and indeed, if there had been no sheep standing nearby, it would have been easy to mistake him for a full-grown horse. Meanwhile, though the Bean goes into paroxysms of joy when he gets to ride anything with wheels, tooling around on George doesn't excite him yet. As a result, George's time has been mostly his own, which has meant lots of slow grazing punctuated by long rolls in the dust and, every once in a while, a quick canter along the fence line.

Spring is the season our horses work the hardest. The deep draws in our north pasture are too rocky and steep for a four-wheeler to navigate, but a horse does just fine. Between checking the cows and going to brandings, the Man of the Ranch doesn't have many days during April and May when he isn't riding, usually on Wallace or Charlie, the youngest geldings, or Carl, our most trusted helper.

Whenever the horses were in, George would reach his narrow nose across the fence and whinny, the long, loud whinny of a gentleman in exile. Because Wallace and Charlie are the lowest in the pecking order, they'd snort and stomp in reply, rushing the fence to chase George away. George would whinny louder his dismay (from a safe distance), as heartbreaking as it was eardrum-splitting.

The drought withered the grass in the little pasture by the beginning of summer, and the sheep have been free-range ever since. I suppose we could have let George roam free as well, but the Man of the Ranch decided to put him in with the horses instead. I was worried he would be ostracized at best, and injured at worst, but the union was achieved without incident. Well, there were some shenanigans at first. George's mournful vocalizations increased in volume and frequency for a time, and then they stopped. I took this as a good sign, though whenever I saw him, he was trotting a few paces behind everyone else. Clearly, he was not quite an accepted member of the string, but at least they were no longer chasing him away.

Yesterday was a long, sweltering day. Roo woke everyone at 5:30 a.m., and the Bean took only a twenty-minute nap, so by evening we were all in a sad state. After supper, I put the kids in the stroller and started walking, hoping they would fall asleep. Instead, we came up to the pasture to see the horses fanned across it, grazing in the cool evening breeze. I stopped and marveled. George stood shoulder to shoulder with Charlie. They both took a few steps toward us, but then decided to continue grazing instead of coming closer. Once again, George's mane was glowing in the last of the light. And if it's possible for a pony to smile, he did.

A drought is a hard time for almost everyone on a ranch, but there is no great loss without some small gain. On this ranch at least, there is one animal who will go to bed joyful and wake the same, despite the heat and the flies and the dry, dusty rations. Oh, to be a pony restored to the heritage of open plains and kinship, his wish to belong granted at long last.

SEPTEMBER 18, 2017

AUTUMN

The sun rises red, a haze of smoke scattering its rays, buffering the light, but not the heat. The smoke is from wildfires in Montana, and it has traveled a thousand miles, maybe more, to get here. For three days it hangs over the ranch, hot and thick as a dragon's breath, and just as foul smelling, until finally the wind brings clear, cool air. And just like that, it's fall.

Well, not officially. This coming weekend is the autumnal equinox, the hour of balance in the battle between day and night. The night will win this round, and we will be headed into our season of darkness. Usually this is a time of introspection—or it always has been for me—but lately my thoughts and I have become strangers. On the rare occasions we have a chance to meet, our conversation is awkward and stilted. The two tiny people who crowd my days are the culprits behind the alienation.

Sometimes I think: What did I do before children? How did I accomplish so little? The answer: It was because I spent so much time lost in thought. These days, I don't even have time to contemplate whether I miss it. There is so much to do. Life is good, but it is fast paced. There is little opportunity to meditate on all its pleasures or its disappointments.

For example, we recently made our yearly appointment to take a cow to the butcher. It's a day I always used to dread. But like many aspects of ranch life, something I thought I would never learn to accept has now become commonplace. And, as I said, I just don't have time to focus on sorrow anymore.

Perhaps not surprisingly, this lack of free time makes writing about ranch life harder, so one day a week a young friend from a neighboring ranch has been coming to play with the kids. Today, we went to town so I could write in the pickup while they played at the park. We brought a big blanket, snacks, and a shovel for the park's sandy ground cover.

My kids are wholly satisfied without me—they love having a big girl to play with—but instead of working, I sit in the pickup's wide driver's seat and look out the window at my children. The baby has on a cotton cap, a gray sweater, striped pants, and soft leather shoes. She sits straight and sturdy, her chubby knees tucked beneath her. The Bean has just learned to play peekaboo, and he covers and uncovers his eyes, shouting "Peeka!" which elicits a shriek of delight from his sister. His cap has recently gone missing, so the wind blows his curls this way and that. He had so little hair for so long that it's never been cut, but I will need to see to that soon.

I try to type a few words, the laptop balanced awkwardly in the space between my body and the steering wheel. Supper is still a few hours away, but already the light has shifted toward dusk. The sun doesn't have time to linger anymore either; it hustles its way toward evening, crossing the sky quickly. The wind suddenly shifts too, and it gets instantly colder. A torrent of leaves, yellow and curled at the edges, lose their collective grip and begin a circling dance downward. The Bean runs to catch one. He is learning words for colors, and I hear him yelling, "Le-low!" over and over. High above his head, one dark bird circles, its long wings heavy with shadows.

It's too chilly now for the kids to play without coats and winter caps, which I have neglected to bring. I open the pickup door and shuffle everyone inside, turning the vehicle on and with it, the heat. As I strap him in, the Bean recaps the afternoon's events for me: "Slide! Shovel! Leaves!" he says. His world is mostly nouns, a conglomeration of objects.

He is still shouting as we drive the few miles home: "Truck! Truck! Tractor! Tractor! Tractor! Hay!" His sister merrily shouts along. Our neighbor chuckles. She has younger siblings, so she's used to the din.

We turn at our gravel driveway, and the Bean begins another list, this one comprised of all the things we will see soon: the house, the dogs, the chickens.

For all things there is a season, and this season, for me, is not about deep thoughts. This season is about jubilant chatter, the purple fire of autumn dusk, and the bright flags of the trees, flaming brilliantly before they drop their leaves, each one a sweet memory of summer.

SEPTEMBER 25, 2017

FOUR ANIMAL CAP

Two weeks ago, I wrote about our mama cat, Esme, who was once again expecting. Soon after, I went traveling for a weekend of shows, and when I returned, she was no longer pregnant. I scoured the barn but found no signs of a litter. Before I left, she hadn't looked very close to delivery to me, so I assumed she had miscarried. I was angry with myself for not realizing her condition earlier and therefore not making sure she got the extra rations she needed—she never really gained back the weight she lost nursing her first litter. I was also the tiniest bit relieved. It would be better for her to go into winter without having to raise another litter of kittens.

Now, if you are a regular reader of this column, you might remember my ineptitude at guessing when my sheep are close to lambing. Because we don't have enough barn space for the whole flock, I would, without fail, move a soon-to-be mama into the barn, only to find her sister had just given birth to twins in the corral. This year, we solved that problem by lambing in May. Thank goodness, because I was still never, ever right about who was close and who was not.

Which is why when the Man of the Ranch came in this morning and said, "You better come out to the barn, there are some short cats running around," I probably shouldn't have been so dismissive.

"No," I said, "there can't be kittens in the barn. You must have seen something else."

"There are definitely kittens in the barn," he replied.

Their cries were unmistakable the second our boots stepped over the threshold. There were three of them: one orange tabby, one misty gray, and one tortoise shell with fur the colors of South Dakota in September. With Emmy Rose on my hip, and the Bean by my side, the Man of the Ranch piled the kittens in the arm I had free. All three snuggled close and promptly fell asleep. The Bean was uncharacteristically gentle as he reached out to pat their fuzzy heads.

"Baby tats," he said. "Tiny baby tats."

When I last wrote of Esme, I mentioned my husband prefers that all non-human animals live outside, and outside only. I trend in the other direction. Now that I dwell in close proximity to droves of baby animals, I try to keep that tendency in check, lest we be overrun, but I am not always successful. This was one of those times, and I found myself asking without even meaning to, "Can we bring them inside?"

"They don't need to come in, honey," my very tolerant husband said, and he was right. Though the weather had turned colder as of late, the kittens were at least ten days old, and they were obviously thriving. Esme didn't look too run-down either; though she was wire-thin, her black coat was smooth and shiny as patent leather.

Unbeknownst to us, the Bean was listening to our whole conversation, and as has recently become the norm, he had his own thoughts to share on the matter. The Man of the Ranch left the barn to grain our weanling bottle calves, and the Bean looked up at me with round eyes. "Baby tats, house," he said firmly.

"Your son has something to tell you," I said when the Man of the Ranch returned. "Tell him what you told me," I said to the Bean.

"Baby tats, house," he repeated, just as adamantly, this time touching the kittens with one chubby finger, just in case his father was confused about which baby tats he was referring to.

So now, we have a mama cat and three kittens cuddled in our bathtub.

They call a mother cat a queen, and curled in one of my soft flannel work coats, Esme looks the part. All afternoon we have been making visits to the little family, bearing egg yolks and kibble and little dishes of fresh water. She lifts her dark head with a regal gesture every time we come in, holding court as we coo over the babies that are nestled in the warm curve of her body. Their eyes, blue as the Dakota sky, are just barely open; her eyes are bright as the sun.

The Bean has always been every bit his father's son, but I guess there is a little of his mama in there too. What does this mean? I predict a subtle shift in the indoor-outdoor animal policy. As the main house cleaner, I fear in the end I may be voting against my own interests, but I can't help it. For today, at least, I am thankful to have a cozy place to pamper a little creature and her brood, and to see the smile that climbs across the Bean's cheeks every time we visit them.

DECEMBER 11, 2017

SORTING SHEEP

December is date month on our ranch—at least where the sheep are concerned. Last year, with a new baby of our own on the way, we decided to try lambing in May. On December 1, the bucks went in with the ladies, and then we waited.

It turned out May was a great time to lamb; it was warm, the grass was green and sweet. Every morning and evening, I'd make a round through the pasture to check the mamas and new babies, my own wee one cuddled close. Other than that, the ewes were left to their own devices, and everyone did great.

So, here we are once again. Things have gotten a hair more complicated, however. A few years ago, when I got my first buck, I had only four sheep. He did his work well, and seemingly overnight our flock more than doubled in size. In the interim, I acquired a few more sheep, including a small flock of Shetlands, so as of last winter we had about twenty girls and two boys milling around.

This year, we have over forty. By the standards of most of our neighbors, this still isn't very many. What makes it tricky, however, is the variety of sizes, and basic genetics—namely, who is related to whom. Long story short, in order for it not to get creepy, we've had to create three different corrals with three different rams. I won't bore you with the details, but it's a temporary solution to a permanent problem. We've been selling wethers and some of the crossbred ewe lambs each fall, but it's clear that some of the beautiful breeding ewes are going to have to go eventually, too.

That's another story, though. In the meantime, we've set up the three pens. Now, about half the flock is "normal" size. These ewes and their ram are mostly Rambouillet crosses. They are also mostly former bottle lambs, and therefore they're as tame as the day is long. To sort them, you just walk past, and they usually follow.

The Shetlands, on the other hand, are as small as badgers and just as wily. We can't keep them fenced for anything, and except for a few sweet-eyed gals, they act like feral range sheep—they see a human and they bolt. You'd think this would make sorting easy, but you'd be wrong.

Sorting day arrived, and the Man of the Ranch was in charge of the gate, while I was in charge of stirring the pot (so to speak), making slow rounds to keep the flock moving. When one of the big sheep neared the gate, I had to keep her going forward faster than everyone else, so the Man of the Ranch could get her out before any of the Shetlands zipped through.

This worked fabulously at first. But, as the big sheep were thinned out and the Shetlands got more agitated, it got harder to keep the latter from slipping through. Strangely, I was enjoying myself. I am not the sporty type, but this did have the appealing edge of a physical challenge, and the weather was fine. Plus, I like looking at sheep, and let's be real, I don't get out much.

The Man of the Ranch, on the other hand, works at a sale barn. If sorting sheep was something he wanted to do for fun, he has plenty of opportunities. Round and round we went, until there were only two ewes left, but we couldn't get those two out for anything. The Man of the Ranch's patience was wearing thin.

When I played music for a living, I heard plenty of colorful language from bandmates and bar patrons, but never have I heard the kind of language that flows from a cowboy's mouth when he's got uncooperative animals running wild. The Man of the Ranch is very calm in most regards, and when dealing with a rapidly deteriorating livestock situation, his demeanor might not change much, but his vocabulary sure does. Suffice to say, "rapidly deteriorating" was exactly what we were experiencing.

Did I happen to mention we were both carrying a child in our arms during all this?

Well, all the sheep are sorted now. And the Bean has a new word. All around the yard and house I hear him say in a deep, gravelly voice, "Dada says . . . 'Gosh-darn it!'"

Once again I am counting my blessings. To have a cowman take on your sheep, help you sort, shear, and breed them, and build pens and fences, and the most he says about it is "Gosh-darn it"? Well, I've said it before, and I'll say it again, I am a lucky, lucky woman.

DECEMBER 18, 2017

ROO

Our little Emmy Rose celebrated her first Christmas at just five days old, in the middle of a blizzard; if you live in our neck of the woods, you probably remember last winter was full of those. During the weeks leading up to her birth, and in the weeks after, storms raged across the prairie, burying us in drifts. We'd dig out, only to be covered again. The snow in the windbreak reached the house's second story before the new year, the tops of the trees peeping through like small shrubs.

Thankfully, Roo had great timing from the first. I feared going into labor during bad weather. Late at night, the wind howling around the eaves, I would awaken with contractions, plagued by visions of giving birth stranded on the side of the road. When I did finally go into labor, it was on a clear night. I looked out the window at the stars, bright as diamonds, not a cloud in sight. What a relief!

But I hated to wake up two households: the Bean was only eighteen months old, and the grandma that was going to come stay with him was two and a half hours away. "Let's try to hang on until morning, okay?" I asked Emmy.

So, she did. The contractions intensified at first light, and by the time Grandma Cheryl arrived, I was a tiny bit worried we'd waited too long. Still, that sweet girl stayed put until we made it to the hospital and got our paperwork filled out. With the last paper signed, the Man of the Ranch went out into the hallway to make a phone call and nearly missed his daughter's arrival. She was born seven minutes later.

All in all, a stormy, snowy winter wasn't the worst time to have a new baby. Other than when I took quick trips to the barn, with Roo bundled inside my oversized parka, she and I stayed home. It's a bit of a blur now—like new mothers everywhere, I never quite fell asleep and never quite woke up that whole long winter. When I look back, I mostly recall so many diapers and so much snuggling.

Like her brother, Roo was colicky, which made those first few months tough, but having gone through it once already, I knew it wouldn't last forever. By spring, she had blossomed into the sunniest baby I've ever met, smiling in her dreams, laughing before she was even fully awake.

So, here we are, one year later. While I was still early in motherhood, people were always telling me, "Enjoy it! It goes so fast!" Exhausted and cranky, I thought they were crazy. Those newborn nights seemed endless. I couldn't wait to get to the next part, the part where sleeping happened.

But it's true, those endless nights end, and your baby is suddenly a toddler. Roo started taking steps a month ago, and now she walks from room to room, a little bobbin in the Bean's wide wake. "Not a baby anymore," he said solemnly the first time he saw her walking behind him. The fact that he can say that is mind-blowing in and of itself—I still can't believe he isn't a baby.

Now, it's time for Roo's second Christmas and her first birthday. She's too young to get excited for Santa, or presents, but her brother isn't. He can't wait to help her blow out birthday candles, though he is a little concerned about the cake. We've discussed it several times, but he doesn't believe me when I tell him that, even though the cake is for his sister's birthday, we will all get to eat it. Instead, he keeps requesting a blueberry cake for his own birthday.

Meanwhile, we still haven't gotten to the part where sleeping happens. (We've been blessed with active, exuberant children who apparently don't think sleeping in long stretches is a necessity.) But we've gotten our sea legs, so to speak. Tired is the new normal, and so is limitless joy, with each day an adventure.

I'll close by saying happy birthday to our sweet December Rose, the rarest of rare blooms and the best Christmas present we'll ever receive. I've always loved Christmastime, but never more so than now, when I get to celebrate my daughter as well.

2018

MARCH 26, 2018

CALVES

"Calving heifers" is a term synonymous with the watchful eye a cattle rancher must keep on first-time mothers as they approach their due date. When calving heifers, the herd must be checked every few hours, day and night, in case anyone goes into labor and needs assistance. It is a grueling time of year.

With last summer's drought (and consequent lack of hay) we didn't keep any yearlings, so, unlike many of our neighbors, we aren't calving heifers this spring. Not to rub it in, but that means we get to stay in bed instead of tromping through damp wind and deep snow all night long. Considering our own children's recent viruses, it is a double blessing—we would really have been getting no sleep at all if we'd needed to keep watch on mamas-to-be in the barn while our own two babies woke us every few hours!

Calving experienced mothers is not without challenges, however, especially when winter hasn't yet loosened its grip on the landscape. Our first calves arrived last week in the midst of swirling snow and icy wind. The Man of the Ranch rolled out hay bales beside the tin windbreak to create some shelter for the herd and dry spots for the babies to nestle, but we still worried. Everyone survived, thankfully.

This week, the temperature is significantly higher but still mostly below freezing. We've had snow, snow, and freezing rain, a terrible combination for wee calves, not to mention the rancher who is out trying to check on them. His diligence is paying off. Three times in the last two days he's saved a calf that would otherwise have died.

The first calf was born into a deep snow drift. His mama paced and called, and tried to rouse her baby, but it was no use. His wobbly new legs were too weak to escape.

The ensuing rescue involved several forms of transportation. First, the Man of the Ranch tried to get to the calf with a four-wheeler, which got stuck in said drift. He walked back, then rode out again in the skid steer. The mama was mad and scared, so in addition to the elements, there was also a charging cow to avoid. After he got the baby in the cab of the skid steer without being mauled and made the rumbling trek across the pasture to the house, the Man of the Ranch dropped off the little one with me (and by little one, I mean huge—that newborn calf outweighed me!) and went to round up a horse to trail the mother on.

All the clean towels in the house and forty-five minutes of blow-drying later, and that little calf was shivering hard—yet a vast improvement over the still, lolling form he had been. His tongue was still cold as ice, and his eyes glazed, but he could hold his head up for a few minutes and even let out a few ear-splitting moos (much to the human children's chagrin, both of whom went running from the bathroom at the noise).

After another hour under blankets, he came around. The Man of the Ranch carried him back out to be reunited with his mother in the corral, and within minutes the little fellow was up and taking his first sips of milk. All in all, it was a very happy ending.

The next day there was more of the same. First, the Man of the Ranch found a very new, very wet calf trapped under a thick bracket of bramble. The poor thing had been born on a slick hillside and slid down beneath the sharp branches of a buffaloberry bush. Once freed, however, the calf was up and ready to chase after his mama.

Then, not more than a few yards away, another unusually large calf was born and got chilled down before his mother could get him up. Fortunately, this mama wasn't as angry, and the snow wasn't as deeply drifted, so bringing him to the house was easy enough. A few hundred more towels, the hair dryer treatment, plus an additional hour wrapped in flannel, and that baby was ready to go meet his mama in the corral as well.

Today, the house is a wreck from muddy boots and muddy animals. The children, for lack of an available tub, have only gotten sponge baths in the sink for the past few evenings, and the mountain of laundry is even more insurmountable than usual. Supper was late; so was bedtime. But I've gotten to watch the light come back into the eyes of two newborn babies. I've gotten to walk across the yard and visit those same babies bouncing on their gangly knob knees, while their mothers call them gently.

There is a reason ranching is considered a livelihood, and not just a way to make a living. When you ranch, you sometimes hold an animal's life in your hands—literally. It's a big responsibility, and when the day is done, it's work you can feel proud of, even if that day lasts well into the night.

I'll tell you one thing, though—the towels are washed and dried, but not folded, and I don't intend to clean the tub until tonight, just in case we have another visitor . . .

APRIL 16, 2018

STORM PREP

Today, the air is heavy with damp wind. I went out to feed the lambs and calves their morning bottles, and immediately regretted forgetting my gloves. The joints of my fingers and knees ache. The dampness feels like getting old; it adds all the creaks that will come with time.

There's another storm on its way. By the time you read this, it will be past. It will live up to the epic, "historic" conditions they are predicting, or it will be just another slap of snow and ice and wind slathered over the still-wintery landscape. Either way, we are weary from worrying, from checking on mamas and babies through the days, and from the long, dark nights. But there's nothing to be done about the worry, except to keep moving.

So move we do, working through the afternoon, trying to prepare. The

Man of the Ranch pushes the yearling heifers into the sheep pen, where there's more cover. Then he sorts the bulls in with the horses, moves a big bunch of expectant mothers into the largest corral, and lures the mamas who have already calved into the adjacent pasture with a bale of rolled-out hay. Everyone is bucking and shoving, kicking up mud, wild and jittery from the impending storm.

The Man of the Ranch goes off to round up one last bunch of cattle, and I try to get my little orphans into the barn. There are three calves and four lambs, including Belle, the tiniest lamb, who fell ill and spent a week inside. She's better now and happy to be back with her twin brother. They are lying curled together in a tight knot, sharing warmth. The two larger lambs, however, are not pleased. They bleat to me through the wooden gate. They'd like to be out running and bouncing, instead of imprisoned in the small pen. They don't know they're the lucky ones, shielded from the wind, with thick straw bedding to snuggle down into.

The human children are similarly ensconced in their own little pen, and they can play without worry of an overly friendly calf knocking them down. Like the big lambs, however, they'd prefer not to be confined, and they watch me with wide eyes through the slats of wood. "Can you find something you and your sister can play?" I ask the Bean as I hurtle past. He'll be three in June, and suddenly he seems so much older—ready to help, ready to be a "big boy."

Out in the small corral, I flap my arms to push Rita the milk cow toward the gate. The mud from melting snow and freezing rain is ankle deep. Every step sucks my boots halfway off my feet, and I'm sweating under my wool coat and soaked-through coveralls. I circle around behind her and swing the long metal gate as quickly as I can to let her out, but I catch her two calves before they can sneak through with her. Inside the barn, Roo starts to cry. She's tired of being a footnote in our storm preparations.

I get Rita and the calves separated and then hustle the calves back to their own pen. The air is dusty from all the bodies kicking up straw, and Roo's face is streaked with dirty tears. The Bean has climbed to the top of the fence and is preparing to escape, leaving his sister behind—which is no doubt the cause of her consternation.

I pick Roo up and take the Bean's little hand in my own. It's time to head in and wait. We'll try not to worry too much, knowing we've done the best we can, and hope that it's enough. It's been said that man's labors, though impressive, fade to insignificance before nature unbound. In our line of work, we know this to be true, but we gather ourselves up anyway. We gather ourselves, our children, our animals—we gather them in the warmth of our best efforts, the labor of our bodies a statement of gratitude for this way of life.

APRIL 19, 2018

LAMBS IN THE HOUSE

First of all, have you noticed I keep writing that it's spring, or almost spring, or sure to be spring soon, and it keeps not being spring? This past week featured record lows all over the state of South Dakota, and it also included a swirl of winter storms. The Man of the Ranch has been checking the herd around the clock, so it's been another string of days that bleed into night. Everyone is blurry, sleep-deprived, and cold.

Which is why I'm not going to mention the weather at all. No, instead, I'm going to tell you the other thing I was wrong about—baby lambs. Remember how I said I didn't feel as attached to my little orphans as I used to? I've had to eat my words in that regard as well. If you happened to stop by our house this week, you could not have helped but notice a small lamb snuggled in blankets by the sliding glass door. I really have to stop tempting fate with these proclamations . . . .

Suffice to say, after writing that I felt my time serving as mother to orphan lambs was past, we found Belle, one of the tiny twins, huddled on the barn floor and struggling to stand. She could lift herself with her back legs, but try as she might, her front legs buckled beneath her. So, she's now snugly ensconced in the house—and just as snugly ensconced in my heart.

Most likely, the cause of her condition is "joint ill," a bacterial infection that attacks the joints of young lambs, causing stiffness, swelling, and lameness. The course of treatment is high doses of penicillin. Normally, we would have treated her in the barn, left her with her brother, and hoped for the best. But the record low temps precluded that, and now we have a house lamb. (Oops, I just mentioned the weather again! That's the last time, I promise.)

Belle is the third house lamb I've had in the five years since I began keeping sheep. A house lamb, in case you're wondering, is different from a lamb in the house—the distinction being that while a lamb may come into the house for a few hours or a night, house lambs come for a day that somehow turns to weeks. The result? A lot of extra laundry, and an undeniable bond.

Like Belle, my other two house lambs also started out okay but then lost the ability to walk within their first week of life. (Which is how they ended up with me; that was back when my house was the hub for injured babies of all kinds.) Another similarity is that all three exhibited a preternatural calm. Usually lambs are frenetic, bouncing, bleating balls of joy and mayhem. These lambs, though alert and affectionate, conserved their energy, turning their wide brown eyes to the parade of daily life as it passed their nest of blankets.

I've learned from mistakes I made with the first two, so even with the wintry weather, we've been taking Belle outside to visit her brother and cousins. We don't want her to forget she's a lamb. While the healthy lambs practice grazing nearby, Belle nibbles at the brambles she can reach with her outstretched neck. All is well, until the others decide to leap away, and then Belle cries out in dismay. She doesn't want to be left behind.

Her distress is heartbreaking, but the Bean has devised a solution: wagon rides. Dragging a sickly lamb over the frozen ruts of mud and snow that serve as our yard doesn't seem like a great idea, but the Bean offers his lap and his warm arms as a buffer. So, I set him in the wagon, then nestle Belle onto the cushion of his thick snowsuit.

From the first, it was clear the Bean was right. Bumping around in wide circles, snuggled close to her human brother, Belle was the lamb equivalent of beaming. The Bean stroked her woolly head softly, and she looked up occasionally to offer a small kiss. "Belle likes me!" he murmured gently, as we continued our voyage.

I've written before that caring for sickly animals, some of whom I knew there was little hope of saving, taught me how to love bigger. It's painful to open your heart to something you will more than likely lose, but the pain is your heart muscle growing stronger, its four-chambered walls hung bright with stars. And watching my small son learn tenderness through his careful attention to this sickly creature has been another unexpected gift.

What does it mean to let yourself get a little broken by loving? Well, I think it means everything.

MAY 29, 2018

FLOWERS AND BIRDS

Birds, birds, birds everywhere! Have there ever been so many birds? Green, green, green—I swear it's never been this green! And there are lilac and chokecherry and plum and crabapple trees all bursting simultaneously into blossom, like a choir full of converts bursting into song.

Of course, it's possible we're experiencing all the normal regalia that accompanies spring, and that the unusually long winter makes it somehow seem extraordinary this year, but I don't think so. I think there's something more going on.

Just this morning, the children and I were sitting in the grass beneath our one big shade tree, while a dozen barn swallows swooped wildly over our heads, catching bugs in midflight. One or two at a time would stop to sit on the peak of our house before taking flight once again. The display went on and on all morning. I've never experienced anything quite like it—it actually felt like we were members of the flock. Meanwhile, meadowlarks, robins, and mourning doves called to one another so loudly that it was almost difficult to get a word in edgewise.

It's a similar story with the greenness of the grass. A neighbor theorized that after two years of drought, perhaps the soil held extra nutrients, and all that abundant nourishment was just waiting for moisture. Whatever the cause, there's no discounting the fact that the grass is almost ridiculously bright, like something from the Emerald City after Judy Garland makes it to Technicolor. It's the purest green I've ever seen.

One very small downside of all this supersized spring glory is the weeds, which didn't take a break for drought but are more than happy to capitalize on the added nutrients as well. The long, hard winter, after a long, hard summer, has meant that many of my perennial herbs and flowers did not return. They've been replaced by pigweed and goosefoot and endless, winding ropes of creeping Jenny. It seems every time we weed a garden bed, we find it has returned to the same degree of weediness by the following morning.

Really, it's a small price to pay, and now I have a garden helper. The Bean is old enough to want to work in the garden too, so I've been trying to explain the difference between plants we want and plants we don't want. We're getting plenty of chances to identify and pull out the ones we don't want; so far that's mostly all that the garden beds contain.

Meanwhile, the pasture is flush with flowers. With each trip out to check the herd, we find a new kind of blossom rolling above the green grass in rollicking waves. Yellow, purple, and white, the flowers are small, and the stems tough and reedy; like most of what grows here, they aren't showy. But the beauty is in the details. Each petal has its own miniature geography. Each small patch of buds is a soft stroke of color on the prairie's canvas. Together they form an ever-evolving masterpiece.

We had some guests over this weekend for supper. There were thunderstorms predicted, but the weather held, and we ate outside under a perfect lavender sky. To the east, the moon rose full as a pink pearl, while the sun began its descent in the west. In the yard, the children played barefoot, a little gray barn kitten romped, and our bottle lambs grazed. I thought of the flowers in the field, nodding their sweet faces as the sun set. Only a month ago, there was still snow on the ground, and it seemed winter would never end. But it has, as it always must, and this, all this, was well worth the wait.

JUNE 4, 2018

GRASS TETANY

Last week I wrote about the beautiful green prairie—a rancher's dream come true. Except when every once in a while, it's not. The lack of minerals in fast-growing spring grass can cause a dangerous imbalance in cattle called "grass tetany." The disease strikes hard and fast—in many cases, the first symptom is death.

Grass tetany is notorious for striking the healthiest, best milkers first, but it was still a shock when we found Zena, our half-Jersey tanker-truck of a milk cow lying in the grass one bright spring morning, barely breathing and unable to move. The Man of the Ranch rushed to the feed store for medication, but even after a full dose, Zena still wasn't able to stand. The prognosis was not good.

I was cavalier at first. Talking to a friend on the phone, I said, "Well, I'm finally accepting that part of ranch life is losing animals you care about. You can't let your heart break over every single one." But when I went out to check on Zena later that morning and discovered her half lying, half sitting on the same matted section of grass where she'd first fallen down, tears sprang to my eyes. "Oh, Zena," I said aloud.

She heard my voice, and her black tufted head wobbled in my direction. She tried to lift herself up, but her legs crumpled, and she fell back limply, her neck lolling wildly. I hurried away, scared that my presence would lead to another attempt to stand. When I snuck back to check again a few hours later, she still hadn't moved, and I slipped away as quietly as I could.

It therefore felt like more than a small miracle when Zena limped into the corral that evening; but her eyes were still glazed, her breathing still labored. It became clear that she was coming in as a matter of habit—this was when she usually came in to feed her calves—and though her body was once again mobile, her spirit was still out wandering. She hobbled in a small circle before heading back through the gate, where she once again laid down and did not rise.

For two days, the Man of the Ranch lugged water and feed to her. The fact that she was still alive was inexplicable. “That’s one tough cow,” he said, shaking his head.

Then, on the third day, a second miracle happened: Zena walked into the corral once more. This time her gait was steady, her eyes clear. She began to call using the soft low all mother cows reserve for their young children. Her two adopted babies came over to the fence line to investigate. Her biological calf did not come, however, but instead turned his back to her. Zena kept calling to him, but he did not respond.

Rita, our other milk cow, came to the fence as well, sticking her long black tongue out to kiss her friend on the cheek and nose. Zena accepted the gesture but looked past Rita to her calf. He did not turn to face her, not even once. She finally stopped calling to her baby when night fell, and she and Rita went back out to the pasture together to graze side by side.

Fortunately, the story doesn’t end there. This morning, the third miracle occurred. Zena’s milk came back, and as I write this, she is nursing her babies once again. After he is done drinking, her little calf stands beneath her, lifting his glossy head up to nuzzle her chin. Zena’s eyes are soft, and she bows her head to nuzzle him back.

I can’t help thinking it was, at least in part, motherly love that kept Zena with us. Whatever the case, there is no doubt my husband was right: she is one tough cow, with a big, big heart, and we are very lucky to have her.

JUNE 25, 2018

YELLOW CAT SOFTENS

Longtime readers of this column may remember tales about our crusty tom, Yellow Cat. Yellow Cat preceded me in his residency here at the ranch, and at seven or eight (or nine, we aren't sure) years of age, he has well exceeded the many lives allotted to his kind. For a feral barn cat, he has achieved near-legendary longevity.

Through the years, Yellow Cat has witnessed many other cats come and go—in some cases, he has even been responsible for their leaving. On moonlit nights, we've heard his yowling when some young upstart passed through and tried to pick a fight. We've seen the bite marks on his flank and the notches taken out of his ears. But, as he remains, and the other cats do not, it's safe to say the other cats looked worse. He's also outlasted many of his own offspring and, sadly, a wife or two as well.

Surprisingly, Yellow Cat is not particularly big or burly, and as the years pass, he has gotten frailer still. He no longer has all his teeth, and his fur often looks disheveled. But, until recently, everything seemed to be as it had always been. Yellow Cat presided over the barn like a shadowy king, slipping in and out as he pleased, fixing us in his stern blue-eyed gaze when we came to deliver kibble, and never once in all these years letting human hands touch him.

Until now. The barn is currently occupied by Esme, our mama cat, a litter of young kittens, and her two teenage daughters. Esme is even smaller than Yellow Cat, as are her daughters. All are gentle and affectionate. They love to be petted and babied, and they generally appear to be the picture of docile domesticity.

Meanwhile, Yellow Cat has grown downright skinny over the last few months. We assumed it was his advanced age, but then we noticed he was never in the barn. Not in the morning when we poured out a few drops for cats from the lamb bottles, not in the evening when we refilled the cat dish. Esme and her brood would circle our ankles, purring cozily, but Yellow Cat was conspicuously absent.

Instead, he began turning up on the porch. One day he even tried to sneak in the house when the Bean left the door ajar. Things were getting weird.

Unbeknownst to each other, the Man of the Ranch and I both began leaving him small piles of kibble on the patio table from time to time, and he gobbled up every bite like he was half-starved. Which he was, as it turned out. Apparently, our tough old man, who regularly routs every roving brute, was not up for battling three demure little ladies. Or maybe he was just being a gentleman.

Either way, since his exile from the barn, he is a cat transformed. Last night, I went to set down his evening snack, and he zipped right past me into the kitchen. When I tried to shoo him out, he began rubbing against my leg. I reached down and touched his head, gingerly at first, and then I started petting him. A real, honest-to-goodness head pet. He began to purr.

I don't think there's any danger of Yellow Cat becoming a bona fide house cat, but it looks like we now have a half-friendly porch cat. Yellow Cat has always been an emblem of strength and stoicism around here, but even the toughest cats sometimes need a little comfort, I guess. And I personally find it wonderful to be reminded it's possible to open oneself up to affection late in the game. After all, everyone deserves love, even (or especially?) old tomcats.

SEPTEMBER 10, 2018

PREGNANCY CHECKING

This spring my mother bought miniature camping chairs for the small fry, and my goodness, if they haven't turned out to be the best gift ever. Those wee chairs have held tiny tushies at campsites and concerts in the park, at wayside truck stops and family potlucks. They have been dang handy.

Their most surprising uses, however, have been ranch related. They've been used during shearing, while freeing a ewe who had gotten herself tangled in some old, half-buried twine, and when I weeded out stinging nettle from the back garden. In other words, anytime I wanted the kids to stay close, but not too close, I've pulled out those camping chairs.

This morning we pregnancy tested the heifers, and once again the camping chairs were parked on the sidelines. It was a strange moment documenting the passage of time. The past four years I've either had a baby in my belly or a baby on my back (or a baby in both places) while we preg-tested. No longer babes-in-arms, my two wildlings instead happily observed their daddy from the camp chairs, their feet propped up on the pipe railing.

My skill set makes me most useful with a paper and pen, so while the men worked, and the children watched, I wrote down all the tag numbers, calving dates, and other relevant info. Since we refer to most of the members of our herd as "mama cow," Roo would shout "Mama!" as each heifer was released from the chute. The Bean just peered through the pipe intently, studying every movement of the process—readying himself, I'm sure, for the day he's on the other side of the fence.

Then the Bean remembered we were going to have a midmorning treat when the men took a break. I had made the mistake of telling him the treat would be chocolate chip cookies, and the poor child was suddenly ravenous, breakfast light-years in the past and nothing, not a banana or an apple, or any other snack I offered, would do. He was hungry for, "Something sweet. Something really sweet, Mama."

His sister soon joined the fray, chanting, "Cookie! Cookie!"

"We have to wait until the break," I intoned again and again, much to their chagrin. The charm of the camp chairs had worn thin, and to pass the time, brother and sister began climbing the pipe fence, bending over the top rung, little torsos swinging recklessly. I did my best to steady them by the loops at the waists of their denim pants, but they kept wiggling away. Meanwhile, the vet kept shouting numbers.

Eventually we made it through the queue, the kids got their cookies, and I finished the books, which I think are mostly accurate. My nerves were frayed, though, and I couldn't help thinking of all the people who told me having two kids so close in age is hard at first but gets easier when the kids start playing together. "I'm still waiting for the 'gets easier' part," I thought to myself as I packed up the camping chairs, shooing the kids toward the house, away from tall fences and discombobulated livestock.

It's hard not to think back fondly on the days when these two could be contained by a backpack or a cloth sling; and it's probably for the best that last year at this time, when I was chasing a two-year-old with a nine-month-old strapped to my body, I didn't know life was actually going to become more harried, not less.

And yet in only a few short years, a mere breath of time, those little chairs will be collecting dust in the corner of the shop, long outgrown, and I will mourn not hearing "Mama, Mama!" a thousand times a day. It is, after all, a name I waited a long time to grow into.

SEPTEMBER 24, 2018

NESTS

Synchronicity: the simultaneous occurrence of events that appear significantly related but have no discernible connection. . . .

One morning this spring my son and I found an intricately woven bird's nest on the ground outside the house. We were delighted. In addition to strands of dried grass, there were tufts of wool and even a few errant strips of unwound baling twine. We brought it in and set it on the bookshelf.

That afternoon I found another, even tinier nest by the clothesline. The next day I found two more. Coincidence? Well, there had been high winds all that week, which surely pulled the nests from their respective branches, but when are there not high winds during South Dakota's springs? To find so many nests in such a short period of time was noteworthy, even if I had no idea what it meant.

This week provided a new set of coincidences to mull over. We had been keeping a lowkey vigil in the barn of late, as we had not one, but two expectant mothers there. Esme, our black mama cat, is as round as a ripe pumpkin. Her daughter, Cheryl Cat, was not nearly as rotund, but also expecting.

When the kids and I went to check last Friday, we found Mama Esme as plump as ever, while Cheryl looked downright skinny. We found her kitten tucked safely beside a saddle blanket in a dark corner of an old feed bunk. Cheryl seemed strange though, and when I felt her tummy, there was a kitten-shaped bulge close to her hip.

After I put the kids in bed, I checked the barn again, and this time I found Cheryl's sister, Aster, curled up with the newborn. Cheryl was nowhere to be found. On the ground, a few feet from the cozy nest, however, was a wet, gray lump, with an umbilical cord and afterbirth still attached.

"Oh, Cheryl," I said aloud as I knelt to touch the kitten. It was cold and didn't move. It had been stillborn or had died from exposure, no doubt. I went back to check on Aster, who purred loudly, holding the other baby in the curve of her hip as gently as if it were her own.

Just then I heard a muted cry. I looked toward the patch of straw where the dead baby lay. There was no movement, but I reached down to touch its body anyway. It still didn't move, but I knew what I'd heard, so I picked the fragile body up. I heard it again—a murmur that couldn't be coming from anywhere but that tiny cold kitten. In the warm shelter of my palm, I felt a tremor of life.

Then Saturday, Roo and I found a two-day-old chick that had fallen in the well of a cement block and was too tiny to hop out. Once again, I heard it before we saw it, its frightened cries so weak they were barely audible. The chick kept chirping when I lifted it from its stone prison, but its eyes were half closed, its body limp. The morning was chilly, too chilly for a newly hatched chick to be separated from its mother's sheltering feathers for long. I tucked it into my shirt, and there it remained for the rest of the morning as it slowly warmed.

At the writing of this column, three days later, both kittens, the chick, and their respective mamas are thriving.

So, I have been a witness to two miracles this week, miracles so tiny I could hold them both in my hand. Was it divine intervention that caused me to be in exactly the right place at exactly the right time, two days in a row? Was it an inscrutable omen? Or was it simply a coincidence, as random as the wind pulling nest after nest from the trees.

Of course I can't say, but I do know that it is always good to be reminded how little we really know of life's mysteries and, my goodness, how wonderful it is to find we can be useful anyway.

OCTOBER 29, 2018

PUMPKIN AND BUTTERNUT

Rita, our Jersey cow, is getting older. She'll be eight years old this spring. That's getting up there for a dairy cow—genetics demand that a dairy cow's body produce a lot of milk, and that takes its toll. Rita still seems plenty spry, but she won't be with us forever.

Meanwhile, our lives have changed a lot since she first arrived on the scene. Most obviously, we've got two kids now. Milking twice a day was a lot easier when I didn't have my little helpers in tow. And it's not just kids—work off the ranch has picked up. I've been traveling more for music, and the Man of the Ranch has two other jobs as well. All summer we discussed the constantly juggled balls that are our current life circumstances, and we agreed downsizing chores was a wise choice at this juncture. Which is why, when we recently had the opportunity to bring home two Jersey heifer calves, we probably should have said no.

If you happened to stop by our place this week, however, you would have noticed two Jersey heifer calves in the corral by the barn. What does that mean? One takeaway might be that wisdom doesn't necessarily come with experience. Another might be that love of a good milk cow cannot be denied, even when one ought to know better. And you know what? I am already thrilled with our decision. Besides, we've gotten pretty good at juggling. What's one more ball?

We named the new gals Pumpkin and Butternut; one is reddish-orange, the other yellow and brown. They have the glossy turned-up noses of their breed and tiny horn buds beside the tufts of hair on their knobbed heads. Their soft brown eyes are as round as full moons, and just as bright. Twice a day we go out to "ooh" and "ahhh" over them, to feed them a little grain, and to slowly but surely convince them that when the time comes, they should share their milk with us.

It still amazes me what selective breeding can do. Jersey cows are famous for the high fat content of their milk (which means lots of butter!), lower feed cost due to lower bodyweight compared to other dairy breeds, and of course, their genial dispositions. Regarding the latter characteristic, Pumpkin and Butternut are quintessential Jerseys—even though they were out to pasture all summer, surrounded only by other cows, after just a few days here they are already gentle enough to come over and sniff our fingers, as interested in us as we are in them. Much like our guard dog's innate ability to perceive the difference between a chicken and a hawk, Pumpkin and Butternut seem born to trust.

Of course, even if Rita is no longer with us by the time these girls are ready to be milked, we still won't need two—there is only so much milk one family can drink! The plan is to acclimate them to life in the barnyard, halter-break them both, and work on their "standing," so they can be hand-milked out in the pasture, or in a head catch, with minimal fuss. Then, when the time comes, we will sell one of them and keep the other for ourselves. The sadness of letting one of them go will be tempered by the knowledge that we are providing a useful and worthy friend to another family.

It's a good plan. A really good plan. So was the plan to downsize chores, which is to say, we'll see how it goes. I think making sensible decisions is important, but so is welcoming joy where you find it. Whatever happens, I already know I won't regret standing in the corral, the last sun-warmed days of autumn pooling around us, telling soft stories to Pumpkin and Butternut while Roo and the Bean bring them wisps of hay by the chubby fistful, time slowing so the many balls of chores and responsibilities hang overhead briefly, almost like stars.

DECEMBER 27, 2018

TODDLERS AND PUPPIES

Christmas was a mix of barely-contained chaos, toddler meltdowns, so much wrapping paper, and even more sweetness and gratitude. Emmy is old enough to really open and enjoy her presents now, and she did so with gusto, chuckling "Oh wow, oh wow, oh wow!" every single time. Today, with the dust finally beginning to settle on the festivities, she has been wandering the house cradling her new treasures, saying, "Oh, I love dem. I love dem." The Bean was equally impressed with his gifts and has already clocked many hours leveling the living room floor with his shiny yellow motor grader.

Meanwhile, after weeks of balmy weather, cold and snow swept in on Christmas night and have left a frosty blanket around our little house. Consequently, the Man of the Ranch and I have been sipping coffee and tea and playing hand after hand of Go Fish with a new toddler-friendly deck of cards. (Instead of the standard suits, it uses food to delineate the different categories. "Do you have any cheeses? If you don't, you say 'go fish,'" the Bean tells me, peeking from behind his fan of cards.)

It all feels a little like having our cake and eating it too. We got to spend the days leading up to Christmas outside, in the wind and sun, and now, with so many interesting new activities to occupy us indoors, we can enjoy the winter weather from the coziness of our own dear hearth.

Of course, we did exit the building briefly this morning, mostly so the Bean could test the motor grader's prowess at plowing snow. But though the flakes were soft and fluffy, the wind was not, and Emmy, who still isn't as mobile as her brother when suited up in full snow gear, deemed it "too cold" about thirty seconds after stepping outside.

In other news, the Christmas puppy I dreamed of this autumn did in fact materialize. She is a fluffy ball of constant, frantic motion, except when she's sleeping. Like all puppies, she has two speeds: on and off. Her name is Hazel, but we've been calling her Zuzu, which is appropriate, as her presence makes our home even more like a cageless zoo than ever. Since the human children seem to run on similar speeds, she fits right into the family.

Getting a puppy in the dark days of early winter could be listed as an example of sheer madness, but again, the weeks of warm weather served us well, and Hazel is already (mostly) potty-trained. Which, coincidentally, I can also say of Emmy. So, while I haven't permanently packed away the industrial-sized bottle of carpet cleaner, I'm not pulling it out multiple times a day anymore, either.

From my vantage point here in the waning days of December, I can see the shape of the rest of our winter clearly: the galloping herd of kids and cats and dogs carving a pattern up and down floorboards, walls clattering with the echoes of "Jingle bells, jingle bells!" —a song that isn't going out of fashion just because Christmas is over. From time to time, the adults bundle the herd in polyester and wool so the galloping can occur, albeit briefly, outside. There will also be couch snuggles, and more card games, and long winter naps, but when we look back, I bet it's the galloping we will remember, in this, our season of puppies and toddlers.

The Man of the Ranch and I are firmly ensconced in middle age, so, left to our devices, we'd probably be running at two speeds these days as well: not-too-fast and even-slower. On long winter evenings, however, I'm betting we join the house-wide gallop parade. How can we resist? The joy contained within our young charges is too great for their small bodies to hold in stillness for long, and our joy in watching them, equally great.

2019

FEBRUARY 4, 2019

BABY FREEZY

When we pregnancy tested our herd last autumn, the neighbor who did the ultrasounds warned that one of the cows would give birth early. "She must have been in the wrong place at the right time," he mused. Since there really wasn't much to be done after the fact, we mentally filed the information away, then promptly forgot all about it.

That is, until this week, of course, when the recorded temperature dipped into the negative double digits. Checking the herd the morning after the deepest cold, the Man of the Ranch was surprised to discover an ice-dusted calf lying beside her mother. She was chilled, but still blinking. The mama's ministrations weren't cutting the mustard, however, so the little calf needed to come in and get warmed up.

As surprised as the Man of the Ranch was to find the calf in the pasture, the kids were even more surprised to see him pulling her to the sliding glass door in their red plastic sled. Usually we put chilled-down calves in the bathtub, but this calf wasn't in terrible shape, so instead the little gal got snuggled under blankets and towels by our propane stove. The kids and I rubbed her dry with rags and got her blood flowing while we discussed names. The Bean proposed "Freezy," and Roo and I agreed it was the perfect suggestion.

Within minutes Freezy was shivering hard (a good sign), and then she dropped into a deep sleep. Our old dog, Lily, gave Freezy a quick sniff before lying down on her own soft bed, and the house cats paid the calf no mind at all. Since the kids' toy kitchen is beside the propane stove too, they went back to making tea and cookies and soup and all their other important work, the snoozing bundle of blankets now an unremarkable part of the landscape.

An hour passed, and suddenly Freezy awoke from her dreams and remembered that her tummy was empty and that she needed milk and she needed it fast. Her first creaking steps were toward us, as I tried to help her gain her balance lest she stumble against the hot grate of the stove. A hasty call was made to the Man of the Ranch, who was out doing chores, while the kids cheered at Freezy's recovery.

The little calf was standing without wobbles by the time the Man of the Ranch arrived, but when he lifted Freezy up to carry her outside, Roo began to weep. "Dada not take Freezy!" she cried. I tried to spin a tale of Freezy's happy reunion with her mother, but Roo wasn't buying it. She had her heart set on Freezy spending the rest of the winter inside with us.

Today, the weather is almost eerily warm. Water is once again running down the ruts in the gravel road, and the steady tick of icicles melting off the roof has the kids laughing and chanting, "It's raining, it's raining!" In the past twenty-four hours, we've made many trips to the far corral to check on Freezy. Each time, Roo is elated to find her pal alert and thriving, but she's equally crestfallen when we leave the corral and Freezy doesn't come with us. Fortunately, the fine weather means the frequent trips are no hardship.

If you were to see Roo riding on her father's strong arm to the corral and back, you'd have no doubt they were father and daughter—every day she grows more like him—but apparently there is quite a bit of her mama present as well. This week it was the Man of the Ranch's birthday, but if you run into him, you may want to offer a sympathetic pat on the back instead of well-wishes. With a wife and a daughter who want to bring in all the babies all the time, the poor man has his work cut out for him.

FEBRUARY 11, 2019

WAYWARD CHICKENS

After weeks and weeks of raving about how unseasonably warm it has been here on the ranch, I can finally report winter has arrived, and apparently it is making up for lost time. The thermometer has not crept above zero in nearly two weeks, and the extended forecast predicts much of the same for the rest of the month. That's a lot of cold weather, folks.

The worst is hopefully behind us, though. Last Thursday, we had record-breaking temperatures—the mercury dove into the negative mid-thirties, the windchill was much colder than that. There was plenty of warning though, so the Man of the Ranch spent the better part of the preceding two days preparing: extra feed, extra bedding, extra care taken to make sure waterers were working for the livestock, and a heat lamp installed in the chicken coop.

There is an old adage: there is no such thing as bad weather, just inappropriate clothing. While the originators of that aphorism might not have taken negative-thirty-five-degree weather into consideration when making such a claim, I can now attest it is true until at least negative fifteen degrees—the temperature on the day I set out for the puppy's evening walk. I was wearing long johns, jeans, insulated overalls, a wool sweater, a down jacket, and a second, much larger down jacket with a fur-lined hood, plus a hat and mittens, of course. The wind blew like a tempest, swirling snow around the circle of my hood, but I was actually quite comfortable.

After I finished the walk, I stopped at the barn. A few weeks ago, I wrote about my two barn chickens, who have shunned the coop to live with the cats. That was all well and good until now, but the barn isn't as warm as the coop, so I needed to move them back, and I knew they wouldn't be pleased.

I spotted my neighbor's hen first—or rather, she spotted me and took off running, somehow sensing my intentions, and that is when my wardrobe choices turned from asset to liability. Round and round the barn we went, my snowman-like proportions slowing my every step, and my fur-lined hood narrowing my vision to a small tunnel. By the time I caught her, I had begun to sweat under my thousand layers, and I was ready to be done with the whole affair.

During the initial chase, I didn't see one of the chickens, Red Molly, anywhere, so I was hopeful she had already made her way to the coop. When I dropped off the first hen, however, Red Molly was nowhere to be found. I feared she had already succumbed to the cold, and I pondered simply returning to the house.

Ten minutes later, I was teetering on the uneven ledge of a feed bunk, reaching up into the rafters of the barn, my ridiculous layers proving once again to be a hinderance. After my guilty conscience got the better of me, I had returned to scour the barn, finally locating Molly in a dim corner, high above my head. Face upturned, waiting to either be pooped on or have Red Molly try to claw my eyes out (while also risking a not-so-short fall to the ground myself), I had a thought I've had many, many times before: "Why am I doing this? This is a terrible idea."

"Why indeed?" I asked myself again when I finally crossed the yard to the coop, a large yellow chicken under my arm. Perhaps I was unkind to animals in a previous life, and thus I am compelled to make amends this time around. Or maybe I am simply accumulating good karma for happy returns in the afterlife. Who knows? But I will rest a little easier knowing my barn hens are safe and warm, and I guess that's as good a reason to play chicken rescuer as any other.

APRIL 1, 2019

BRING MUD BOOTS

I am as big a nature lover as they come, but even I have to admit that early spring on the Dakota plains is not Mother Nature's most attractive season. In wet years, this is mud season; in dry ones, it's plain dirt. But either way, what is uncovered when the snow melts ain't pretty.

For starters, the grass is long dead. Autumn grass is glowy and golden, and it waves from the fields in a friendly wash of warm light. The prairie in early spring does not glow. The grass looks gray and tired—and rightly so. All winter the stems are battered and blasted by arctic winds, buried, crushed by drifts of ice and snow, and of course, nibbled to nubs by cattle, sheep, deer, rabbits, and every other hungry critter that has passed through. New growth needs some sun and warmth before green emerges. In the meantime, it's muck and rotten stems as far as the eye can see.

Dead grass is not all that reappears once the snow melts. Anything that's died in the last six months is abruptly excavated. This is especially true if you have a dog or two monitoring the melt. More so if your dogs are the generous sort, who believe in bringing their findings to the yard to share, display, and, revoltingly, snack on. Deer antlers still attached to a skull, all manner of hooves still attached to the legs, tufts of moldering feathers still attached to a wing—the dogs drag it all back from the pastures and draws. My kids are growing up with this as their "normal," but for me, it still feels a bit shocking.

Additionally, when I say "mud," I'm not talking about dirt and water. I'm talking about dirt and water that runs in small rivers from the corrals or the cozy spots in draws where the livestock huddled during the rough weather. I'm talking about "mud" that is actually mostly manure.

Unlike the animal remains, these cascading torrents of dung-water are something I *have* gotten used to. So much so that I feel confused when someone who doesn't live here, like my visiting mom or sister for example, walks gingerly through the corral, while the rest of us just tromp straight across.

"Oh, that's right!" I have to remind myself. "I used to be like that too. People who don't live on ranches or farms aren't used to being ankle deep in poop all the time and find it unsavory."

Which is why, when two of my very best friends in the world, one who hails from Boston, the other from Seattle, asked about coming to visit us on their respective spring breaks, I was a little worried. Well, not at first . . . at first I was overjoyed, forgetting about "mud" and animal excavation season. Plus, sometimes April is snow from start to finish, so there was always the chance of a soft white blanket still covering the worst of winter's leavings.

Fine weather since the spring equinox and unseasonably high temperatures next week mean a sanitizing, frosty blanket is unlikely. My friends will get to see our ranch in all its early spring glory. And what a sight it will be.

Thank goodness for baby animals, especially ones that need bottles. Cuddling the sweet softness of lambs and goat kids and little bottle calves makes up for what this season lacks in aesthetic pleasures. Or at least that's what I'm banking on my friends thinking. It certainly is true for me.

Meanwhile, my friends have been warned. When asked what they should bring, I said, "Jeans you don't mind getting dirty and mud boots. High boots. No, really, the highest you've got." So, we'll see how it goes, and perhaps if they ever decide to come back, I'll suggest they come in June, when the grass is knee high and shimmering like emeralds in the warm sunshine, undulating like ocean waves all the way to the horizon.

APRIL 14, 2019

LAMBING

The past week has been a master class in the perils of shepherding. We spent the first half of the week getting ready for a major winter storm, the second half weathering it, and now we are digging out. I don't think I've ever been this physically or emotionally exhausted before (and this comes from a woman who had two children in the span of eighteen months).

A blizzard is never a welcome thing in our line of work, but late-season storms are especially dreaded. It's hard on the mamas, it's harder on the babies, and serving as midwife to animals giving birth in the cold and snow is no fun, either. This year has been exceptionally difficult because in addition to the nasty weather, after never having triplets born into my flock before, I've had four sets this season already.

Triplets, I'm learning the hard way, are no boon. For one thing, I've twice wrongly assumed a mother was done laboring, and I left thinking everything was under control. In one instance this led to another ewe "stealing" the first baby. I returned to find the newborn following around a ewe who had yet to lamb and therefore had no milk. In the other cases it has simply meant I've been scrambling to decide how to give them all the best start, knowing that a ewe often can't produce enough milk to nourish three babies.

Moreover, the first hours on the ground are the most important of a lamb's life. The beginning milk from the mother, called colostrum, provides essential nutrients. Without it, a lamb's outlook is bleak. Lambs also arrive earthside slippery and wet, and it's the mother's job to lick them dry so they don't get chilled down. A ewe has to work fast in the temperatures we've been enduring, no small feat when she's busy giving birth to another baby. It's that much worse when she stops to give birth to a third.

While they wait, the first babies expend the precious energy they need to get up and start suckling just trying to keep warm. As you might expect, triplets also tend to be smaller and weaker than twins and singles. It's no wonder, then, that without careful and timely intervention one or more of the triplets usually will not survive.

So, in addition to a body that's exhausted and aching from trudging through wind and knee-deep snow all hours of the day and night, my heart is aching too. I've had to make some tough calls the past few nights, and honestly, I've not been making good ones. I'm new to shepherding, and I've never experienced lambing in a blizzard. Plus, I'm overly sentimental, hating to separate mothers and babies. Sentimentality can be a liability, and I've lost babies as a result.

There's nothing to do but keep on keeping on, however. I don't have the luxury of regret just yet, because lambing is far from over. I'm writing this column in between trips outside. Most of the mothers and babies, and the ewes still waiting for labor, are lounging in the big corral, chewing their cud or dozing in the first sunshine we've seen in days. A few of the pregnant ewes look like they won't last the day, let alone the night, so I need to keep a close eye on them.

Meanwhile, I have two sets of triplets still with their mothers in the barn, as well as another baby from a different set curled up in blankets in the laundry room. Our laundry room guest is black with a narrow white crescent on her forehead, and she is tiny and frail and oh-so-sweet. We've named her Luna, for the light that shines in darkness, a reminder to hold hope like a candle, while the moon glows like a lullaby above the prairie's long embrace.

APRIL 29, 2019

FIBER FLOCK

This week the final lamb of the season was born, which means I can finally take a breath. What a whirlwind! Mothers and babies are fanned out across the greening pasture like fluffy white clouds, and although the weather is cold and rainy, everyone is happy and thriving.

Since beginning this shepherding adventure seven years ago, I've only had two bottle lambs come out of my own flock. Both times, the lamb in question was a twin, and the mother either didn't want two babies or didn't realize she'd actually given birth to two. Either way, when the babies rose on their wobbly legs to nurse for the first time, they received a headbutt instead of milk. Thus, they became my babies.

As last week's column described, however, I've always found myself with extra bum lambs; I am no stranger to the care and feeding of those babies who, for whatever reason, don't have a mother. In fact, bum lambs are the foundation of my flock. With the exception of a handful of Shetland ewes, every sheep in my flock is either a bum lamb or is the descendant of one.

The result is a motley, ragtag bunch. There are white-faced ewes and black-faced ewes, short ones and tall ones, long-wooled, fine-wooled, and every variation in between. Some grow even, well-curled fleeces and have slender, elegant silhouettes. Others are stout and as wily as badgers. Most are unlike any sheep seen before—rare combinations that will probably never be repeated.

My original intent in breeding sheep was to start a business selling fiber and yarn to hand spinners and knitters. This was partially because I love to knit, but mostly it's because when you think of your sheep as friends, you don't want to think about people eating them. Using their wool to make warm, beautiful garments, on the other hand, is quite appealing.

Most fiber shepherds still cull for quality, which obviously is not the kind of program I've been overseeing. So, while we do sell our wethers and some of the ewe lambs in the fall, if they've been named or were one of my bottle babies, they stay.

Between consigning the lambs and the occasional fleece sale, the flock does turn a profit, but no one would mistake it for a money-making endeavor. The early mornings and late nights during lambing season alone mean that I earn pennies an hour for my labor, not to mention the labor of my poor husband, a cowman through and through, who doesn't even like sheep. Thank goodness he likes me, or did before we brought those fence-crawling Shetlands home. Now he's stuck with both of us.

And I'll admit, there were a few times this past month I contemplated throwing in the towel. Between predation, bad weather, and the simple fact that if you keep your aging ewes, they are going to have more health problems, this has been the hardest year of shepherding, culminating in the hardest lambing season yet. I keep saying I either need to run a lot more sheep so I stop caring so much about every single one, or I need to run a lot less.

In the meantime, four little bottle babies are waiting for me in the barn, which means there are still early mornings and late nights as long as they need milk delivered several times a day. But this part is sheer pleasure, and I am rewarded by their devotion and eager lamb nibbles. Plus, with the help of a talented fiber artist friend, I am finally getting that fiber business off the ground. What our fleeces lack in breed conformity, they make up for with their one-of-a-kind quality, and when folks buy fleece or yarn from us, they will know, if nothing else, it comes from a sheep that is well-loved!

MAY 6, 2019

MOTHER'S DAY

Mother's Day is this coming weekend. It's only my third as a mother, and I am experiencing the same pleasant shock I had the last two years when realizing that this holiday is now about me. After all, I spent a lot of years celebrating mothers before I actually became one.

This is a good time of year to celebrate motherhood. All across the prairie, mothers and new babies are beginning their own unique rituals of care and bonding. Robins are piecing together their intricate nests of twigs and mud. Fawns lie hidden in the grass while their mothers graze nearby. Cottontail dens teem with tiny newborns, their eyes still sealed shut. And of course, the cows, sheep, and horses are spread across the greening grass, their babies running and bucking and playing nearby.

My thoughts on motherhood are simultaneously too big and too small to fit in this column, which is rather like motherhood itself. Motherhood is full of an overwhelming amount of minute tasks, such as finding your kids' matching socks and clipping their toenails, as well as gigantic responsibilities, like shaping a human being (with his or her own unique thoughts, needs, and proclivities) into a healthy, productive member of the bigger human family. It's easy to get bogged down trying to attend to the former, but too much time considering the latter can lead to complete paralysis.

Currently, there seems to be a consensus among social scientists that parenthood has become more labor-intensive than ever before. Perhaps this is true, though I can't imagine parenting has ever been "easy." Nor should it be. The undertaking is awesome in every sense of the word.

Certainly, animals are no strangers to the intensity of parenting. For example, lambs and calves nurse a lot. And they headbutt their moms when they do it. Both my kids went through a stage where they reminded me of baby wolverines while nursing. Tempted to feel sorry for myself, I would think of one of my favorite little ewes in the meadow, her half-grown twins running full speed across the grass toward her and nearly lifting her off the ground as they dove under her to get their hundredth drink of the day. The ewe, for her part, kept calmly chewing, unflappable in the aftermath of the onslaught.

Much like in humans, there is also a lot of variability in livestock in parenting skill and style. First-time sheep and cow mothers can often be seen nervously following their offspring around the pasture, calling to them in anxious tones. An experienced mother, on the other hand, will let her baby wander farther, but when she calls, you better believe that baby comes running. Some mothers keep tabs on the babies, lifting their heads often as they graze; others seem to forget their babies even exist until they hear the young ones calling out from across the pasture. Then the poor absent-minded mothers begin running around in a panic, shouting, "Where are you? What's wrong? Ahhhhh!"

These observations allow me to grant myself a little more grace when it comes to parenting foibles. I truly believe most of us are doing the best we can most of the time—at parenting, and at life in general. Sometimes our best looks like a sloppy mess, but we keep trying. I mean, I try really hard to be an alert, attentive mother, but at least once a day I find myself running around the metaphorical pasture shouting, "Where are you? What's wrong?"

So, if you can, hug your mom this week. If you can't, give yourself a hug from your mom. I know she'd want you to have it.

MAY 24, 2019

RELENTLESS RAIN

Two weeks ago, we had a date for the shearer to come and shear the flock. We'd already enjoyed a string of beautiful, warm days—too warm for the sheep in their overgrown wool coats—so I was very thankful for the appointment, worrying we'd already waited too long. Then, the day before shearing, it began to rain. Since you can't shear a wet sheep, we tentatively rescheduled for the next week.

"We might want to wait a little longer, though," said the Man of the Ranch. "It's supposed to get cold again."

Since then, it has rained or snowed every single day, sometimes both at the same time and often without stopping all day long. The yard and corrals are a sloppy mess. Creeks are rising, roads are washing out, nobody can do much of anything until the rain stops. So we wait.

Every animal we have looks miserable, including our sheepdog, Ellie. She has dry places to rest, but her work as ranch guardian keeps her out in the elements all night and much of the day. Like everyone else, she hasn't been dry in a long time. She has just turned five, and her years of service are starting to show in a slower gait and a world-weary expression. The rain after a long, cold winter hasn't helped. Like most folks who work in agriculture, she doesn't get a vacation from work when the weather's harsh; her job just gets harder.

The sheep look the worst of all the critters, though they probably have it the best. Their wool hangs in dirty, sodden clumps, but the lanolin in the fleece keeps them drier than everybody else. After all, the Cotswold and Shetland genes, two breeds that figure heavily in my flock's heritage, hail from England, a country renowned for its dampness.

So, it's good we waited to shear, except for one thing. Many Shetland sheep, including several of mine, "roo" their fleece in the spring, which means the fleece loosens and is therefore easy to pluck or cut off. If a shepherd does his or her own shearing, this is a great quality; as soon as the sheep starts to roo, off comes the fleece, sometimes with relative ease.

If, however, the shepherd is beholden to someone else's schedule for shearing, or, say, he or she has been experiencing relentless, unending rain, then rooing becomes a liability. The pasture is currently dotted with muddy chunks of Shetland fleece, so you can guess which category I fall into. Every evening when we bring the flock into the corral for the night, I see another ewe who has started to roo. Much like a farmer watching seeds rot in the field, that fleece—the fodder for my fledgling yarn business—is a whole year of product lost. It's disheartening, to say the least.

But it's also the reality of this line of work. Two years ago, we were deep in drought, begging the sky to open up and offer us a few drops of moisture. This year we'd do well to start raising ducks instead of ruminants with so many pastures under water.

The rich man gets his ice in summer, the poor man in winter, and the rancher hopes for moisture all year long. I'll take the sweet green grasses the rain nourishes over fleece any day of the week, but it just goes to illustrate the challenges inherent in a livelihood so wholly dependent on forces beyond human control. It's humbling, it's stressful, but it's what we've chosen and what we love. So, out into the wet and cold we'll trundle to do our chores, knowing that, like everything else, this too shall pass. And the sunshine will be all the more welcome when it finally returns.

JUNE 23, 2019

WEST OF 20

Across our north pasture, and on into our neighbors' bordering pastures, abandoned homesteads dot the landscape at regular intervals. Some feature old houses and windmills that are still standing despite years of neglect. Others are nothing more than brick foundations that rise out of the grass like miniature fortresses. Often a rusted piece of antique farm equipment is nestled nearby, waiting patiently for its farmer to reclaim it, or bedsteads with springs still intact, the mattresses long since rotted away; all evidence of plans laid and left unfulfilled. These scenes are a testament to the way farming and ranching has changed but also to the difficulties of working the land in this place.

Our county was established in 1908, during the second wave of immigration to the Dakotas. By 1909, the area was flooded with hopeful pioneers. They had harnessed their futures to land "West of 20," where the average annual precipitation amounts to less than twenty inches, or near-desert conditions. That first year, however, homesteaders found themselves living in a verdant paradise. Rain was abundant, and consequently, so were crops. At the time it was believed rain would "follow the plow." For that first year, it appeared to be true.

The year 1910 dealt a blow to this fantasy. Whereas the first year had been unusually wet, many homesteaders lost their investments of time and money during the second year, when the area failed to receive even its average of fourteen inches of annual precipitation. They learned, as I have, that "average" doesn't mean much in these parts.

And it didn't end there. After the first year of drought, according to Paula M. Nelson in her book *After the West Was Won*, the spring of 1911 "arrived early and was unusually warm and much too dry. It was the beginning of a growing season that would exceed all others for drought, heat, and wind."[1] Scores of families had no choice but to abandon their homesteads. They had no financial wiggle room to stick it out, having already mortgaged their land for what it was worth. Dropping from a population of 11,348 in the 1910 federal census, our county was listed as 7,641 people in the state census conducted just five years later.

My residence on the ranch has mirrored those original homesteaders' experiences exactly. My first summer here boasted regular intervals of gentle rain, green grasses, waist-high clover, and cool breezes scented with prairie roses. In the fall, cattle prices also happened to be at an all-time high, so we sold our calves with a healthy profit margin and didn't have to buy winter hay. Everyone told me this wasn't normal, but like those early settlers, I couldn't quite believe it. Abundance was all I had ever known in my adopted home.

The years since have taught me otherwise, and I've learned firsthand that if you crave predictability, western South Dakota is not the place to settle. Every time I think I've got our climate figured out, the weather gods send a season of weather so unexpected I have to admit I've got no idea what to plan for next.

Here is a case in point: After several years of hot, dry conditions, I started fifty tomato plants in the greenhouse this spring. I figured that would give me plenty of extra tomatoes to sell at our local farmers market. Other than a brief spike early in the spring, the mercury has barely climbed to seventy degrees so far. Not surprisingly, my tomatoes are languishing. Meanwhile, the grass is once again abundant due to the unprecedented rain, so I'm not going to complain about the tomatoes.

JULY 15, 2019

DAKOTA MOSQUITOES

When I was thirteen, my family moved from Michigan to Minnesota. Our new home featured an expansive wetland bordering the modest backyard, a not uncommon sight in eastern Minnesota. Upon arrival, my sister, then five, went running through the house, and after seeing the backyard through a window, she shouted, "You guys, our house has a park!"

The wetland was beautiful in every season, and we loved living next to it except for one thing—it came with an annual infestation of the Minnesota state bird, a.k.a. the mosquito. Of course, we were not entirely unfamiliar with the nasty critter; we had mosquitoes in Michigan, too. In fact, some of my earliest summer memories are of lying in bed, long after dark, scratching and scratching at mosquito bites.

But, as we soon discovered, those early experiences with Michigan mosquitoes in no way prepared us for the Minnesota mosquitoes living in our backyard. They arrived daily in an abundance we had never seen in our original homeland. During the daylight hours, one was usually safe from their pesky bites, but once dusk hit, all bets were off. The mosquitoes would descend in giant droves, swarming any warm-blooded body they could find. Kids playing in the yard, parents visiting with a neighbor in the driveway, a slump-shouldered teen dragging the trash to the curb, no one was safe from the swarms.

They were unavoidable and ubiquitous and annoying, but as long as you kept moving, they didn't actually bite, thus giving rise to what my dad called "The Minnesota Polka," an elaborate dance that involved jumping, kicking, swatting at the air, and smacking one's own face, arms, and legs. It wasn't pretty, but it was effective.

Years later, I heard a scientist explain this phenomenon. Mosquitoes can't land if there is more than a slight breeze. "A small fan is more of a deterrent than any bug spray on the market," he expounded. This was certainly true with Minnesota mosquitoes.

Which brings me to the final chapter of my story. Mosquitoes breed in standing water, which is why they love Minnesota, and they especially loved the beautiful wetland in our backyard. Most of the time, western South Dakota doesn't feature much standing water, and consequently, it doesn't usually have many mosquitoes. When I first arrived here on the high prairie, the seeming lack of mosquitoes was a very welcome change after so many summers in Minnesota.

However, the third summer I spent on the plains happened to be rainy, and that was when I discovered that Dakota mosquitoes are nothing like their Minnesota counterparts. As with the human denizens of this region, Dakota mosquitoes are tough as nails, and they are wily. The Minnesota Polka is useless, as is brisk walking, running away, or even, as I discovered one evening, biking. Apparently, science has not studied the Dakota mosquito, because, perhaps not surprisingly, wind is decidedly not a deterrent for our particular strain of the pest.

Nor do they confine themselves to the evening hours for hunting. In the dewy morning, and the bright, shimmering heat of midday, and the deepest dark of night, Dakota mosquitoes will find you and they will extract their weight, many times over, in your blood. And it makes sense, doesn't it? When there's only a summer or two per decade you can thrive, you've got to take full advantage.

I'm reminded of all this because it's another wet year, so in addition to enjoying beautiful tall grasses and wildflowers galore, the kids and I are sporting a few hundred mosquito bites each. The three of us look like we've contracted some kind of rare skin disease. It's not a good look.

You know who isn't getting constantly bitten by mosquitoes, though? The Man of the Ranch—thus proving the only thing tougher than a Dakota mosquito is a Dakota cowboy.

SEPTEMBER 23, 2019

MOTHERING

It's 11:00 p.m., and I'm sitting on the bathroom floor with a rumpled towel on my lap and a needle-less plastic syringe in my hand. My other hand cradles a tiny orange-and-white-spotted kitten. Her eyes are barely open, and her body is so frail in my palm it feels more like an autumn leaf, as if the slightest breeze could carry her away. She doesn't want to drink from the syringe, but it is the only way I can get milk into her belly—she is too weak to suck it from the tiny bottle I bought at the farm supply store. She mews as I put the syringe tip in her mouth and squeeze out one tiny drop at a time.

How many times has this same scenario repeated itself in this bathroom? I've never bottle-fed a kitten before, but the count of newborn lambs I've nursed now numbers in the dozens, not to mention the baby birds fallen from the nest, the chilled-down chicks, and, once, a newborn bunny rescued from our dog's mouth. Each time the work looks surprisingly similar: me hunched over on the bathroom floor, willing the little ones to swallow, fretting about them choking, trying, trying, trying to get enough sustenance in them so they can survive.

Most of the time there is not a happy ending. More often than not they are sickly or born with some kind of defect (otherwise they wouldn't be in my bathroom) and they fight me. I am not their mama, and they know it. Cross-species mothering is a gamble even with a healthy, thriving baby. And yet I stay, late into the night, or early in the morning, unable to walk away until I've gotten as much nourishment as I possibly can into their small bodies.

My husband will tell you I do the same to him. Before we had kids, I was constantly asking him when and what he last ate. I know he is quite thankful that now two small children take the focus off his eating habits. Still, when the three of them head out for an adventure in town or to the pasture to check cows, I am often found chasing the pickup down the driveway, waving a bag of healthy snacks and a water bottle, just in case.

It's gotten me thinking about what comes naturally. For the orphan babies in my care, a connection to their biological mother comes naturally. When I pet this little orange kitten's ears, as weak and sickly as she is, she starts to nuzzle and purr, looking for a nipple. She knows what she should be doing, which is why the syringe is such a disappointment.

As for me, my penchant for taking in baby animals started in childhood, but it wasn't until I became a mother that I finally understood this tendency. Apparently, my maternal instincts extend to almost every creature that crosses my path, but when I had my own babies, I experienced a fulfillment that my other forms of mothering never achieved. Sometimes, such as right now, when my warm bed is calling, those nurturing instincts feel like a burden. I would rather be sleeping than caring for a kitten that has little chance of surviving even with my ministrations. But it's who I am, so I let go and lean in.

In pursuit of a purpose-driven life, I think we all question the wisdom of the patterns that emerge over the years. Some habits are worth breaking, or, at the very least, refashioning; but there are certainly aspects of ourselves that are intrinsic, and those are worth celebrating. We each have gifts to offer, and a world that is hungry to accept them, even if it sometimes requires late nights and a tiny syringe to get the job done.

OCTOBER 7, 2019

GOING TO THE FARM

When I was a youngster, I had a black-and-white Manx cat named Manny. He was an easy cat to love. He had a jovial disposition and slept beside me every night. He probably would have lived with us until a ripe old age had we not moved into a house that had once been home to an incontinent dog. My parents pulled up the carpet and laid down beautiful wood floors, and to our human noses that solved the problem. Unfortunately, Manny's olfactory abilities surpassed ours, and as a means of ensuring the offending dog did not return, he began marking the same spots around the house the dog had used. Soon after, Manny was sent to live on a farm.

I was devastated, but I understood my parents' position on the matter. Anyway, I agreed with their assessment that he would probably be happier on a farm. What cat wouldn't be? Years passed, and though I still pined for Manny, he wasn't a topic of general discussion.

Then one day during my freshman year of college, a few of the kids in my hall started discussing taking pets to "the farm" as a euphemism for having them put down or dropped off at the Humane Society. I laughed along with their tongue-in-cheek tales of woe about parental deception, but I couldn't help adding, "Well, I actually had a cat that my parents took to a farm when he started peeing in the house."

The circle of kids stopped laughing for a moment, glanced around at one another, and then started laughing again twice as hard. And that's when it suddenly occurred to me that my parents had never known a farmer.

A few weeks ago, we were getting lambs ready to send to the sale barn.

Beatrix, one of our teenage goats, got mixed in by accident. We had intended to sort her off before we put the lambs on the trailer, but between a naughty dog, a toddler meltdown, and the general mayhem that is sorting sheep, she ended up on the trailer after all.

"Do you want me to get her out?" the Man of the Ranch asked, a look of sad desperation in his eyes. We both knew that would mean unloading and reloading all the lambs again.

"Yes! Yes!" shouted the kids.

"Oh, that's okay, just bring her home at the end of the day," I said. Then, because my husband works for the sale barn, I jokingly added, "Do you need a goat for work?"

"We actually do," he said. "She can help lead the sheep."

"Perfect! She can work for a few weeks, and then you can bring her back," I said.

He left, and the kids and I went about our day.

The following week, I asked after Beatrix. "How's she doing?"

"Fine," he replied.

The week after, I asked again. "Does she miss us?" I said.

He gave me a funny look before replying, "I think she's okay."

I thought the funny look was in reference to her missing us, but when I asked him about her again a few days ago, this time not in the presence of the kids, my husband shook his head.

"Honey, she's sold. I thought when you told me to take her to work, it was a wink, wink, nod, nod situation."

"What?" I said, the horror plain in my voice. "Why didn't you tell me sooner?"

"Well, the kids were around, and I thought we were still playing along . . . Although last time you asked, I was starting to get the idea we weren't."

So there you go, folks. It's been almost three decades since my parents took my cat to "the farm," and not much has changed except now it's my husband taking my goat to "work." Which just goes to show, growing older doesn't always mean growing wiser.

OCTOBER 14, 2019

GRATITUDE

After the Atlas blizzard six years ago, even the whiff of October snow strikes fear into our hearts, so last week when the forecast began predicting anything from four to sixteen inches of snow, we hoped for the best, but planned for the worst.

By the time the snow began to fly, the hatches were as battened down as they could possibly be. The cows were trailed to a pasture closer to the house, with deep draws for cover from the wind and snow. The sheep were in the corral closest to the barn, a bale of hay and a big tin windbreak at their disposal. Chickens and barn cats had their own indoor spaces to occupy and plenty of food to nibble should the storm rage for a few days.

As expected, we woke up Thursday morning to a world of white. The kids were thrilled. While I made breakfast, they donned snowsuits and went out to check if it was "snowman" snow. It was. "I hope it never melts!" my son shouted when they came back in to eat. All morning they were in and out with their dad, who was on "rancher's vacation" (the hidden benefit of bad weather), while I processed the last of the herbs and vegetables I had pulled from the garden the day before.

Late in the afternoon I took a break to join them and do my little rounds as well. Snow was still falling sideways due to the stormy gusts of wind, but within the shelter of the yard and barn, it wasn't too bad. The sheep looked annoyed, but not miserable, the barn cats the same. Heading toward the chicken coop, however, I discovered something was amiss.

The previous day I had noticed two young chickens wandering around outside. They were both hatched this summer by an exceptionally sneaky hen, and they are now only half-grown. Since the rest of the flock had already put themselves in the coop in preparation for the storm, I was a little worried about the pair being outside, but neither seemed distressed. They were scurrying around, hunting and pecking, happy to scoop up the vegetable odds and ends I'd thrown over the garden fence. On Thursday, however, nearly twenty-four hours after the storm began, with snow still flying, I rounded the corner by the coop to discover the pair roosting outside on a steel fencing panel, feathers fluffed. Each gust of wind shook the poor creatures, so they wobbled and teetered, scrunched and trembling.

After a few rounds of me chasing them and tripping through deep drifts of snow, it was clear they weren't going indoors without a fight. I went to the shed to get the large fishing net used for tasks such as this.

Back at the coop, I caught one of the chickens immediately, and once in my arms, the exhausted bird snuggled down and shut his eyes, clearly relieved. I took him to the barn to wait out the storm (since I suspected they were avoiding the coop because of internal flock politics) and gave him some food. He radiated contentment, and he even let me pet his head.

The second chicken was a different story. I chased her across the yard and through the corrals. I kept stopping to climb over fences she could slip right under, so she had the advantage. When I finally captured her by the windbreak, she squawked and carried on, flustered with anger and terror. Pinned under my arm, she continued to shout, and the second I released her in the barn, she flapped away from me, still yelling, "Get away, get away!" The moral of the story: not everyone who needs our help wants it, and while I normally believe it is advisable to wait to be asked before offering aid, there are circumstances where plowing ahead is the better course. Don't expect to be thanked, however!

OCTOBER 28, 2019

HALLOWEEN

I've been knitting, cutting cardboard, wielding a hot glue gun, and wrapping stuff in duct tape all week in preparation for the spookiest holiday of the year. I am proud to share we now have a knight in somewhat-shining armor and a fairy butterfly in our family. The kids couldn't be more excited, and I'm having a blast, too. What can I say? After all these years, I love playing dress-up just as much as I did when I was their age.

Meanwhile, we are nearly four and a half years into our parenting journey, and it feels like we are arriving at a new and very exciting part of the ride. During the first few Halloweens of dressing up, for example, the kids seemed more bewildered than anything. As we had be snapping pictures and zipping them into costumes, they'd look at us with big eyes and blank stares. It was pretty clear that dressing up was more for us than them. Likewise, my kids, who are both reserved and shy with new adults, found strangers offering them treats off-putting instead of exciting. Either my husband or I would have to take the offered candy, prompting, "Say 'thank you!'" while the kids stood motionless, like deer blinded by oncoming traffic.

Last year, the Bean was old enough to have an opinion about his costume. "I want to be a red cat," he told me firmly. He did not waver in his decision, despite significant attempts at redirection from me. ("Are you sure you don't want to be a black cat? A gray cat? No? Just a red cat . . . Are you really sure?")

So, I knit a long red tail and sewed it to the back of a pair of red pajamas, then knit a red cap with pointy red ears. I was pleased with my work, but the Bean was not so impressed. When we put the costume on him, he was dismayed to discover he was not, in fact, transformed into a red cat but remained merely a boy in red pajamas and a red knit cap.

This year was quite different. After he decided on being a knight, he and his dad got a book about knights from the town library. He pored over the book for hours, planning exactly what kind of knight he would be. We gathered supplies, drew designs, gathered more supplies, and then got to work. When our work was complete, he said it was just as he'd hoped, his face beaming with pride.

His sister has been even more pleased with her fairy butterfly costume. So pleased, in fact, that she's worn at least some part of the costume, usually the wings, every day for the past two weeks. At first I thought we should "save" the costume for Halloween, and then I thought: Why? Unlike eating vegetables or brushing one's teeth, dressing up for Halloween is about pleasure and doesn't need parental regulations. Consequently, the yard and pastures are now routinely graced by a brightly colored, winged creature, who flits and flutters amongst the autumn grasses.

Yes, this is certainly the other side of the sleepless nights when a little one is sick or sad. The other side of the tantrums that result as they try to find their independence. The other side of battles about wearing socks—sweaters, pants, any clothes at all sometimes! The other side of the struggles involved with helping someone grow up is getting to be there while the world unfolds for them, getting to relive the fun of all those firsts, getting to work with them to see their carefully laid plans come to fruition.

Oh, and it's also getting to eat some of their Halloween candy after they go to bed. I mean, that's way too much candy for a small child. Really, it would be irresponsible not to!

NOVEMBER 11, 2019

SLEDDING

Greetings from the future! The calendar currently states that it's the beginning of November, but as all of us living in western South Dakota can attest, it's actually January. At least that's what the view of snow-covered fields and ice-crusted branches seems to suggest. The thermometer reading of one degree above zero this morning was further proof that we've skipped ahead a few months.

This may appear to be a depressing turn of events, especially since I suspect our sojourn to the future will not result in a speedier entry to spring. Something surprising is occurring, however. After I spent the last month of summer absolutely dreading cold weather and then the tiny sliver of autumn feeling sorry for myself because my fear of many, many months of cold seemed to be materializing, winter's premature arrival has been, well, magical!

I wish I could explain this change of heart. Part of it could be that the more you dread something, the more likely it will not be as bad as you feared. Part of it could also be that the beginning of winter is never as weary as the end. In truth, both these things are certainly true; however, I am choosing to believe a different story. There is magic afoot, I just know it.

Yes, there is magic in the sparkles Jack Frost has been painting on our windows and on the grass and leaves. There is magic in the dawn as the sun rises, those sparkles glowing with its first soft rays and then blazing bright as the sun pulls its fullness over the horizon. And there is certainly magic in the dusk, which colors the sky every shade ever painted and many shades that will never be caught on a canvas.

Also, with all this winter ahead, I decided we really need to find some outdoor fun. We've been following the Scandinavian adage that "there is no bad weather, just inappropriate clothing," and we spend some well-bundled quality time outdoors every day. We've also started doing something new: sledding.

Now, I have a terrible fear of going fast down hills. I discovered this the first time I tried to ski. I rode the lift up the hill, took one look down, and then went right back to the chalet to see if I could get a refund on my ski rental. There was no way I was going down that hill other than on foot and slowly.

The fear continues to this day and includes riding down hillsides on horseback or even in a pickup. Who knows, maybe I fell off a cliff in a former life. Either way, sledding is not something I ordinarily enjoy. Even the thought of it gives me shivers. But the kids are at an age when sledding sounds fun, but they aren't ready for anything too steep. In other words, they are ready for exactly the kind of sledding I can do.

So, last week the kids and I started testing any place within walking distance that displayed even the slightest incline. Which is how we discovered the gravel road that leads to our house is the perfect slope for a gentle meander, provided someone strong gives you a good push to start.

Down the hill we softly slid, then back up it we ran, laughing. Because it wasn't very steep, running back up was just enough exercise to keep us warm, but not enough to wear us out. We have only one sled, so the kids rode together, or with me, or singly, while whoever was left out ran beside, "racing" the sled.

All around us dusk fell, first gold, then amber, then peach, then the faintest rose, while our laughter echoed over the snow. And every moment of it was perfect, and singular as a snowflake.

NOVEMBER 18, 2019

BEST COOK IN THE COUNTY

There are a few yearly events on a ranch that require a crew. Branding in the spring and "preg-testing" in the fall are two such events. Preg-testing (a.k.a. doing ultrasounds on the mamas-to-be to make sure they are pregnant) can be a joyous event, or a somber one, depending on the results, but either way it requires extra hands and a vet.

The other thing these events require is a hearty meal when the work is done. While there are plenty of husbands and wives who work side-by-side at chore time, many households still follow a more traditional distribution of responsibilities for the meal, where the man of the ranch leads the outdoor work, while the woman of the ranch readies the home and food. Wives often gain a reputation based on these meals, the vets invariably performing the role of informal judge. One woman may become known for the most tender roasts, another for decadent dessert spreads.

Now, being as I was not raised on a ranch, and I'm neither very strong nor very handy, I'm a mediocre ranch hand on my best day. I can, however, hold my own in a kitchen. Still, when the big meals come around, there's always some anxiety attached, and it's hard not to have my competitive side come out a little.

Well, one of those big meals came around this past weekend, and I started mentally preparing my menu a week in advance. My plan was to keep it simple, let the ingredients shine, and most importantly, not make anything I wasn't already familiar with. Tried and true recipes only!

Of course, that never works out for me. I can't stop myself from improvising and changing plans at the last minute—and this meal was no different. By midmorning, with dinner still a few hours away, I was in great shape. My girl is just a month shy of three years old, but she loves to work in the kitchen and can do a few tasks reliably enough that I can truthfully call her helpful. Meanwhile, her brother was very happy to be outside with the other workers, so the house was quiet save for the soft sounds of kitchen work. "We are going to be done in plenty of time!" I thought to myself, having daydreams of the extra things we could accomplish.

Soon after, the Bean decided he had had enough watching and came inside to check on us. About the same time, Roo started getting a little tired and cranky. Things were beginning to get stressful for me, too, as I realized, despite assurances from the internet, that the brisket was not going to be done in time.

"Mama needs to concentrate!" I told the kids, and I asked them to work in their play kitchen. That went great for about three minutes. Then they started to fight.

Inconsolable after her "brudder" wouldn't let her finish mopping the floor (he thought it was his turn), Emmy spent the final hour of meal prep riding in the backpack I used when she was a baby, while I raced around, sweating under her weight.

Sadly, that was not the end of my trials, and by the time the men came in for their meal, we'd had a fairy sprinkle rice all over the floor ("Mama, it's fairy dust!"), requiring a second round of vacuuming, and an overcooked dessert plus a brisket, singed on the edges, but still tough, emerge from the oven.

Nobody complained, but there definitely weren't any "best cook in the county" proclamations delivered over the meal. As I sit writing this later in the day, however, my back still aching from Emmy's weight, my shirt still smudged with whipped cream and flour and who knows what else, I have to say, I don't think any of those hard-working men worked harder than I did today.

NOVEMBER 25, 2019

GHOST CHICKENS

Ever since Halloween, the kids have been obsessed with "Spookables." They love creepy tales where shadows lurk long and two children must bravely confront things that go bump in the night. So, while everyone else is preparing for Thanksgiving, or starting to decorate for Christmas, I am still telling ghost stories.

In the past month I've regaled them with tales of ghost cats and ghost children, but their favorite is the story of the ghost chicken. That's because it's all true, and it took place exactly six years ago this month, not far from where I sit typing this today . . .

It all began with the Great Chicken Massacre of 2013. I was living alone in a little house at the end of a long gravel road then, teaching school and practicing being a homesteader in my free time. I had an old chicken coop that I had tried to predator-proof, but like many undertakings in my early attempts to be a back-to-the-lander, I didn't do a very good job. Unfortunately, this fact didn't become clear until one night in late fall when a raccoon ripped through the chicken wire I had nailed over a broken corner of the coop's lone window.

When I opened the coop door the next morning, I found the raccoon had killed all my chickens except for one tiny bantam hen, who was hiding in a pile of feathers. I brought her inside to live in my bathroom (which is another story for another time). I mourned the flock I had lost, all of whom I had since their first days of life, and all of whom were tame as puppies, and tried to figure out what to do with the remaining hen.

In the meantime, life went on, as life must. Every morning I fed my little hen, then took my dogs out for a walk before I left for the school day. I'd watch the bands of light rise on the eastern horizon while they'd run and cavort. It was a beautiful way to start the day.

One morning, about a week after the massacre, I was walking with the dogs, when they took off running ahead. The first full rays of sun caught the dusting of snow that had fallen the night before, and the dogs stopped to sniff something on the ground. I came up behind them to see what they had found, and there, glistening in the new snow, were the perfectly preserved tracks of a single chicken.

I stood dumbfounded for a moment, looking all around me. Had one of my hens survived but been so traumatized she was now in hiding?

No, I'd seen the remains of my flock in the coop. There had been no escapees. I followed the tracks, the dogs racing ahead, barking. The chicken tracks went on until the path crested the hill and then they abruptly stopped. The field before me stood gleaming in the light, and as far as the eye could see, there was not a single footprint, save the ones left by my gallivanting dogs, marring the bright whiteness.

So, who left the mysterious tracks? The answer was obvious: a ghost chicken.

When I went to check for the prints again the next day, the warmth of the previous afternoon had melted them, so they were no longer recognizable. The next time it snowed, the mysterious prints appeared again, and then again nearly every other time it snowed for the next several months.

Now, there are some skeptics who might say chicken prints and pheasant prints look very similar. But I'm unconvinced. In all those early morning strolls, the dogs never flushed a single pheasant from the tall grasses along the path. I expect if you went there yourself, you would see the prints, too—evidence that my ghost chicken haunts the prairie still.

DECEMBER 9, 2019

WETHERS AND WEATHER

Many of the biggest decisions on a ranch are made well in advance. So far in advance, in fact, that we often don't know if it was a good decision for half a year or more. There are always many factors to consider, and most of them are beyond our control—weather and market trends being the two biggest.

Well, we made one such big decision this week. We put a ram in with the sheep. Assuming all goes as it should, come May we will have wobbly lambs taking their first steps across the newly sprouted stems of green grass. Or, it could be like last year, and those new babies will be born in our drafty barn during an epic snowstorm.

The memory of trudging through the sideways blasts of ice and wind, snow drifts higher than my knees, trying to get to the barn to check on mamas and babies has me shivering even now. I was honestly tempted to try lambing even later this time around. I mean, we can't possibly get snow in June, right? Of course, there are risks to having animals labor in the heat, as well (as any woman who has been pregnant during the summer months can attest). Since no one knows what the weather will be like in the spring, especially here in western South Dakota, I didn't know what to do.

However, a scrappy little Shetland "wether" (a male sheep that lacks the equipment to procreate) made the decision for me. You see, we recently sold most of our Shetland sheep, a beautiful breed that is famous for its soft fleeces. They are also tenacious and tough, make good mothers, and have babies that grow fast and strong. And they are small, which, when I was researching the breed, I thought would make them easier to handle.

In reality, they are as wily as badgers and just as feisty. Unfortunately, they are also ill-suited for rangeland because in addition to being small-framed, they scatter instead of bunch up when they sense danger, so they are easy targets for coyotes. Our poor guard dog was run ragged every night chasing predators and still couldn't keep them all safe.

In their place, we now have a flock of Targhee sheep, a breed much more appropriate for our situation. I did keep several of the Shetlands, however, who were more pets than livestock, with the idea that in the spring they will reside in a small fenced-in area beside the yard, close enough to keep them safe and out of trouble. I figured they could live out their days as fancy lawn mowers/wool growers, and I wouldn't worry about breeding them. To that end, I kept a wether because he has the most stunning cinnamon-colored fleece I've ever seen, as well as perfectly formed round horns.

Well, Dear Reader, as is often the case with the best laid of my plans, things didn't work out as I had hoped. It turned out that the wether's gorgeous, fluffy fleece was hiding evidence of . . . ahem . . . a late-to-descend ram-part. Which I didn't find out until I was walking past the corral the other day and saw him acting decidedly un-wether-like with one of the new Targhee ewes.

There won't be any way to tell until May how much potential the aforementioned part contains, but after that sighting, there was no longer any sense in waiting to start "date month." We put the Targhee ram in with the Targhee ewes the next day, and only time will tell the results. Hopefully, there will be more tall, leggy white lambs than little, burly brown ones. Honestly though, as long as the ground is green and not white when they arrive, I won't complain!

DECEMBER 16, 2019

ONE EGG A DAY

Last week I wrote about a ranch-related venture that didn't work out as planned. This week, I will share a plan that did work . . . too well. It concerns our chickens.

Before we brought our guard dog, Ellie, to the ranch, I lost two separate flocks of chickens in two years to predators. This was before I had human children, back when I had a lot more time and energy to devote to the animals under my care. Each one of those chickens had a name, and my Facebook page attested to the excessive amount of time I spent at the coop documenting every movement. Suffice to say, the loss of those chickens was devastating. So, while the proposed reason to bring Ellie to the ranch was to guard sheep (since the monthly expense of feeding a giant dog would far exceed the monthly cost of store-bought eggs, I could hardly justify her as a poultry guard dog), I secretly hoped she would keep the flock safe as well.

Boy, has she! We quickly became victims of our own success. The first chicks on the ranch post-Ellie arrived via the USPS. That little flock of eight blossomed to a flock of eighteen literally overnight when a clever hen appeared with ten wee chicks in tow. She had managed to hide her nest from us for the requisite month, and the result was a more than doubling of our chicken population.

Since then, the number of chickens on the premises has ebbed and flowed, but mostly flowed. We've lost a few chickens to accidents and old age, but never once to a predator's sharp teeth. Meanwhile, we've given a dozen or more away to neighbors and friends whose coops were empty, and I even butchered some young roosters (while I was eight months pregnant) because they were harassing the hens.

The flock now stands at thirty strong. This is officially too many chickens, especially considering we are getting one egg a day. You read that right: one egg a day. ONE EGG. A DAY.

Other than a few chicks purchased from the local farm supply store in moments of weakness, the rest of the flock is the result of our unintentional breeding program. We've tried every means we can think of to keep broody hens from sneaking off to create secret nests. Nothing has worked. Ellie is just too darn good at her job. We may not know where those hens are, but she certainly does, and she keeps them all safe.

Butchering would be a simple solution to our situation. There are quite a few older hens whose egg-laying days are probably long in the past, but, though ranch life has toughened me up considerably these last few years, it hasn't toughened me up enough yet to think of those sweet old girls as supper. Nasty roosters are one thing; hens who have given us years of service are quite another.

Meanwhile, the feed bill has become a topic the Man of the Ranch and I dare not discuss, but I'm considering asking for chicken scratch from Santa this year. And maybe for my birthday. And our anniversary. And any other holiday for which chicken feed might be gifted.

In the meantime, we will be thankful for our one egg a day. After all, it's a 100 percent increase over the number of eggs we were getting for most of the fall when many of the younger hens were molting. One egg a day is half a loaf of banana bread. Or half a glass of eggnog. Or a teeny-tiny omelet. If we hoard them for a week, we could even have bacon and eggs for breakfast one morning.

The solstice is only a week away, and since daylight is one of the factors that affects laying eggs, we can only hope a return of the light will mean a return to productivity. If not, well, anybody need some pet chickens?

DECEMBER 27, 2019

YELLOW CAT

Longtime readers of this column may recall tales of Yellow Cat, the lone cat in residence when I arrived on the ranch six years ago. Gnarled and bedraggled, he appeared to have used up most of his nine lives already. As an inveterate cat-lover, I took over barn cat duties, determined to win Yellow Cat over. He was not impressed. He would hiss and spit every time I entered the barn, refusing to eat the kibble I put down for him until after I had left his sight.

Very slowly, he began tolerating my presence. I didn't dare touch him, however. One glare from those slightly crossed blue eyes made it quite clear he was not going to be tamed by anyone, and especially not by a greenhorn like me.

Many tomcats have come and gone since then, but Yellow Cat, against all odds, remains, and while the years have not improved his appearance, they have softened him considerably. That's because, while we've had quite a few female cats take up residence in the barn since small-but-mighty Mama Cat Esme began her reign, Yellow Cat is no longer welcome in the barn much of the year. A king without a kingdom, he was forced to come to us for aid.

When it became clear that Mama Cat was chasing him off, we took pity on the old man and began leaving his food on the patio. That was all well and good until the chickens discovered his dish. Cats are relatively tidy patio guests. Chickens are not. So, when Yellow Cat spontaneously decided to follow us inside one day and raced right over to the indoor cats' food dish, we let him. He ate his fill and raced back to the door, desperate to be released once again to the wild.

Over the past year, these comings and goings have become a regular part of our household. Once or twice a day, Yellow Cat will appear at the door asking to be let in. If we open the door and there are strangers in the house, he will immediately run away, not to be seen again for hours. Otherwise, he will zip past us at top speed, gobble up as much food as his belly can hold, then hide beside the shoe basket until someone opens the door to let him back out.

More often than not, one of his visits occurs when I let my ancient dog, Lily, in after her last bathroom break before bed. Unfortunately, there have been a few evenings recently when I accidentally locked Yellow Cat in overnight. (He has gotten so stealthy he can sail in under Lily's legs without me realizing it.) During those nights it did not escape his notice that the house is much cozier than the other buildings on our place. Consequently, on particularly cold nights, he no longer races to the door after his meal, but hides behind the washing machine instead.

Meanwhile, our puppy, Zuzu, is experiencing the first flames of young love, and Yellow Cat is the object of her affection. She wants to be wherever he is. So, at the end of the day, when all I want to do is to go to bed, I find myself chasing a feral cat around the house with an exuberant puppy behind me. When I do finally get Yellow Cat corralled by the door and try to shoo him out, Zuzu jumps forward and blocks his exit. Back between my legs he runs, to the laundry room, and the whole fiasco repeats.

All of which is to say, Dear Reader, that my New Year's resolution should definitely be Stop Letting Outdoor Animals in the House. What are the chances I would be able to keep such a resolution, though? They are zero, of course, so I won't even bother. Hopefully you will have better luck with your resolutions this year!

2020

JANUARY 13, 2020

REAL WINTER

I grew up in Michigan, where winters were a brown and sloshing affair punctuated by a few snowy episodes. It was damp and chilly there, rarely bitter, with cold breezes instead of cold winds. Early last winter I kept having sense memories of my childhood because, for the first time since I arrived in South Dakota nearly ten years ago, winter was settling in mild. By January, however, any suggestion that we were going to be in for easy weather had vanished and winter stayed hard and cold all the way until mid-May.

This winter started much the same as last. Snow came early and fell often, but it would immediately melt back into puddles, keeping the farmers from their fields. "Once it freezes up hard . . ." was a refrain repeated across the countryside, until finally everyone gave up and either harvested in the mud or stopped mentioning it altogether.

Meanwhile, every freeze and thaw was accompanied by dense fog that frosted the trees and grasses with silver. A winter wonderland to be sure, but also, if you believe the old-timers (and I do) a harbinger of spring storms to come.

During the mild weather of the last few months, I almost forgot why I spent all summer dreading winter, but I am starting to remember. Three months after our first snow, winter is in all likelihood just beginning.

Yes, the deep cold is upon us, the forecasted temperatures running the gamut from abysmal to whatever is even worse than that. The silver lining is that I can finally turn my attention to the house. With such fair days, it seemed wrong not to keep plugging away at outdoor jobs, and the housework suffered. Christmas clutter didn't help. Our living space is small, so every time something comes in, something else must go out. This week there was a mass exodus of the old to make way for the new, with the happy result that at long last we can move from one side of the house to the other without the sensation of running through an obstacle course.

In other news, our young dog, Zuzu, met her first porcupine this week. Never a good thing, but it could have gone worse. After the unhappy exchange, she came to the door sporting only a handful of quills in her poor nose. Enough, hopefully, to dissuade her from attempting a similar interaction with porcupines in the future. At least in the near term, the cold and her sore snout are keeping her close to home, which is for the best. I like having her around.

She and I still walk every evening we can, watching the sun wave goodbye with its wagging scarves of color. I'm back to wearing snow pants, sweatpants, long johns, and just as many layers on top. The thin strip of skin visible between my many scarves and hats can feel the difference between this week and last, but the rest of me is quite toasty even with the turn the temperature has taken.

Zuzu, for her part, simply wears her glossy coat of white, gold, and dark brown—perfect camouflage for the winter prairie. Ellie, the Great Pyrenees, usually joins us for a stretch as well, but as soon as coyotes start their howling, she's off to work.

Zuzu follows Ellie, barking, but only for a minute. Then she circles back, her bright eyes lively and focused. Ellie's job is to guard the place; Zuzu's job is to guard me. The Man of the Ranch suspects Zuzu actually thinks it's my job to guard her, but I disagree.

She is a good dog, and I'm lucky to have her, even if only for company during that one mile a day at dusk. That one quiet mile when I gather the comfort of the colors in a prairie sunset, warm and bright, even on the coldest of cold South Dakota evenings.

FEBRUARY 3, 2020

THAW

It is widely understood that as we get older, time moves more quickly. As I age, I have found the truth of this to be quite shocking, and doubly so now that I have children. Just days ago, my kids were tiny infants, and in a few more minutes they will be heading off to their own adult adventures. Their respective childhoods are flashing by, just as everyone warned they would.

There is one exception to the rule, however: January. One month ago, we celebrated entry into a new year, and now, 3,362 days later, it is February. Even though this year's January was quite mild compared to most, I still ended up leaving the month feeling a bit wounded.

Perhaps it's because by January we've been living with so little sunlight for so long. We are bound to get a little shriveled. Many plants and animals go into hibernation during these cold, dark days, but not us humans. (Thanks a lot, evolution.) We persevere and plow ahead, though not literally (the ground is usually too frozen for plowing), waiting and dreaming for the return of the warmth and the heat.

Depending on how far north one lives, it can be quite a wait, though. The first day of February marks winter's halfway point, a time of celebration in many agrarian cultures because it means the march toward planting times has begun in earnest. Even for those who don't make their living based on the seasons as we in agriculture do, it is a cause for celebration. However, when winter sometimes starts in October, and it's still snowing in May, halfway isn't as reassuring.

But, just as there's no use crying over spilled milk, there's no sense in lamenting the habitual lack of early spring when one lives on the northern plains. So, what is one to do when a hardcore case of the "Januaries" flows right into February?

Yesterday, in the midst of a lovely, sunny day with above-freezing temperatures, I decided a thorough airing out of the house might be the cure. Last week was almost ceaselessly gray and damp. Even with the change in weather, I was crabby, the kids were crabby, and nothing, not bright skies or fresh air, seemed enough to improve our foul moods.

I figured it was worth a try, though. I put the kids in their thickest sweaters, turned off the furnace, opened the windows and the sliding glass door, and got to work. I vacuumed and shampooed the carpets while the cool air pooled around us. Somehow the kids' shouts as they played pirates, jumping from couch to armchair and back again, weren't nearly as deafening with the open windows. By the time I was done, I felt a lot better, as is almost always the case after some exercise. Plus, we now had clean rugs and clean air.

The next step in the "February Feel Better Initiative" was some time outside in the sunshine.

It was great, although when we returned later, the kids' boots and coveralls, plus the dogs and a few marauding house cats, made short work of the newly vacuumed and shampooed floors. The fresh air and light had worked their magic however, and I didn't mind. Well, not too much. Fresh mud is preferable to old dirt, right?

Today, the weather is warm and sunny again: not Florida warm, of course, but South Dakota warm, which might be even better. The yard and the corrals are all mud now, and little rivers of the melt-off are flowing through the pasture grasses on their way to the dam. The sheep in the front corral, hoof deep in muck, are enjoying the sweet sunshine seeping through their thick fleeces. In other words, despite Punxsutawney Phil's prediction, this thaw is as close to an early spring as we are likely to get, but we will gladly take it.

MARCH 23, 2020

ANXIETY

As a child I was prone to anxiety. In first grade, during a unit on fire safety, my teacher told us we should go home and plan emergency escape routes with our families. I ran home that day and told my parents, who offered a few thoughts on the matter and then moved on to other things. For weeks afterward, however, I lay in bed at night imagining my role in the escape: how I would run from my room to my brother's bed, fling open the window, push out the screen, then help him through it before jumping after him into the darkness.

For better or for worse, this is my personality type, and I've come to accept that being in a state of high alert is how I naturally operate. It has its assets. Rarely one to stray from the prescribed path for fear of calamity, during high school I made many good, responsible choices, which led to acceptance at an excellent college. As a result, when I graduated, I had plenty of job prospects. But, of course, I was also a wreck—unmoored, exhausted, and in desperate need of a vacation from myself.

During the intervening decade I found healthier ways to handle my penchant for anxious thoughts, or "catastrophizing" as I now describe it. Spending time outside, getting plenty of physical activity, and having routines that draw me out of the spiral of worry are all helpful, and they're no doubt the reason ranch life suits me so well. I've often wished that all those who suffer from anxiety or depression had the opportunity to try living rurally. I don't know if it would help everyone, but I know it has helped me.

Perhaps the best antidote for my fears, however, has simply been getting older. I've learned life does not present itself as endless progress, but endless possibility. There is always more to discover; every crossroads contains a gift destined to unfurl in its own time. And I've learned not to put too much stock in my very active imagination when it comes to risk assessment—it's a great attribute for my writing practice, but not as helpful for making decisions.

Until two weeks ago, that is, when a phone call from a dear friend who was supposed to come visit us from Italy left us reeling. His report of what was happening in his country, as well as an admonishment to "Stay home," was terrifying. For the first time in a long time, I felt my senses ramping up to high alert, and each day since, as reports of fresh recommendations clamor ceaselessly, has felt like a mini-marathon of stress escalation.

At the time of this writing, the news continues to be bleak. For our part, social distancing on a ranch during calving and lambing season is effortless. Stemming the tide of worry over far-flung friends and family is not as easy. So, I turn again to what has worked in the past. I listen for the meadowlark's trilled greeting. I look to the pasture, ripe to awaken with the first blush of green splendor. I watch while newborn calves, wet as dew, lift themselves on wobbling legs to catch sips of their mother's sweet milk. I tell myself to keep moving—to chase the children and the baby goats, to catch them and cradle them, then release them to run, once more, laughing across the yard.

To discover again and again how little control we humans actually have of outcomes, but how much control we do have over cultivating wellsprings of joy, well, that's the work of a lifetime. The work does not cease, but flows onward, catching us in its current, offering us up as guardians of our own sense of wonder, until, even in the deepest dark we discover the firmament of stars twinkling high above our heads, a blessing and a benediction.

MARCH 30, 2020

CLAUDIO AND VIRGINIA

Before my husband moved back to his hometown, he worked for many years at a guest ranch in Wyoming. He was in charge of the cows and horses, not the guests, but he still had ample opportunity to meet folks from all over Europe, the origin of many of the ranch's visitors. One of those visitors, an Italian man named Claudio, became a dear friend.

Over the years, the Man of the Ranch and Claudio have kept in touch, and when the Man of the Ranch moved home, Claudio even came back to the states for several extended visits. During the last visit, seven years ago, there was a late calf born in the night. I am the surrogate mom for calves these days, but this was before my time here, so when the calf's mother decided she didn't want the baby, Claudio took over. He named the little one Virginia, after his beloved grandmother.

The baby was weak, wobbly, and unusually small. Her prospects were bleak because even healthy calves don't do as well as ones raised on their mothers' milk, and this calf was far from spunky. But Claudio loved that little baby and gave her the best care he could. She fought the bottle at first, but he gently persisted, ministering to her many times a day with nourishment and kindness.

By the time Claudio left to return home, Virginia was doing beautifully. Over the course of the next year, she grew into her knobby frame with a fine crown of gleaming horns and a shiny red-and-white spotted coat. She was feisty and robust, bucking and tossing her head as she played in the long dusk of prairie evenings. Every so often we sent a photo or video of her to Claudio, who remained the proud papa, and it wasn't long before we were sending him photos of her babies as well.

Now in her middle age, Virginia remains a magnificent creature, and she carries herself with a royal dignity. Because of that, and the crown of horns, we call her queen of the herd, and she's often spotted leading her herdmates across the pasture. She's a great mom, too, even though she never had one herself, perhaps because she had such a great dad during her first month of life.

This week, Claudio was supposed to arrive on a plane from Italy. The ticket was purchased in early January, back when most of us had only heard about coronavirus in passing. The idea that Claudio's whole country would be on lockdown by the date printed on that ticket was unthinkable, but that's exactly what happened as the date approached.

"We'll change the ticket for later in the summer," we all agreed, knowing that probably wasn't going to happen.

"Be well, friends," Claudio told us before hanging up, and there were tears in his voice as he said goodbye.

Meanwhile, because Mother Nature stops for no one, calving has started in earnest at our place. Yesterday, the day after the plane carrying our friend would have landed, the Man of the Ranch went out for the daily sweep on horseback to make sure all was well with the herd in the north pasture. That's where we let our older mothers labor, as its deep draws give them more privacy and protection. Since they are experienced, they rarely need interventions when the weather is fine—a daily check usually suffices.

The Man of the Ranch spotted Virginia's strong, curved horns and smooth, shiny coat right away. She was standing, back legs spread wide, on the canyon's rugged edge. Beneath her, a tiny red-and-white calf lay, still wet, but with head lifted and eyes alert. From atop his horse, the Man of the Ranch snapped a blurry picture on his cell phone, then sent it across the ocean to his friend—a reminder that our kindnesses multiply, as well as the hope that we will indeed all be together again soon.

APRIL 27, 2020

LEMMINGS

We were listening to an audiobook this week that mentioned lemmings. "What's a lemming?" my son asked when the story was over.

"It's a monkey. A very small monkey," I replied, then paused. "No, maybe it's more like a squirrel. Wait, no . . . I think it's a cross between a squirrel and a very small monkey."

Both kids looked at me with confusion and something akin to distress. Was Mama joking? My son's mouth opened with a question he couldn't quite bring to fruition, while I continued to babble.

"What are you even talking about right now?" he asked finally.

And that's when I had to confront the reality that, in fact, I had managed to make it four decades without knowing what a lemming is.

My shameful lapse in knowledge aside, this type of information is easily accessible with modern technological advances. After a quick search of Wikipedia, I was able to tell the kids that lemmings are a type of rodent that dwells on the tundra and burrows into snowpack instead of dirt. Definitely not tiny monkeys.

Where I got the idea that they were in the primate family, I do not know, but my search revealed that the only other thing I thought I knew about lemmings—that they purposefully and regularly jump en masse to their deaths—was also untrue. The origin myth of lemmings' lethal cliff-diving behavior, I soon learned, is in fact quite shocking. Apparently, Disney produced a series of nature documentaries in the 1950s, and one of them featured a segment using faked footage of lemmings jumping into the ocean. In reality, the lemmings were not acting of their own volition but were forced over the cliff by the humans filming them. While lemmings will attempt to swim when migrating to find food and do sometimes drown, it is accidental, not intentional. Yet the idea that lemmings are suicidal persists to this day. Such is the power of well-crafted misinformation.

The whole episode reminds me of how much I had to unlearn about rural life when I first moved to South Dakota. There were many preconceived notions and anecdotal half-truths I picked up from books and movies over the years that I discovered bore little resemblance to the reality of living closer to the land. My homesteader fantasies were just that—a fantasy.

That does not mean the reality of this lifestyle was a disappointment. The shift from urban to rural came with many blessings, and not the least of them was a dose of humility. It was good to be reminded at that point in my adulthood how much I didn't know, and it continues to be helpful to this day. I am better for being humbled by my inexperience.

This week also marked the start of lambing for our flock, and it was a chance to learn again another, much harsher lesson. As of this writing, one baby has already been born and died, its body malformed, unable to draw a single breath. What a way to begin. And yet, as I've shared in this column before, confronting death regularly is part of ranching.

And that's the other blessing that, even now, I struggle to accept: there's so much more uncertainty and loss inherent in human experience than modernity acknowledges or prepares us for, but prepare we must, lest we spend all our time trying to avoid the inevitable truth that life is sometimes brutal.

So, friends, let's do the best we can to remain open to all we don't yet know, and all we may never know. There is a comfort to be found in stripping back the armor of our misconceptions—the shield of certainty that separates us from the tenderness we all knew as children, when the world was fresh as the prairie in spring, and just as wide and green.

MAY 4, 2020

NEW YORK TIMES

Two weeks ago, I decided I was going to write an opinion piece for the *New York Times*. Never mind that I didn't have any reliable way to reach them, nor was there any reason to think they'd be interested in hearing from me. It was a crazy idea. But, as I told my husband, "I have some things I need to say. I know they probably won't even read my email, but I need to write it anyway."

He lifted his eyebrows. "You should," was all he said.

I stayed up late to write, and I woke up early to keep working. I sent it to a few trusted friends who offered edits. I wrote on and off all day while the kids systematically destroyed the house. When the Man of the Ranch returned from building a fence at a neighboring ranch late in the afternoon, he looked at the counter piled high with dishes, the hurricane of blocks strewn across the floor, and the sofa liberated from its cushions, and he merely lifted his eyebrows once again.

"I've been working on that piece for the *Times*," I said, glancing up from the computer.

He nodded his head solemnly, then went out to start chores.

There's only so much ruin I could justify to myself in the creation of a piece of writing with little chance of being published, so I polished it just enough to make supper late but not enough to miss milking the cow, then sent it off, expecting that to be the end of the story.

Well, in a plot twist I did not expect, they did read it, and today that piece landed on doorsteps across the Eastern Seaboard and beyond.

In my twenties, when I lived in New York City, being featured in the *New York Times* represented the very pinnacle of success. Scribbling in my journal while I rode the crowded subway to my dismal temp job, the idea of my byline gracing those fabled pages was the stuff of fairytales. Back then, I couldn't imagine ever mustering the courage to share those scribbles, and perhaps rightly so. They were the scribbles of a young person taking tentative steps toward something still too tender to be exposed to scrutiny. In this age of social media, we sometimes forget not everything needs to be shared, and that the privacy of notebooks and diaries can be a gift—the chance to test our words carefully; the opportunity to explore who we are meant to be without worrying too much about how it looks to everybody else.

Yesterday, while we waited for the digital version of my piece to be posted online, my husband read me the stats for the *New York Times* weekend circulation. "Whoa," I said, and I felt an old fear surge through my body. "That's a lot," I mumbled. But I was thinking, "That's *too much*." The idea of so many people reading my words was terrifying.

But what could I do? There was no turning back. So, I finished cooking supper. I went out and milked the cow. I watched dusk spread across the prairie in a blanket of rosy light while I checked the flock. I bottle-fed a lamb as the first pinprick of an evening star peeked through the purpled sky.

This morning it was back out to milk the cow, make breakfast, feed lambs, fret over one who wasn't doing well, then open the greenhouse so the seedlings didn't get burned in the first heat of the day. Meanwhile, my email inbox filled up with messages from people all over the country. Some were sweet, some were strange, and one was mean, but mostly they were simply people who wanted to share their stories, just as I do with you, Dear Reader, every week.

MAY 18, 2020

SAD TOMATO

One of our first ewes to lamb this year gave birth to premature triplets. One was stillborn, but two, though tiny and extremely weak, survived. Perhaps because they were premature, the lambs' mother had no milk, so they became our babies instead.

The kids decided to call them Maaaa and No Maaaa because one had a loud and raucous voice, while the other was as quiet as a field mouse. Once she was able to walk on her own (which took a few days), Maaaa followed us everywhere. If I was working in the garden, she would try to climb in my lap. If we were eating outside at the picnic table, she would curl on top of one of our feet. If she was separated from us for even a moment, a loud "Maaaaaaaa!" would echo out across the prairie.

No Maaaa, on the other hand, would frequently get lost. Although she also rarely strayed more than a few feet from us, she still managed to find awkward places to get stuck. Noticing she was missing, we would wander in circles calling and calling until we stumbled upon her twisted and tangled around the roots of a lilac bush, or over the rung of a chair. Despite her obvious discomfort, she would never make a peep.

I saw the writing on the wall, but as No Maaaa still ate with vigor, I held out hope she would outgrow this odd quirk. Instead, she grew weaker. It wasn't long before the worst occurred, and Maaaa became an only child.

My kids and I love brainstorming names for our animal friends, and while mourning for No Maaaa, we all started to quietly advocate for renaming Maaaa. Meanwhile, a different ewe developed an infection after giving birth, and quite suddenly Maaaa had a new name, Nell, and we also had a new baby to feed.

Because we were already in the habit of naming and renaming, the new lamb was first called Eggplant because her ears were "big as an eggplant," then Bunnyhead. Next, someone changed Nell's name to Fat Tomato because after a week of careful tending, she had traded her birdlike frame for a round belly. Just like that, Bunnyhead became Tall Tomato, since she towered over her older, but smaller friend.

The day they were called Fat Tomato and Tall Tomato was the day we had to bring in one final bum—a huge ewe lamb whose mother didn't have enough milk for her and her equally giant twin. This gangly lamb was even taller than Tall Tomato, but she carried herself with a posture of defeat—ears dangling low, woolly brows furrowed, thick head hanging down. Her name was obvious: Sad Tomato.

Tall Tomato has since returned to being called Bunnyhead, and Fat Tomato is once again called Nell, but Sad Tomato remains Sad Tomato, perhaps because it would be impossible to find a better name for her. Despite her daily rations of warm milk and snuggles, her legs are still too long for her body, her ears too heavy for her too-heavy head, and her general attitude suggests an overwhelming pessimism that things won't improve.

Bum lambs were my gateway to ranching; after acquiring two soon into my tenure here in western South Dakota, I knew there was no going back to city life. In them I saw the shape of my future and a way to be of service. Perhaps I also saw a bit of myself—I spent quite a few years as a sad tomato, wondering when and if I'd ever belong anywhere.

Thankfully, the gate of the world opened wide for me, as it someday will for these lambs when they discover they belong to the grass and to one another, the green arms of their mother beckoning, the soil beneath their hooves their home.

JULY 6, 2020

MILKING

The abundance of flies on a ranch in midsummer makes milking then a wildly different experience from early spring. The sizzling, dusty heat of the prairie is a fly's favorite weather, especially when the hot winds die back in the early evening. In other words, evening is a buggy, sweaty disaster of a time to be milking outdoors.

Morning is only slightly better, as the sun's heat starts to spread the second it peeks over the horizon, pulling the dew right back into the shimmering air. A recent series of midnight thunderstorms have kept us sleepless and groggy during daylight hours, wilting from the heat, but thankful for the moisture. It also ensures, however, that when we walk the cows in, they are plastered with drying mud and manure, and so are we by the time milking is complete.

We keep dairy cows with their calves, so we only milk once a day. Last week we switched over from evening to morning sessions. What a way to start the day. The insistent biting and buzzing of flies means I have to tie a long string from poor Pumpkin's halter to her strong whip of a tail. Otherwise, I get slapped in the face every thirty seconds as she attempts to sweep the pests off her flanks and back. Her only means to defend herself therefore is to kick, so milking becomes a very mobile experience for us, her kicking up dirt and dust, and me weaving back and forth to avoid her hooves. There's no point in trying to sit if I want to end up with anything left in the pail—it's a nonstop, full-body endeavor.

And through it all, her calf paces and bellows on the other side of the fence. Little Carrot wants her turn. I get through two udders' worth of milk and call it good enough. That leaves plenty of milk for the baby, and it leaves me with about one shred of sanity intact.

I mention all this because a semi-famous, pseudo-homesteader woman I follow on social media recently posted pictures of her new milking parlor. It is the palace of milking parlors, with gleaming floors, flawless white walls, and a pristine, stainless-steel milking machine, and it is so far away from any facility Pumpkin and I will ever experience that after scrolling through the pictures, I couldn't decide if I wanted to laugh or cry.

Do I sound a little bitter? Because I'm not—I want this woman to have the milking parlor of her dreams. I just want one, too! Instead, Pumpkin and I are destined to emerge from every milking dusty, sweat-slicked, and fly-bitten, locked into a conflict that won't be resolved until snow falls and fly season comes to a close.

If a state-of-the-art milking facility isn't an option, what are my choices? First and foremost, by longing for what I don't have, I miss out on appreciating the beauty that's in front of me—what a shame! Better to lift my head up from the screen and look around when I'm starting to feel glum.

That can be hard to do, though. Back at the house I strain the milk and put it in the fridge, but not before skimming the foamy layer from the top of the pail and plopping it into my coffee cup. A milkmaid cappuccino—simultaneously the easiest or hardest cappuccino to prepare, depending on how you weigh things out. Either way, it's delicious. Layered like a creamy pillow against the rim of my favorite sea-green mug, it's also beautiful.

So, I snap a picture and post it online. Someday in the future, when I am feeling down, instead of scrolling through someone else's social media posts, I will scroll through my own, marveling at the bounty of my life. The flies will be long forgotten by then, leaving only the sweetness of a well-tended cow's good milk glowing in the summer sunshine.

OCTOBER 19, 2020

AN UNEXPECTED VISITOR

In the long winter nights preceding my daughter's birth, I would often lie awake, too uncomfortable and restless to sleep, and listen to the voice of an owl softly calling just outside my window. I found the sound very comforting and a bit exotic; I had never heard an owl that close before.

We've not had another owl roost by the house since Emmy Rose's earthside arrival, but coming in from some late-night chore, I've caught the murmured question "Who-who?" in our tree breaks many times. Once or twice I've even spotted a large owl silently gliding between branches, its wide brown wings moving through the air without sound, a marvel of physics.

Last week, the kids were playing in the yard when our young dog Zuzu started barking. She was using her familiar "Danger! Danger!" bark, and I immediately went to investigate. She glanced at me then looked up into a tall ash tree beside our house, clearly concerned about what the branches contained. But try as I might, I could not see what she deemed so worrisome. My son came over too, and together we walked around the tree several times while Zuzu continued to bark. Eventually my son went back to his game, and my attention began to flag as well, but Zuzu insisted there was something noteworthy, so I kept looking.

After several more turns around the tree's trunk, I spotted her—a giant great horned owl. I called the kids over to look, and Zuzu stopped barking. She seemed relieved we had finally figured out what the fuss was about, and she lay down beside the tree, calm, but alert.

The owl was so still she looked like a nature photograph. Her camouflage was impressive, the dark and light variations of her brown plumage perfectly coordinated with the dappled sunlight passing through the tree's shade. We yelled up to her, "Hello, Owl!" and her only movement was a barely discernible tilting of the head to better observe us.

Meanwhile, the yard was crawling with an abundance of kittens and chicks, all of whom were playing out in the open without a care in the world. Now, as I've written many, many times before, I love the abundance of babies on a ranch, but at a certain point, usually when everyone hits adolescence and starts pooping in the sandbox, or rushing to the door every time we try to enter or exit, I am reminded of the error of my ways in treating them all like beloved friends. My husband, on the other hand, never forgets kittens will become cats, and chicks will become chickens, and every autumn our marital bliss is tested by the terrible decisions I've made earlier in the summer.

So, while I was delighted at the opportunity to see an owl close up, and having her around was certainly one solution to the chick and kitten conundrum, the possibility of watching that owl swoop down and carry off one of our playmates was less thrilling. My son, wise beyond his years, was also concerned. Once the initial wonder of having an owl visitor waned, he proposed we pretend to be coyotes and howl at the tree. His sister and I agreed to the plan, and the group howling commenced for several minutes—but to no avail. The owl was unruffled. In fact, the only change in her demeanor was a glacially slow blink of her round yellow eyes.

Next, my son decided to up the ante and insisted we continue howling while he banged the tree's trunk with a long stick. That did the trick. After a few crashing blows, the owl looked down, this time with disgust, and then pulled herself silently into the air and sailed away.

My son, victorious, gazed upon his many chicks and cats and beamed proudly. The crisis was averted. And I, for my part, was reminded of the complications of the web of life on a ranch, which exists on the edge of a wildness we humans sometimes long to forget.

NOVEMBER 7, 2020

YARD CAMPING

After a week of winter, we found ourselves fleetingly returned to autumn. The cows and horses and sheep shook off the chill of the previous days and returned to grazing the patches of grass that emerged from the melting snow. The chickens poked their heads from the coop in wonder and returned to chasing insects and fighting over scratched-up seeds. And my kids returned to the yard whooping with joy.

For the adults, a return to warmth meant trying to finish up all the chores we'd skipped in anticipation of the October snowstorms. I planted garlic and crocus bulbs while the kids crafted tiny snow sculptures in what remained of the blizzard, wearing mittens and short-sleeves at the same time, leaving barefooted prints in the fast-fading snow. We also sorted calves to be sold at the sale barn, preg-tested the mamas, and started weaning the calves we will keep.

"No way," I told the kids, every time they wanted to play inside. "We need to enjoy every minute of this weather!"

Which is why, on Friday, when the kids suggested we go camping, I started to say no, then paused. The chore list was still long, and overnight temperatures were predicted to be in the mid-thirties.

"But, Mama, it's our last chance!" my son said, repeating a line I'd used all week.

He was right. I hemmed and hawed until a compromise was reached—we would camp, but in the yard.

Camping in November is different from camping in July, as we quickly learned, and not just because of the weather. By 5:30 p.m. it was full dark, so after roasting marshmallows in the firepit, we climbed into our tiny teardrop camper, read a few books by flashlight, and then snuggled under the piles of blankets for the earliest bedtime ever.

Outside we could hear the coyotes' lonesome howl and our guard dog Ellie's bellowed reply. The cows and their newly weaned calves kept up their own chorus of dismay. The night was alive with animal music. We humans listened, huddled beneath the electric blanket, our bodies warm, our noses already chilly, and both kids fell immediately asleep.

The slumber that started early ended early as well, unfortunately. Every hour or so, one or both kids restlessly kicked off covers, then woke in shock at the rush of cold air. When the first hint of dawn poked above the horizon, my son turned to me and croaked a blurry "I didn't sleep very well."

"I noticed," I replied.

He and his sister lay for a moment, blinking in the weak, milky light. Then they sat up and peeked through the camper's round windows. Their faces broke into grins at the sight of the wide prairie enveloped in thick ribbons of white, the warmth of the previous day transformed by the chill of night into fog.

"Let's make pancakes in the camper!" my son said suddenly.

Now, cooking "in" the camper when the camper is a teardrop, means outside the camper, as the kitchen is in a small galley at the rear. Once again, I felt a "no" rising to my lips, but then I stopped. Why not?

We walked back to the house and got the pancake batter I had made the night before, then bundled up against the damp cold. We trailed back to the teardrop and fired up the camper's propane burner. The kids sat in their camp chairs, wrapped snugly in blankets while they waited, marveling at the fields and grasses and the unfamiliar pearly sheen. I was cold, but not too cold, standing by the stove, watching steam rise from the frying pan. We talked and giggled as the pancakes sizzled to a golden brown, then I laid them on plates. For once, they weren't too hot to eat straight from the griddle.

The next day the real cold arrived with rain and wind. The kids played inside with the little wooden family of dolls from their dollhouse. The dollhouse family was not in their house, however. They went camping, laughing and playing together, making the most of the weather while it lasted.

NOVEMBER 30, 2020

THANKSGIVING

When I was a kid, I prayed all the time. I prayed on the school bus. I prayed in the school lunch line. I prayed beneath the shade of the towering maple tree in my front yard. I tried to pray about the things I thought I should pray for—comfort for people who were in crisis, health for ailing family members, or the big-ticket items like world peace and an end to hunger. But I also did my share of praying for more mundane concerns like Christmas presents, good grades, and snow days.

I prayed enough to accumulate a body of evidence that did not support the power of prayer as reliable wish fulfilment. Wars continued, people still went hungry, I didn't get a talking Julie doll for Christmas even though I had spent months quietly negotiating with God about all the reasons why I needed and deserved one. People I loved died in terrible and unfair ways. It grew harder and harder to believe in the power of prayer.

Over the years I lost my faith and found it again many times over. I stopped praying for the things I wanted—even the altruistic requests. Instead, I started a prayer habit based on what a favorite writer of mine, Anne Lamott, says are the two best prayers she knows: "Help me! Help me! Help me!" and "Thank you. Thank you. Thank you."

Last week, our family tested positive for Covid. Ten days in and neither the kids nor my husband have had symptoms other than a slight cough, as well as being a little more tired than usual. For this I have been using the "Thank you" prayer daily. I am even more thankful that we decided to get tested because we were seriously considering spending Thanksgiving with two older family members. "We've been so careful," we thought. "What are the chances that we'd be infected right now and not know it?"

My symptoms were also mild but a little more intrusive. Every once in a while, I experienced a pressure in my chest and the sensation that I couldn't quite catch my breath; it was scary enough to remind me what a miracle it is simply to breathe in and out without worry.

Then yesterday, I watched a news story about Covid in the Dakotas. In it, they interviewed an eighty-eight-year-old man lying in a hospital bed in Rapid City, his face partially obscured by tubes and wires. The camera went in for a close-up, highlighting wet streaks running down the deep creases of his cheeks, his mouth open as he struggled to breathe. At that moment, while also carrying the disease but still relatively healthy, I was overwhelmed by grief for this man's suffering.

When he spoke, his voice was weak, his words nearly inaudible: "It's been a good life. These tears in my eyes are happy tears." Lying in a hospital bed, laboring to bring breath into his chest, he was gazing back over a long life well-lived, and he was thankful. "My father told me, you know, everyone's got troubles, you've got to help if you can, and I've done that all my life."

The camera cut to a shot of the nurse's gloved hand holding his bent and gnarled one.

"And now they're taking good care of you," said the journalist interviewing him.

"They are, they are, thank God," the man whispered in reply.

In my fourth decade of life, I know now what I could not as a child: prayer does not guarantee protection from grief and tragedy. Instead, prayer offers us wellsprings of grace to endure the inevitable hardships of life. Today, as I breathe in and I breathe out, it is a prayer. I am reminded of the man weeping tears of joy even in the midst of great suffering, the answer to his prayers the discovery that in his hour of greatest need he found himself surrounded by love.

DECEMBER 7, 2020

AUTUMN CHRISTMAS

It's been unseasonably warm here the last few weeks. We do our morning and evening chores in coats and mittens, but during the middle part of the day no more than a sweater is necessary. Considering subzero wind chills and blizzards often arrive this time of year, this weather is quite dreamy, but it has made Christmas preparation feel odd. Decking the halls and baking holiday treats with the windows open? It just seems wrong!

We've not entirely let the weather keep us from being jolly, of course, though it has been hard. Warm winter days are for cleaning barns and outbuildings—fixing, puttering, rearranging—doing all the little jobs we never get to during spring, summer, or fall. Meanwhile, the cozy fire in the propane stove, the smell of cinnamon and sugar, and the slight spice of pine boughs make the short indoor days sweet and special, and decorating for the holidays is woven in seamlessly. This year, the ornaments sat in boxes beside the hearth for a week before we got around to opening them—there were so many outdoor jobs to do instead.

And I kept thinking of last year, when we went to cut down our family Christmas tree. It was our first time doing it together, as the kids' legs were finally long enough to hike back to the vehicle through the snow while the grown-ups lugged the tree, and it was a highlight of the season. I had wrapped up cookies straight from the oven and filled a thermos with hot cocoa. After returning with the tree, we had put down the tailgate of the pickup, and the kids sat enjoying their warm snack, Jack Frost nipping at their noses, steam rising picturesquely from their tiny cups.

Which is why, last week, when we made a plan to once again cut down a Christmas tree, I felt a little crestfallen. Cocoa was out. It was not cool enough to warrant a jacket, let alone a hot beverage. Cookies we could still do, but again, it just felt weird to be biting into a frosted snowman while also wearing a sunhat. I was imagining the perfect white Christmas while simultaneously kicking myself for not being more thankful for the warm weather.

When the big day arrived, the weather was the least of our problems, however. My daughter had woken up with growing pains in the night, so she and I were both crabby from lack of sleep. I scrambled to pack a very mundane, not-at-all festive snack while my husband hustled to get chores done, and the kids fought in the background for no reason other than being siblings. Things got better once we buckled into the pickup and started driving, but the day took another sad turn when, upon arriving at our destination, Emmy Rose fell and scraped her hand. She began to cry, and the tears that started with the tumble continued because she had also gotten sap on her hand, because she didn't want to walk, because her socks were too bunchy, because her legs were soooooo tired.

Her brother, in an exasperated tone, finally said, "If you don't stop crying, we can't get a Christmas tree!" which led to a fresh round of wailing.

In the end, she and I stayed by the pickup and played her favorite game, "Lost Little Girl and Big Sister," and gathered "wildflowers," a.k.a. dried grass, while the boys ventured forth to cut the tree. On a colder, snowier day, this would have been misery, but with the sun shining, and the breeze tender and mild, wandering in circles pretending we couldn't find our way home was not an unpleasant occupation.

Tree, kids, and adults all loaded up, and while bouncing down the gravel road, everyone contentedly munching their not-at-all-festive snacks, Emmy suddenly intoned from the back seat, "This was the best day ever!"

My husband and I shared a glance and a little chuckle, and I said a silent "Thank you" that sometimes when we don't get what we want, we instead get exactly what we need.

DECEMBER 14, 2020

THE KINGDOM OF SILVER AND GOLD

This week, temperatures finally dipped below freezing for the first time in a month. With no moisture in the forecast, a chilly, but mostly gray and brown Christmas season appeared inevitable. The sled we had taken out after the first blizzard sat forlornly by the porch, the frosty holiday decorations we had hung oddly incongruous with the view outside the house. Then we woke up on Saturday to a fog so thick it had painted every bush and blade of grass a shimmering white, pearling the pastures and tree breaks for as far as the eye could see. The kids were thrilled.

"Let's take a little hike after breakfast," I said, which they thought was a great idea until we began the arduous task of putting on winter garb—still a labor-intensive chore for them at ages five and almost-four. Where were their mittens? They couldn't find their mittens! Did they really need to wear socks? What about hats, did they really need to wear hats?

Outerwear at last located and begrudgingly donned, we tumbled out the door just as the sun was beginning to break through the mist. Residual crabbiness from the complications of winter attire was stalking us, however, and I decided we would need the element of surprise if we were going to escape it.

"Let's go this way!" I shouted to the kids, pointing toward the blue yard gate that leads to the Tall Grass Forest (a.k.a. the north tree break). "I have a story to tell you about the Kingdom of Silver and Gold." And this was what I told them as we walked:

"A long time ago, long before I'd traveled to the prairie, and fallen in love with the grass and the wind, back when you were both still twinkling stars in the sky, I lived near a wooded strip of tall old trees. I walked there almost every day, or every day I could, and on those walks I listened to birds, and leaves, and the stories ferns tell crocuses in the spring.

"One day in early winter, I went walking in the first light and found the forest silent. The branches of the sleeping trees were covered completely in frost, as were the piles of fallen brown leaves, and the fallen branches that were making their slow return to the soil. It was so silent and still that I could hear the sound of my own steps like an echo from some other place.

"I had only made it a few steps, however, when the first rays of sunlight broke through the cloudy cover and suddenly turned the forest from white to silver. I stopped in my tracks, breathless. For as far as I could see, everything was alive with bright light, the whole forest transformed completely.

"As I stood marveling, the wind, perhaps feeling jealous, let out a sigh—just enough to shake a bit of shimmering frost down to the forest floor. Then, amused by the trick, the wind came up a bit more, sweeping through the trees, filling the air with swirling jeweled flecks.

"While the sparkles flew madly around me, the gap in the clouds widened, and the frosted bark of the branches closest to me burnished by the sun, warmed to a soft glow. As the wind moved, the clouds moved, and light passed gently from east to west, changing silver to gold as it did so.

"And that was how I discovered that existing alongside this world there are two hidden kingdoms: the Kingdom of Silver, and the Kingdom of Gold. They are always there, but only occasionally are they revealed to us."

As I told this story, the kids turned their heads left and right observing the tree break. They could see the silvery frost gleaming brightly on the tall grass and old elms, and they could also see the muted gold color peeking through the layer of frost. Yes, they nodded, yes, they knew exactly what I was talking about—beneath what is expected, there is almost always more magic than we might suppose.

DECEMBER 21, 2020

SORROW AND JOY

Two years ago, on New Year's Day, I went out walking to the small pasture where our horses run wild during the winter months. The day was cool but not cold, snowy but not so snowy that I couldn't hike comfortably across the fields, breathing in the crisp, fresh air. It was the middle of the afternoon, and the sun hung low in the sky. There was a ceiling of pearly gray clouds above me that left only a thin strip of blue for the light to slip through, but the golden beams shimmering below the cover of clouds illuminated the fields and the sparkling crust of snow. In the distance, the horses galloped across the convergence of land and sky and light, their tails lifted high with the delight of their own powerful movement.

I walked back to the house smiling, and that night I wrote, "2019 . . . I have a good feeling about this year . . ." And I meant it.

I've thought often of that day and of writing those words. What I didn't know then was none of the secret dreams I was harboring, or the plans I was laying, would come to pass. Much of 2019 was spent doing the sacred work of grieving, as well as the sacred work of discovering the person I would become in the aftermath of loss.

When I was a young woman, I remember reading the words of the poet Kahlil Gibran, "The deeper that sorrow carves into your being, the more joy you can contain," and feeling frightened.1 I did not want to be pierced by the sharp knives of grief even if it increased my capacity for joy. Young and mostly untested by life, I hoped there could be a way to get the joy without the suffering.

Ruminating from the vantage point of middle age, I have experienced the truth of Gibran's words now, and I am no longer frightened by them. I am not frightened because I have also experienced the peace that comes with that truth. I am a different "I" now—and I am deeply thankful for the person I have become. I am kinder to others and to myself. I am quicker to forgive. I am unendingly thankful for the circle of my husband's arms and for the laughter of my children, for the quiet sweetness of our life here on the prairie, and for the earth and its heartrending beauty. All of it is a gift. I am thankful for the holiness of the spirit that sometimes arises and guides us through darkness. I am thankful even for the darkness, which allows us to know the blessedness of light.

With all this in mind, last month I took my children down to the north pasture to search for materials to make an advent wreath: a wreath to light us through the darkness of midwinter, the wreath's light expanding as the tired year wanes. Down in the snaking cover of the draws, we gathered silver sage leaves, striped turkey feathers, scarlet buffaloberries dried on their slim thorns, and the golden ghosts of asters' stems. Back at home, I molded a wide ring with salt dough, and we added the items we'd collected to the circle. The children both suddenly seemed so grown up, working busily, chatting quietly with each other. We added the candles and then lit the first one.

Behind us, our Christmas tree twinkled with color. The reflections of the tiny bulbs were sprinkled across the shadowed kitchen window like a thousand bright stars, carrying the warmth of our little house out into the long, deep night—a reminder that darkness cannot hold us forever. The time is fast approaching when we will once again turn, turn, turn toward the light.

DECEMBER 28, 2020

YOU'VE ARRIVED

Ten years ago this week, I left Minneapolis and rolled into a tiny town on the prairie. It was meant to be a temporary adventure, but when I crossed the Missouri River and the landscape abruptly shifted to moonscape, I started to cry. I didn't know where I was going, but I knew that what I was leaving behind, I was leaving behind forever.

I was thirty-two, and the third decade wasn't going much better than the second one had. Just a few years before, on the eve of my thirtieth birthday,

I was living on the coast of Maine. I worked as a cook in a café during the day, wrote songs at night, and walked my dogs by the ocean at dawn and dusk, watching the tides roll in and out.

My tiny studio apartment had a postage-stamp-sized yard, and I woke one morning to find a red-tailed hawk perched on the ledge of the garden gate. It was tearing a small songbird apart.

"This doesn't seem like a great omen," I thought grimly. In truth, I already felt a little like the songbird, the circumstances of my life the hungry hawk.

But I kept hustling, writing songs, touring, hiring booking agents and managers, until I was making enough money as a musician to pay my rent—most months anyway. For every success that glittered and jangled during that time, however, there was a much louder howling that never ceased. I was not where I was supposed to be, and I knew it.

Contrast that with the morning before my fortieth birthday, when I heard my livestock guard dog Ellie barking her customary warning bark from the front yard of our ranch house. It was the bark reserved for coyotes, raccoons, and other would-be intruders. Since most of those creatures do their hunting at night, I was surprised, and I went to the window to investigate.

A giant golden eagle was perched on the telephone pole by the yard fence, balancing awkwardly, her curved talons too large for the top of the narrow pole. The kids and the Man of the Ranch were tucking into plates of pancakes still hot from the skillet, so I slipped through the sliding glass door in my sweater and house shoes to get a closer look.

As I approached, the eagle cocked her head to fix me in her gaze, then lifted herself slowly into the air with the heavy beat of her elegant wings. It may sound silly, Dear Reader, but I have no doubt she came specifically to visit me, and I also have no doubt what she came to share: "Sister," she told me as she took flight, "you're ready."

She was right.

Most days I still feel like I am hustling. I try to get a little writing done between chores and mealtimes and reading stories to the kids and vacuuming. I stay up too late answering emails, bake our bread at midnight, and forget to clean the bathroom for a month. In the evening I go running across the prairie with my dogs so I can get a break from the relentless to-do list, and I watch the bright globe of the sun transmute into bands of color. I get back to the house pink-cheeked and still a little tangled in starshine just in time to empty the dishwasher and start supper.

At twenty-nine, I felt like a small bird, defenseless and tattered, a victim of circumstances beyond my control. Now, I feel a lot more like an eagle, with wings stretched wide and strong. Circling above, I can see our little town, and the pointed peaks of our house. I can see the pasture full of beloved creatures, and the rolling prairie tumbling toward the horizon—the endless hillsides, the endless song. The only howling I hear these days is the mighty prairie wind, and when I get tired, I let it carry me, smooth and certain, so I'm not too breathless to sing along.

2021

JANUARY 18, 2021

PRAIRIE FIRE

I'd just started supper when the phone rang. My husband answered. "Really?" he said with the hard laugh he often uses when receiving bad news. "How big are the flames?" he asked, then paused for a beat. "Well, I better go look," he replied, before hanging up his phone and grabbing a coat from the hook by the door. "They can see a fire from town. Looks like it's farther north than our pasture, but I'll go check," he told me before heading out to drive up the gravel section line to the winter feed ground.

It's been dry this January, unseasonably warm with no snow. The grasses, always brown and brittle this time of year, are desiccated as aged tinder. The wind had been blowing hard for days, gusts up to seventy miles per hour, rocking our old house, overturning buckets, even flipping over the painted barn quilt we'd wired to an outbuilding a few years back. And now, it was pulling fire across those dried grasses faster than any human could run.

Upstairs the kids were playing a joyous game, and their merry shouts echoed down through creaky floorboards. I stirred my pot of soup and checked the biscuits baking in the oven. The fluffy black barn kitten who wasn't supposed to be in the house jumped on the counter, purring, hoping for a splash of broth, I suppose. And I thought, "What if this all burns? What if when he gets back, he says we have to leave and say goodbye to all of this?"

Prairie fires move fast in any conditions, but high wind makes them invincible. They do as they please. They have no care for the concerns of humans or beasts. They jump highways, gravel roads, and rivers, and they don't stop if they don't want to, until the whims of the landscape say, "Enough." So, I stood in my kitchen and contemplated the end of life as I knew it.

My husband returned. "It's far away, maybe thirty miles, and heading east. But it's so big you can see the flames from here." He picked up the phone and started making calls, to see who needed help, to find out what to do next.

In the end, what started from a small spark burned twenty thousand acres in a few hours: outbuildings, barns, historic homesteads, winter feed, thousands of pounds of hay reduced to ash, the prairie itself left shadowed with soot and blackened stems. A testament to our isolation, no one was gravely injured, no homes were lost, no livestock harmed. We were lucky.

It will be winter for a few more long months here on the northern plains. It is a rare year that April or May doesn't offer blizzards, and while we curse the fast-forming clouds and hustle to trail in mama cows and sheep from the pasture with their babies newborn and still so fragile, we are thankful for the moisture when the snow melts into the dams and creek beds. This year, dry as it has been, we will be even more thankful when spring turns grasses burnt to the roots green again; the soil will be richer for the devastation wrought upon it, the prairie blessed into new life by the fire.

Here is a quote from Father Richard Rohr's recent blog post on the Center for Action and Contemplation website: "If we trust the universal pattern, the wisdom of all times and all places, including the creation and evolution of the cosmos itself, we know that an ending is also the place for a new beginning. Death is followed by a new kind of life."[1] What we lose in the fire, we will find in the flood: the crested shoulder of the blackened hillside misted with emerald, the damp belly of the spring-fed marsh renewed, the wind as it calls through the valley inviting us to be buoyant as the dandelion's soft seeds, carried forward to regeneration. Carried up toward the heavens, then back to the earth, to be replanted as seedlings with deep roots and blossoms as bright as the sun.

FEBRUARY 22, 2021

ASHES

I sit down to write with a nubby afghan draped around my shoulders. The deep cold of last week's polar vortex has passed, the nights of worrying about double digit negative temperatures over, hopefully, for a while. Other than a few chickens with frostbitten combs, all the creatures under our care came through the dangerous cold unharmed, and when the temperature climbed out of the negatives for the first time in a week, it felt momentarily like spring. Until, ensconced in my chilly writing closet, with an ancient space heater roaring at full-blast, I remembered ten-plus degrees is still very, very cold. Spring in western South Dakota is a long way off.

The temperature is not the only reason I feel chilled. It's Ash Wednesday, the first day of Lent in the Christian tradition, and it's also the twentieth anniversary of my father's sudden death. I was living and working in New York City, attempting my first foray into adulthood, when the call came one morning at dawn, my mother's weeping voice breaking the news. I flew home for the funeral, but the ground was too frozen to bury him. "What will they do with his body?" I asked. No one knew for sure. It was the beginning of a Lent that would last for years.

A decade later, I found myself in South Dakota; avenues swirling with human activity were replaced by wind-soaked grass and the slow dance of ruminants grazing. I tell people who incredulously ask how I've ended up here that of all the places I've lived, Manhattan and South Dakota are the most similar. They never believe me, but whether lost in a river of bodies at rush hour or in an ocean of grass in late spring, the scale is the same, the magnitude a reminder of my own minuteness.

I recently heard somewhere that we have become a ritual-poor people. Most of our holidays revolve around consumerism rather than connection, the roadmap through grief truncated into clichés that alienate as much as they comfort those who are grieving. Sometimes it seems we've forgotten that the journey through the valley of the shadow of death does not follow a straight or clear path. It is a wilderness.

This winter feels more like Lent than usual. It has already been a year of ashes, but traditions like Lent offer an opportunity to practice walking through the wilderness while in community. We don't have to do it alone.

When Lent ends, there will be a celebration of rebirth. Of resurrection. Of spring and new life. But for now, it's okay to recognize that darkness still encircles us, that the earth still slumbers frozen beneath our feet, that the seeds are stirring but have not yet sprung forth. For now, it's okay to dwell in the gathering twilight of early evening and remember: from ashes we are born and to ashes we shall return. It will be spring soon, but it's not spring yet.

In less than a month we begin calving. Acting as a midwife for livestock is a grueling, round-the-clock job. It is the time of birth, new life, exuberance, and exhaustion, but it is also a time of death. Whether it's because of birth defects or troubles during labor, some of the babies born don't live long. They become part of whatever grows next—the blades of grass that feed the other lambs and calves, the leaves of the towering ash trees, the thicket of brush where a doe hides her fawn.

I shrug off the afghan. The wind has picked up, and it's rattling the panes of the south-facing windows. It's a chinook wind; the weather's changing again. By week's end my kids will run across the yard in sweaters. It will be too cold to leave off coats, but I'll let them anyway so they can remember how it feels to move unencumbered by layers of heavy polyester and wool. And when they return to the house later, red-cheeked and shouting, telling me they are "cold, too cold," but laughing as they say it, I will smile, lift them into the warmth of my arms, and remember how it feels to run unencumbered too.

MARCH 18, 2021

KITTENS AND CATS

Over the years, our Mama Cat's many kittens have been a source of joy and consternation. They've been silly and sickly, tough, aloof, gentle, playful, and feral, depending on what personality quirks genetics awarded them. Most have gone to live at neighbors' barns or friends' houses. A few we've kept around here, but as is the case with most barn cats, they disappeared after the passage of a few seasons.

Through these many litters, Mama Cat, though small in stature, has been the reigning queen on the ranch, even the toughest tom afraid to cross her. Until this past summer, that is, when a similarly demure female cat from the previous summer's litter decided to challenge her mother's authority and unexpectedly prevailed. The result: Mama Cat took to prowling the fields and tree breaks, no longer able to shelter in the barn for fear of retribution. We kept trying to make her a new haven in a different outbuilding, but apparently none suited her. When it was time for another batch of kittens to be born, she instead birthed and hid them in the shelter of the tall grass beneath the rotting branch of a fallen tree.

These homeless babes became our special charges. Mama Cat, still a relatively attentive mother, had lost some of her zeal for parenting over the years, and she was happy to let us help. Meanwhile, my kids were finally at an age where pet ownership actually meant something to them, and out of the litter of kittens they picked two to be their favorites.

My son picked the runt. Long-haired and black as coal, like her mother, but with a coat that was oddly tufted and greasy looking, this kitten's eyes were nearly as big as the rest of her face. Her personality was also big. She was wild and mischievous, the kind of cat who could break every dish on the counter by jumping up and running full tilt amongst them, not even slowing down as they all crashed to the tile floor. (Ask me how I know.) My son named this irrepressible bundle Fluffs, and despite her naughtiness and constantly bedraggled appearance, he loved her without question.

My daughter's pick was the second smallest in the litter. Unlike his rambunctious and incorrigible sister, this little boy was the sweetest dream of a kitten you can imagine. Because he was also black as coal, but short-haired, my daughter named him Not Fluffs.

So, while Fluffs rampaged through the house and yard destroying everything in sight, Not Fluffs was the perfect wee gentleman. He would allow his adopted caregiver to dress him in doll clothes and cart him around in a tiny stroller or carry him slung over her shoulder across the yard and through the house without so much as a meow.

At first, we worried my daughter's ministrations were akin to low-level torture, but if she put him down, he would follow right behind her waiting to be picked up again. To this day he greets even the sight of her with the loud rumble of his prodigious purring. Meanwhile, Fluffs only let us pet her when she slowed down, which was never.

And so we headed happily into fall—two kids and two kittens, the rest of the litter rehomed to other ranches. As winter neared, I began to worry about keeping the kittens (who were still small for their age) warm and safe, as they, along with their mother, continued to be personae non gratae in the barn. Once again, however, all attempts to make another living area for the little family were unsuccessful.

Fortunately, it's been a mild winter. Unfortunately, it's not been mild enough. Consequently, we now have two mostly indoor barn kittens in addition to the two house cats we already had, plus Mama Cat, who is a frequent visitor. Guests often marvel, "Oh look, you have another cat . . . and another. And another?"

To which I reply, "It is an embarrassment of riches . . ." and never have I meant a phrase more completely!

MARCH 22, 2021

LOST WORDS

Yesterday, the robins returned to our yard. We saw them through the living room window on the western side of the house, a small flock of them flitting between the branches of the tallest ash in the tree break. It was a damp, gray day, and they were far enough away that it was difficult to make out the burnt-orange feathers of their breasts, but the plump curve of their bellies and the stuttered swoop of their flight were unmistakable after watching a winter's worth of sparrows.

"Let's take the binoculars upstairs and see if we are right!" I told the kids, and we tromped up to look. I threw open the window, and the cacophony of robin song filled the room even before we spotted the telltale coloration through the binocular's lenses. The kids, satisfied, went back down to their Lego table, where they had been working on a waterpark that included a hot dog stand and nine waterslides. I stayed to marvel. "Hello, friends," I called out the window.

In 2018, Robert Macfarlane and Jackie Morris created a children's picture book called *The Lost Words*. The impetus of the book was the editing of the Oxford Junior Dictionary, which had removed many words used to describe the natural world—some of them relatively common words, such as *acorn, fern, dandelion, raven, goldfinch, gray seal, otter, and kingfisher*. The editing body of the *Oxford Junior Dictionary* determined that the excised words were of increasingly less importance to the modern child and removing them made room for newer words with greater relevance like *blog, broadband, database*, and *voicemail*. The editors argued they couldn't include everything, but Macfarlane explained what was being lost this way: "We find it hard to love what we cannot give a name to. And what we do not love we will not save."[2]

Today the weather is warm and bright. The robins that gathered beneath the chilly clouds yesterday are scattered across the yard now. We hear them calling from every direction. A giant plume of red-winged blackbirds swoops down to occupy the tall ash, their coarse whistles and trills even louder than the robins' chatter. They move on quickly though, our tree break merely a short respite in their journey. We see a downy woodpecker skipping along the bark in a tree by the patio, and then a single goose honks past, so low to the ground we could practically reach up and brush our fingertips over her feathers. "Birds, birds everywhere!" I tell the kids, and they smile at me before returning to draw with chalk on the cement.

The one bird we don't hear is the meadowlark, whose bright song, ubiquitous once the weather warms, is usually how western South Dakotans know that spring has arrived. In total, we've lost nearly three billion American birds since the 1970s, and the meadowlark population in particular has seen a precipitous decline in the last decade, though their numbers in our region are still strong. Or have been. "Where are the meadowlarks?" I whisper aloud, suddenly worried.

Evening begins to settle around us. The shadows are long and stark across the first brushes of green rising softly from the dusty field. The sun, resting just above the horizon, is pure gold. I go out for a run, and I am just about to turn back when I hear it: two long notes followed by a dizzying avalanche of trills. It's a meadowlark.

We live surrounded by a wilderness of grass. Although the land has changed, it still looks surprisingly similar to the way it did a millennia ago. And yet my children, children of the prairie winds and grasses, would rather listen to birdsong on YouTube than out in the pasture. Unlike the editors of the *Oxford Junior Dictionary*, I've tried to give them words for both the world of human creation and the world in which humans are simply one voice in a marvelous and ancient symphony. But I fear Macfarlane may be wrong: What if the things we name and love are still not loved enough to save?

Perhaps it's time to stop saying those names quietly. Perhaps it is time to start shouting, lest we discover what we've lost we've lost for good.

APRIL 26, 2021

WHAT DO YOU NEED?

I met Mason in college. He was athletic, charming, and played bass in the coolest band on campus. I didn't know him well, but I liked him. Everyone did.

One night at a loud, crowded house party, we ended up in small group talking about music.

"The Stones were really onto something with that lyric: 'You can't always get what you want, but you get what you need,'" our mutual friend Tracy shouted, trying to keep her drink from sloshing out of her cup as someone squeezed past her. "It's really true."

"Totally," I shouted back, partially because I agreed but mostly because Tracy was from Manhattan and was much, much cooler than me.

"Hmmmm . . ." said Mason, "I don't know . . . because I feel like I've gotten pretty much everything I've really wanted, and almost nothing that I really need."

He didn't sound sad or angry, just matter-of-fact, his gaze calm as he took a long sip from his drink. "Wow," I said into the long pause that followed his words, and in that moment I felt a seismic shift in my understanding of my own life. Was it possible that I also was mostly getting only what I wanted, and rarely what I needed? That would explain a lot.

This time of year is by far the most intense on a ranch. Lambs and calves are born at all hours and in all kinds of weather, and we need to be close by in case the cows and ewes need help. That means checking on the herd and the flock regularly throughout the day and the night. Life narrows down to the confines of our barn and pastures, the hours filled past brimming with chores and obligations.

Meanwhile, here on the northern plains, winter and spring can never seem to decide who is actually in charge of April (and sometimes May, too). One day I'll be sweating in short sleeves, trying to turn a lamb that's in a breech presentation, the next day my husband will appear on the porch, his coat soaked through from sleet and snow, carrying a chilled-down newborn calf in his arms.

On a ranch, loss and worry are bundled into the joys of seasonal rebirth. For all the many successful births, there are also inevitable deaths. Lambs and calves born during foul weather in particular have a lower chance of survival. On the other hand, when the weather is warm and dry, as it has been this year, we fret over the lack of moisture and the threat of prairie fires.

But during this time of year more than any other, I can easily see the distance between what I want and what I need—something that was much harder to observe during my suburban upbringing—and that has been a gift beyond measure.

And what do I really need? I need to believe my labor has purpose. I need to see that the animals under my care are thriving, and that our stewardship allows the other members of this ecosystem to thrive too. I need to be out in the hard wind and rain, my frozen fingers fumbling to milk a cow or bottle-feed a baby lamb, so that when I return to the shelter of my house I am flooded with gratitude for the warmth. I need to know there's a good neighbor a phone call away who will offer a piece of hardware to fix a broken water tank, or a tube of ointment to treat an infected udder.

In the summer, the new babies won't be so fragile anymore. The herd and the flock will graze in the pastures. The chickens will chase bugs across the yard. We will ride horses under the colored flag of evening just for pleasure. There will still be plenty of work to do, but we will have time to limn the expanse between what we want and what we need with the laughter of our children playing nearby, the animals healthy and thriving, and the stars that rise over our heads as the sun sets on another day.

MAY 3, 2021

RAINDROPS TO ROOTS

It's before 5:00 a.m., and murky gray light creeps beneath the curtain of the bedroom window. Outside, the robins are sharing their first exchanges of the day, while the flock of grackles that congregates in the western windbreak replies: "Hush up, hush up, we've heard enough."

I peek out. There's a fine mist hovering over the prairie grass, brushed to pearl by the imminent arrival of dawn. It's raining enough to get everything damp, but that's about it.

I think about going back to sleep. I haven't been in bed all that long. I did my last check of the flock around midnight, just in time to watch one of my maiden ewes give birth to twins. She was unsure about the first one, especially when it stood up and started trying to nurse. Her maternal instincts instructed her to clean the baby off, but her survival instincts made her wary of the small, wet, and very insistent stranger. When the second one arrived, well, then the survival instincts took over and she ran away from her babies, who called to her in despair with loud, keening cries.

The other ewes, huddled nearby, exchanged worried glances. "Somebody should probably do something," they opined amongst themselves. But who? And what? A few glanced at me with reprimanding looks.

"Let's give her a little more time and extend some grace, my friends," I said, hoping that was the right decision, extremely thankful the night air was unseasonably warm and languid.

An hour later, the first-time mama was settling into her new normal. She had realized that the babies were hers and seemed more concerned than terrified by their presence. "All's well that ends well," I thought as I finally went to bed.

Now, the rain has me worried. An experienced mother would have her babies cleaned, with full tummies, and resting in a sheltered spot. But new mothers, still adjusting to parenthood, aren't always so conscientious.

Meanwhile, in the barn, two orphan lambs wait for their breakfast. Much like my own children when they were brand new, the lambs' bodies aren't built to accommodate a full night of slumber. So, I get up even though I'd rather not. I make bottles in the half-light, fumbling with milk replacer and rubber nipples.

I pull on my flannel barn coat and jam the bottles into its deep pockets. There's enough light to see across the yard, and I follow the path to the corral where the flock rests. As I approach, the ewes stand, leaving behind dry, dusty sheep-shaped marks on the otherwise damp dirt. In the far corner, the ewe who gave birth last night watches me. The babies are wet with rain, but their bellies are round and plump atop the spindly stilts of their skinny legs. Their mother speaks to them softly, reminding them to stay close.

In the dark barn, the two orphans greet me with bleats and tail wags and wobbly nuzzles. They drink their bottles down in seconds flat and then let me scratch their chins for a few minutes. One of them reaches up to nibble on my cheek. He's probably just looking for more milk, but it feels like a kiss. I pet his fluffy head and marvel at his bright, gray eyes, at his fleecy whiteness, at his soft, knobby hooves, still a bit too big for his body.

I stay with the lambs a few minutes more, then walk back across the yard. The horses nod at me as I pass, the scent of sage and fast wind rising from their wet manes. The sun appears just before I reach the house, his arrival heralded by a narrow band of gold visible between clouds and horizon. And out across the meadow, the grasses gather the raindrops to their roots, as joyful as children waking from sweet dreams.

MAY 10, 2021

SO MUCH TO LEARN

There are a lot of ways for a lamb to end up as a bottle baby. Its mother gets sick, and it is orphaned. It is born with a physical problem, or the mother's body doesn't produce enough milk. There's so much that can go wrong, sometimes it amazes me that it ever goes right.

We started lambing last week. So far, we've had three sets of triplets, too many babies for a single ewe to raise. We also lost the first ewe that lambed to a mysterious illness. She was fine, her babies happily nursing by her side, and then within a few hours she sickened and died. All of which means we currently have a barn full of bum lambs.

Now, I love bum lambs. I thought my adventures in South Dakota were temporary until I volunteered to take in two bums from a friend. Everything changed when I fell completely in love with them. Lucky for me, the next time I fell in love it was with a cowboy willing to accommodate me and my shepherding habit.

That was nine years ago. Since then, I've learned a lot about sheep, but there is much that remains a mystery. Sheep are stoic to a fault. It's a liability for prey animals to outwardly display illness, but it makes it challenging to care for them. And while lambs are a little less secretive than adult sheep about their ailments, once they take a bad turn, they tend to take it fast.

Cold, wet weather is especially treacherous on new babies if the calories required to stay warm overtake what they can consume. They will stop trying to nurse and simply curl up somewhere to conserve heat. Unless a watchful shepherd comes along, they will fall asleep and never wake.

Last week, all across western South Dakota, people cheered at a weekend forecast predicting the moisture we so desperately needed, but I am sure I wasn't the only shepherd grimacing while she cheered. Some of that moisture was going to be snow accompanied by high winds—the worst possible weather for those of us in the middle of lambing.

The cold, wet weather arrived on schedule, and on Sunday, I carried a tiny ewe lamb into the house, her body so still and cold that I thought she might already be dead. I watched from afar as she struggled to stand after birth, wondering if I should intervene. The baby's mother was the worried sort, and I've learned the hard way that interrupting the bonding process, especially if the mother is already agitated, can cause irreparable harm. So, I waited too long before interfering, hoping the mother would be able to rouse the lamb herself.

Miraculously, the baby recovered, and we named her Fiona—Finny for short—because Fiona means white in Gaelic and she is the whitest lamb I've ever seen. She is thriving now, and in years past that would have been enough—the satisfaction of rescuing her despite my mistake, a windfall of grace, a temporary reprieve from the demands of mortality. But this year it isn't enough; a rescue no longer feels like a reprieve. It seems I am finally accepting that no matter how hard I try, and how knowledgeable I become, I can't save all the lambs, and there is grief and loss in that realization.

The last of the snow and sleet passed over this afternoon. The sky is still gray, but the air is warmer, and the grasses in the pasture are growing so fast we can almost hear the crinch and squeak as they push up, up, up toward the light, millennia of wisdom held in their quiet roots. Tomorrow the sun will return and the whole prairie will be singing with green, the same hymn of thanksgiving it always sings at the gift of moisture, new life brought forth from the decay of what came before. And I will be listening, because there is still so much to learn.

MAY 24, 2021

PLAINSONG FARM AND FIBER

Small-scale shepherding is not a lucrative undertaking, especially when one has a fiber flock composed mostly of pets. In an effort to not lose money on my shepherding habit, I started a business with an old friend a few years ago called Plainsong Fiber. My friend lives in the Pacific Northwest, where there are fiber enthusiasts aplenty, as well as an abundance of fiber festivals and yarn shops. Once or twice a year, she comes out for an extended visit to help with the sheep, to skirt and sort fleeces, and to spin wool before taking the pick of that year's shearing to Seattle.

My friend and her daughter arrived this week for their annual visit to bright sun and high temperatures, but Seattle missed them, and almost immediately the dry heat shifted to rain and mist. We aren't complaining, and neither is the grass after the last few months of drought. Even the sheep and the lambs, damp through their fine, curly coats, don't seem to mind. They are happy to be out nibbling on fresh stems instead of the last wisps of winter hay.

It also means we are spending a lot of time in the outbuilding we've been slowly converting to a fiber studio. The building had long been used as a storage shed, but I saw promise in its concrete floor and sound structure. Over the last few years, we've tinned the roof, added a small lean-to greenhouse, replaced the ancient, impossible-to-open garage doors, and put in an old woodstove. While aesthetically it still looks more like a shed than anything else, calling it a studio no longer sounds aspirational.

I was contemplating this progress when we lit a fire in the woodstove this morning. My friend had set her spinning wheel up next to the stove, and the wheel's quiet whir accompanied the snap and crackle of the logs as they burned. Mama Cat and her latest batch of kittens have a cozy bed in the studio as well, and the kids played with the chubby babies while I sorted wool, rain tapping gently on the roof.

I'm a person with lots of ideas—too many ideas, it often seems, the capacity of my imagination always bigger than the time, energy, or resources at my disposal. This tendency leaves me feeling that no matter how fast I run, I am always running behind. Our fledgling fiber business is a perfect example. We could be hustling harder, posting more cute pictures and fun stories to social media, working to cultivate relationships with shops and online influencers to build our "brand." But between ranching, mothering, and my work as a writer and musician, I can't hustle any harder for the business—I'm already overextended.

When I was younger, I imagined I would eventually figure out how to reach the end of a daily to-do list with time left over to sit outside and sip an artfully concocted beverage in my well-tended garden. Now, firmly ensconced in middle age, I consider it an accomplishment to drink a full glass of water, and I've had to admit that if I want any garden at all, it will never be well-tended. Looking over at my friend and our children using this space just as I imagined we would, a dream growing, albeit slowly, toward fruition should feel like a victory. Instead, I see the cobwebs and unfinished walls, the tubs of dirty wool, the hours of work ahead, and I am exhausted before I begin.

The real work of my adulthood, it turns out, is not learning how to do it all. It's about learning how to joyfully leave work undone. It's about looking at an unfinished project and seeing all the progress instead of all that's left to do. It's about carving out space in the relentlessness of my own expectations to be still.

Outside, the rain falls steadily, seeping through dusty soil to roots that have been waiting patiently for a drink. It's a drink that arrived later than expected, but still in plenty of time to grow a prairie's worth of summer blooms.

JUNE 14, 2021

WESLEY JUDE

In the middle of June six years ago, my first child arrived into the world. There were some very minor complications that resulted in major implications, and we ended up in the NICU. After a week of hushed voices, kind nurses, beeping machines, and more tubes and cords than we could count, we got to take our little man home. I cried a lot during the drive, but when we reached the cool quiet of our house, the only sound was the wind in the trees and the voices of birds. I was the happiest I've ever been. Our baby was home and healthy.

The cool quiet didn't last long, however. We had barely settled in, our hospital suitcase still sitting by the door, when the weather took a sudden turn, and my husband hustled us all into the basement. "I don't like the look of that sky," he said.

A few days later, a friend reposted a video from a storm chaser who had been in our area that afternoon and had pulled over to film a swirling cloud. The cloud roiled with a sickly greenish hue, ready to funnel down to the ground at any moment, the wind from the clouds already whipping the tattered prairie grasses around in circles. Off to the side of the shot stood a simple, wrought iron sign. The sign trembled and quaked in the wind, too, looking like it might get pulled from the ground by the gale at any moment. I lifted my hand to my mouth in horror as I watched. It was the sign for our ranch.

Looking back, the sign might as well have said "Welcome to Parenthood." The ups, the downs, the dangers miraculously avoided, the dangers you must face head on—it can all feel relentless and daunting. And I was told, but could not really understand before my son was born, that once I became a mother my heart would live outside my chest forevermore. Who I am no longer stops at my flesh and bones but extends beyond the boundaries of my body. In our six years together, I have already experienced the beauty and the terror of this reality many times.

Our boy is named Wesley Jude. Wesley means the "west lea," a western meadow or grove of trees. We have just such a lea of elms to the west of our house. Wesley is named for the wind and the trees and the birds in that lea, and the dappled sunlight that passes through the branches. Jude is for Saint Jude, the patron saint of lost causes, because neither my husband nor I thought we'd get the chance to be parents. Yet, here our boy is, growing straight and tall like a sturdy young sapling. What a wonder. After six years the miracle that he is has not lessened but grown exponentially.

I still often think of those first days. Much of the time I should have spent sleeping I spent watching him sleep instead, his tiny feet curved inward, his tiny fist pressed snug beside his smooth cheek. Sometimes he'd cry out in his sleep, a sharp sound, full of terror, and I'd think about the week in the NICU when I wasn't allowed to hold him while he slept. I made up for it by barely putting him down the whole first year.

That ended after he started walking. Now, he'll briefly sit in my lap for a little comfort after a bike wreck, or slow down long enough for a short hug every once in a while, but mostly he is in motion, greeting the world with every step. My arms are no longer his home, and that is as it should be.

But I still like to watch him sleep. In those quiet moments I can see the baby he was and the man he will become, and I am so thankful—so very, very thankful—for every moment of this journey.

JUNE 21, 2021

HEAT

The high temperatures early in June meant we put our two ancient air-conditioning units in the windows early, too. My husband says he starts dreading this yearly procedure the moment he takes them out in the fall. In addition to mounting the bulky units on the sills, the operation requires the creation of carefully constructed shields of duct tape and cardboard to fill in the gaps between the unit and window frame, followed by a lengthy search-and-rescue mission for the indoor extension cords that always manage to migrate outdoors.

When all is said and done, we've got a unit upstairs and another downstairs. It's not enough to keep the house really cool, but it's more than enough to keep it from getting really hot, assuming we don't use any kitchen appliances, of course. (And thus, grilling season commences, too.)

Like the deepest cold of winter, these days of extreme heat always get me thinking of our homesteading forebears. Forget about air-conditioning, an electric fan was an unimaginable luxury when my husband's great-grandparents built this house one hundred years ago. And the trees whose shade keeps the worst of the day's heat from the house and yard didn't exist yet either. The Almen family planted our beloved windbreaks, then meticulously tended the saplings for years while they were still too short to offer any respite from the weather. As with so much we take for granted here, their labor paved a pathway for our comfort.

The same is true of the thousands of lilacs and rose blossoms that encircle the yard during early summer, although they are less of a physical comfort and more of a spiritual one. The blossoms offer their beauty and their enchanting scent freely, a memory of the hardworking gardeners who tended them so well that despite our harsh climate they have thrived. Did whoever planted those glorious shrubs guess at the abundance they were granting future generations?

I certainly hope so. Despite its age, this house is surprisingly low-maintenance due to the careful work of our predecessors: those trees, a cool sanctuary; those flowers, a beautiful gift every summer. It's how we can stay cool using only two AC units even when the outdoor temperatures soar into triple digits.

During the years this property has been under our care, we've added a few improvements of our own here and there, and we work hard to maintain what already exists. This year we've added a few pear and apricot trees, as well as some currant bushes to the line of shrubbery that shades the front of the house.

Ironically, our greatest legacy may be to leave as much of this land as unchanged as we can. After all, Mother Earth does a pretty marvelous job without our interventions. We humans might be wilting in the heat, as are the domesticated plants in my garden, but the native prairie grasses are doing just fine. Even if they aren't as tall as they would be in a year with more abundant moisture, the fact that they are growing at all is quite amazing, considering how hot, dry, and windy it has been for weeks.

This past weekend the weather finally modulated a little. It was still windy and dry, but one could walk out across the pasture without fear of being baked alive. It felt great. So great, in fact, that I took the kids camping.

I learned a long time ago that chasing perfection is a fool's errand—in work, life, and weather. But sometimes I find myself cradled by moments so flawless it takes my breath away. Hiking down to our campsite at sunset, a rainbow of pastel colors filling the prairie's wide horizon, the air pooling around us at the exact temperature of a warm bath, was just such a moment—made all the more wonderful by the days of heat and wind and endless sun that preceded it. Perfection, like grace, arrives unexpectedly on the wings of gratitude.

SEPTEMBER 27, 2021

EQUINOX

Walking on the gravel toward the draw, I am surprised by the tops of the ash trees nestled in the folds of the land. They are burnished shades of glowing amber, ochre, and lemon-yellow, brighter than any autumn since I moved here. Against the gray sky and dead prairie grasses, they shine like a vein of gold in a granite hillside. It's easy to imagine, while walking north of our house, what the view would have looked like one hundred years ago, when my husband's great-grandparents arrived here and started building their home. It is easy to imagine because it probably looked exactly the same: hills, valleys, a few trees, a lot of grass.

It is also easy to imagine how those first homesteaders would have felt about the drought that has gripped our region this summer, leaving the grasses bent and tattered. It would have meant ruin for them, or near ruin. Drought is one reason there are, to this day, so many abandoned homesteads dotting the landscape. Then, as now, this place required fortitude, hard work, and luck. Then, as now, a year with so little rain often meant a year with no profit, a heavy burden to carry into a long winter.

Last week was the fall equinox, the exact moment that the shadow cast on the earth is perpendicular to the equator, dividing the globe in half. For an instant the day and night are equally long. And then, just like that, there is a shift—suddenly the night is longer than the day. The equinox is a rare moment of balance in a universe that is always tipping one way or another, because although nature is always trying to reach equilibrium, it is seldom achieved.

I am thinking of those relatives and their journey into winter, and I am feeling trepidation about what lies ahead as well. The heat we endured this summer (which is still lingering—it is ninety degrees right now in the early evening), the constant fear of fire, the ever-present reality that the only constant is change—it all feels heavy. And I am so tired.

Which is why I find myself reflecting on balance. In years past I have written about trying to find balance in motherhood. Trying to find the time and energy to still do my creative work—or any kind of work—when my children were so young. Now, they are finally at the point that kindly people predicted would be my salvation. They play together for an hour at a time with no intervention from me: elaborate, high energy games that require every cushion be removed from the couch and all beds. Or, when I banish them outside, they take armfuls of their toys and bury them in the deep mine shaft they've dug in the front yard. There's an underground laboratory, a house in the forest, a hospital for dinosaurs and unicorns. Suddenly I have these pockets of time that would have felt like grand expanses a year ago, but the world has risen up to fill them, and there's still never enough time to do all I had planned.

So, I go out walking. I walk all the way to the farthest draw and stand beneath a thick-trunked cottonwood. Her leaves rustle loudly; it is impossible not to hear laughter in the sound. She never offers complicated advice, but she already knows almost everything I am trying to figure out. With her deep roots, and branches that bend and don't break, she tells me, "As long as you have, that's how long it will take." And I listen for as long as I can. I wish I could learn all these things faster, but of course, that just shows how slow a learner I am.

I head back to the house in the gloaming. It's still hot. I sweat as I walk, even as the sun sets beside me, a banner of colors, bold and bright, the balancing point between light and dark.

OCTOBER 10, 2021

"IT ALWAYS HAS BEEN SO, AND IT ALWAYS WILL BE."

A neighbor says, "If we get heavy snow this winter, we are in real trouble. And if we don't get heavy snow, we are in real trouble . . ."

"True," my husband replies, nodding his head.

"What does that mean?" I ask my husband in private, later.

"Everybody's got just barely enough hay to get through the winter. If there's a lot of snow, we'll need more feed and there's no place to get it. Everyone is in the same boat. But if it doesn't snow the dams won't fill and the grass won't grow in the spring. Then we'll still be scrambling when the hay runs out," he says.

"Oh, dear," I reply. "That's definitely a problem."

And thus, we find ourselves once again in the kind of frying pan to fire situation that so often defines ranching. Too dry in the spring and the grass won't grow. Too wet and the lambs and the calves will fall sick with pneumonia. We cheer for fresh, green grass until our strongest, best cows get grass tetany from the abundance of minerals saved in the stems. It sometimes seems we can't win for losing, and it's hard to even know what to wish for when every blessing comes with its fair share of curses.

This ongoing dilemma reminds me of Ma Ingalls's words in Laura Ingalls Wilder's *Little Town on the Prairie*. The character of Laura laments that their beautiful fields of nearly-ripe corn are being decimated by blackbirds and crows before they can be harvested. The Ingalls family are the first of the homesteading farmers in their area to have such a large, productive planting, and therefore it is the most delicious and irresistible field the birds have ever encountered. When Laura begins to complain, her mother says, "This earthly life is a battle. . . . If it isn't one thing to contend with, it's another. It always has been so, and it always will be. The sooner you make up your mind to that, the better off you are, and more thankful for your pleasures."[3]

Virginia Driving Hawk Sneve outlines a similarly stark reality in a story about her Lakota ancestors that she wrote for the January/February 2020 issue of *South Dakota Magazine*. Instead of counting how many years old they were, people counted how many winters they had survived. "Winters were hard times for people on the plains," she writes. "Only the hardiest survived the winters."[4]

The truth that life can be hard and full of uncertainty is not news, but it is a truth many of us don't know how to embrace. Ease, material comfort, and constant abundance were never our birthright, but modern life has made it a little easier to pretend that they are, especially for those of us raised far away from the rhythms of the natural world. Thankfully, most of us can expect to survive even a harsh winter, but the reality is we will still lose everything we love eventually—not because we've done something wrong, not because we haven't worked hard enough, buf because "it always has been so, and it always will be."

Today it is raining, really raining, for the first time in over a year, with steady, pattering drops that started this morning and are still falling now in the middle of the afternoon. The trees in the yard and windbreak are full of birds shouting and singing along with the lively rhythm. The puddles forming on the gravel are brimful with flocks of robins splashing and playing. I have never seen birds so giddy about bath time, but I guess I shouldn't be surprised—it has been a long, hot summer for them as well.

Do the robins worry about the uncertain future? Do they ruminate on the difficulties of the past? I don't know, of course, but I can now say with absolute confidence they do rejoice in the rain as it falls after so long a time without, giving thanks with their whole bodies, voices raised, baptizing themselves in the mud before stretching their wings and flying up toward heaven.

DECEMBER 27, 2021

JOVI

This morning, as I sat down to work on my column, I found a small scrap of paper on my desk with the following words scrawled on it:

See Joy

Seek Joy

I had written the words a few days before, contemplating New Year's resolutions, and then forgotten all about them. In truth, I'd only meant to write Seek Joy, but a slip of my pen had made me write See by accident, which is why I'd written it again, correctly, just below.

In the interim, we had gotten a puppy. A puppy my children (especially my son) had been imagining for quite some time. He wanted a small dog who liked kids and wanted to play games like fetch and tug-of-war. A dog who would snuggle. A dog who knew how to play just a little wild and how to have fun, something ranch dogs, like parents, weren't always good at remembering how to do.

I was not, however, ready to take on a puppy, so I had decided the small dog of my son's dreams would have to wait until he was older and able to do more of the puppy-rearing himself. Then, a few months ago, we suddenly lost our English shepherd, Zuzu. I was heartbroken, but he was devastated. Though we've lost pets before, this one cut deeper, probably because he was finally old enough to understand the permanence of the loss. Every night for weeks he'd lie awake asking me through tears, "I am thinking about sad things. How can I stop thinking about sad things?"

I often had to answer, through tears myself, "Sometimes we just have to let ourselves be sad." But I was also reminded of a quote I read on the internet, which says that grief is love with no place to go. Which is why, when we found out a neighbor had a litter of corgi/miniature Australian shepherds that were born at the exact time—almost to the minute—Zuzu died, I couldn't help but think one of them was meant to be ours.

Even before we brought him home, however, I was worried this new puppy was a bad idea. Zuzu was the dog of my dreams. She was a second mother to my kids, my constant companion, as loyal as she was sensitive and intelligent, and her only fault was being so good I didn't sufficiently appreciate her because she so rarely required anything of me. How could a new dog ever live up to that?

My fears were well placed. We picked up our new puppy the day before Christmas Eve, and whereas Zuzu had snuggled peacefully on my lap on her first ride home, Jovi McWaddles howled nonstop. And he kept on howling. After a few hours he finally curled up on my shoulder and fell asleep, but I was already exhausted and dreading the long night ahead too much to appreciate his sweetness.

The next few days unfolded much as you might expect. Jovi got used to us pretty quickly. The howling abated. He is absolutely adorable with his short corgi legs and Australian shepherd floof, and everyone who sees him can't help but giggle. He floats across the floor like a furry Roomba or a feather duster with no handle and already comes when he's called, mostly because he rarely leaves our sides.

Meanwhile, he is less than a foot tall but still has managed to overturn houseplants and chew tiny, pinpoint-sized holes in nearly every surface that's chewable, and he is the reason we will have our Christmas tree undecorated and out the door before New Year's Eve for the first time ever. In other words, he is both the best of times and the worst of times all rolled into one hilarious, exhausting disaster.

He is also the reason I chuckled when I found the scrap of paper I'd left on my desk. Seeking joy is a bit like seeking perfection: it's an endless quest. Seeing joy is a different thing altogether because it's always there if we remember to look. And sometimes it looks just like a rambunctious, short-legged puppy chasing his favorite humans across the yard, barking wildly while they laugh in delight.

2022

JANUARY 10, 2022

GOODBYE, ORVILLE

We are only halfway through, but this has already been the January-est January we've had in a while. Day after day of deep cold, high winds, no new snow but plenty of new drifts, and we are all feeling chilled to the bone and more than a little weary.

Or maybe it's actual sleep deprivation that's getting us down. Though our new puppy is doing great with potty training, we are still on the late-night and early-morning potty break schedule. Thankfully, the cold has actually helped to make outdoor trips brief, but in the days after the New Year, the kids briefly reverted to middle-of-the-night waking. Between bouts of growing pains and a few bad dreams, it has been restless nights all around, and mounting crabbiness as a result.

Then, just when it seemed we were all getting back on schedule, there came two nights where the windchill dipped to negative forty and negative fifty degrees respectively. I find it almost impossible to sleep on nights that cold, even without puppy and kid problems. Lying in bed, listening to the wind howling around the corners of the house, feeling the creeping chill of icy fingers through the doors and windows, I worry about all the animals outside. I know they are hardy, well-fed, tucked into barns, coops, and behind windbreaks, but still, fifty below? That kind of cold seems impossible to survive.

I'm always amazed to go out after these arctic nights and see all the animals standing together patiently, and except for a little frost around their nostrils, looking none the worse for wear. Sometimes the horses or the yearling heifers will even be running and kicking around, seemingly enjoying the inhospitable temperatures.

I've been on the ranch long enough now to know, however, that it's often not the day after the deep, deep cold, but the day after the cold finally breaks when one discovers the toll the weather has taken. While most of the animals are able to do fine, the very old and very young or the otherwise compromised are vulnerable. Vulnerability is a liability for herd animals, and therefore it is often hard to tell weakened livestock from their stronger peers until it's too late.

Everyone was reasonably healthy going into the cold snap. Still, we do have quite a few elderly among us, including three senior citizen sheep who have been taken out of breeding rotation and now do as they please, and a cadre of retired horses who are spending their twilight years ambling around together, kings and queen of their domain. So, on the coldest nights, I lie awake and worry about them.

Today, the first "warm" day we've had in weeks, it was not an old horse or an old sheep that I found lying down as though asleep, but our ancient donkey, Orville, one of the pair of aged miniature donkeys my husband gave me as a wedding present. We lost his brother, Wilbur, during a similar cold snap two years ago, and though we thought about finding Orville a new companion, he seemed happy enough to integrate with the flock and become a somewhat ineffective sheep livestock guardian. He took the new role seriously, and at all hours of day or night he could be heard screaming that singular "Hee-haw" gifted to donkeys whenever anyone or anything approached his sheep friends, whether that be me, a cat, or the actual livestock guard, our Great Pyrenees, Ellie.

Orville was old, and I'd like to think he lived a good life; still, it's always hard to say goodbye. In some ways these goodbyes have gotten easier as I've become more accustomed to the losses that accompany a life so full of animal companions, but in other ways it's gotten harder. I'm getting older, too, and the view from the middle of my life doesn't look as expansive as

I thought it would. Hours become days become decades so quickly. Thank goodness for the beauty that remains: the grasses moving as one in the breeze, the wind humming its favorite songs, and the bold winter sparrows that are brave enough to sing along.

JANUARY 31, 2022

BOO THE GOAT

January and February are difficult months on the plains of the Upper Midwest. The sky provides a gorgeous light show in mauve, peach, lavender, and gold twice a day, but the rest of the time the moonscape of gray, brown, and white can get monotonous. There's also the cold and the relentless wind and the tyranny of winter chore clothes that must be laboriously donned every time one wishes to go outside. As the days tick slowly by, it gets harder and harder to believe spring will ever come.

In an effort to combat the winter doldrums, I am overtaken most Februarys by an overwhelming desire to acquire new animals—specifically new baby animals. What better than something cute and cuddly to carry us through to warmer weather?

Baby animals are not ubiquitous in deep winter, but they are not completely impossible to find either. A few producers in our area still lamb in January, so for several years in a row, overcome by baby animal fever, I ended up with bottle lambs rejected from the flock. The extra work and the extra snuggles were a perfect antidote to the malaise.

Two years ago, the fever happened to coincide with an extended arctic blast that resulted in two newborn Nigerian dwarf goats needing a home; I was only too happy to step in and take them. My kids, then three and four-and-a-half, promptly named the goats Honeybee and Bucky the Woodpecker. An explanation for those names would require an entire column, but suffice to say, if you've not spent a week of double-digit subzero temperatures indoors with two small children and two baby goats (the latter clad in diapers and onesies to keep said diapers from falling off) have you really lived? It was adorableness overload and total chaos—just what we needed to make it to spring.

This year, I hoped our Christmas puppy would keep the pangs to a minimum, and so far he has. However, the memory of those baby goats' goofy antics, plus the rising price of milk, started me dreaming and scheming recently. Honeybee is now old enough to be a mother herself, and the combination of spring babies and fresh goat milk was too powerful to resist, so last weekend we brought home a visitor named Boo.

Like Bucky and Honeybee, Boo is a Nigerian dwarf goat. He is short and personable, with longish white-and-black hair, and thick, curving horns, and like all billy goats, he is accompanied by an aroma so powerful it would be best categorized as "reeking to high heaven." Since his arrival, no matter where one goes on the ranch, Boo's scent is sure to follow, and the closer one gets to him, the more powerfully one is reminded of his virile presence.

Perhaps it's a good thing. Honeybee hasn't gone into heat since Boo arrived, and feeling lonely and a little bored, he broke out of their pen late yesterday afternoon. I happened to be out walking through the adjacent pasture at dusk, and I smelled him before I saw him. His escape efforts earned him a ride home in the back of the pickup and a night in the barn while we reinforced the fence of the pen, but despite having washed my hands and changed my clothes since then, I swear I can still smell his singular odor clinging to me since I lifted him into the truck bed.

So, there you have it: instead of spending February making bottles and washing the diapers of two cute baby goats, I will be chasing a super stinky baby daddy around. If excitement is what the second half of winter on a ranch usually lacks, I guess we've got it now. And for my husband, who like most other civilized people disapproves of barnyard animals in the house, it's a welcome alternative. So, Happy Early Valentine's Day, my love, and to all unexpected visitors, sorry about the smell!

FEBRUARY 21, 2022

HONEYBEE

Last week I had the honor of giving an author talk at the Matthews Opera House in Spearfish, South Dakota. If you've never been to the opera house, it is a beautifully restored building that hosts all kinds of arts and cultural events. It has high ceilings, glowing murals, and a grand staircase. Even the bathrooms are fancy.

I was thrilled to be invited because it's a great place to spend time with great people, but also because I was suffering from a massive case of the Februaries, and doing anything out of the ordinary was very welcome. Putting on some pretty clothes, chatting about books, seeing some new faces, it all sounded wonderful. I was worried about weather—the main reason we don't plan many events off-ranch this time of year—but the day in question arrived clear and unseasonably warm.

"Finish your morning jobs and then get your car bags packed up!" I told my bed-headed kids as I went out to finish chores. "We need to leave as soon as we are ready."

To my daughter, instructions like these mean to make your bed, get dressed, brush your hair, collect some books and toys. To my son they mean to begin to invent a Lego masterpiece and then be totally devastated when your mom returns and tells you that you will have to stop working on the masterpiece because you have to get ready to go "Right now. Right now!"

"Right now" meant another forty-five minutes of low-level grumbling—a little from the kids, but mostly from me as I remembered why I don't usually put on pretty clothes. It's a lot more work! Confronting the hair situation was similarly daunting. By the time I was ready, the kids had long since completed their own preparations and had moved on to other adventures, which once again proved devastating to have interrupted.

But interrupted the poor kids had to be, and then shuffled, with much consternation, toward the car. "I don't want to wear a coat!" my daughter said as I tried to jam her arms into her jacket. "It gets too bunchy!"

"Okay, fine, let's just go," I replied, yanking the coat back off as gently as I could, my panic escalating with each passing moment. I grabbed my own coat, and my son's, and added them to the giant purse, the tote bag of books, and the small cooler of snacks already piled in my arms. "Let's just go. Go! Go!" I calmly shouted again.

Departure finally appeared to be imminent, and I was jamming bags and coats in the car when I heard my daughter say, "Look, there's Honeybee," referring to one of our Nigerian dwarf goats whom we had recently moved to a pen by our big barn.

"Okay, sweetheart," I said. "Say goodbye to Honeybee and get in the car."

"No, Mama, there's Honeybee," she said, pointing west.

My eyes followed her finger, and I let out a long sigh. There, indeed, was Honeybee, not in her pen at all but jauntily skipping down the driveway to parts unknown.

As anyone who has ever lived on a farm or ranch can tell you, once you've put on your town clothes, you cannot, under any circumstances, do anything farm or ranch related unless you want to be immediately covered in dirt, hay, or worse. This is a time-tested fact, as certain as gravity or taxes. I looked down at my nice shoes and my clean sweater (which was white—white! —of all colors) and seriously considered leaving Honeybee to her own devices.

Ten minutes, and ten years off the end of my life, later, I hoisted that naughty little goat up and into her pen, saying aloud to no one in particular, "Well, at least I have a column for this week." And so I do, which is almost as good as arriving on time with an undefiled sweater and, all things considered, far more interesting.

FEBRUARY 28, 2022

NEXT YEAR

Last winter, it didn't snow. The kids waited and waited to take out their sled, but they never got the chance. The dams that usually fill with spring melt stayed empty, the grasses that usually get their first start the same way stayed gray and brown. Spring turned into summer, and no rain fell. By the time autumn rolled around we'd been on fire watch for months, and neighbor after neighbor loaded their breeding stock onto trucks because no grass meant no hay for winter feed.

Early in December we got a few dustings of snow, but it was barely enough to scrape together a shovelful. The sled stayed in the shed. In January, we rejoiced when we finally did get enough snow to turn the fields white, but nobody relaxed. We knew it wasn't enough to get the grasses growing when the time came.

Last week an actual winter storm was forecast, and the number of inches predicted grew as the storm approached. "I hope we get a foot!" our neighbor texted as the snow began to fall on the expanse that divides our pasture from his. Ranchers and farmers across the county pulled their chairs up to the window to watch the fine white flakes fall sideways with the wind, and they prayed it wouldn't stop for a long time.

It snowed on and off for two days while the temperatures hovered in the negative double digits. It's always hard to measure snowfall on our patch of the prairie; the high winds make great glaciers of packed ice while leaving other spots bare. All told, we probably got five or six inches of snow, but it was dry as sand, a fraction of an inch of actual moisture.

Today, the weather warmed. My husband plowed out the part of the road that always gets drifted over, and now the kids have their own private snow mountain. They spent the morning sledding down it and the afternoon digging a tunnel through it. "This is the best day ever!" my daughter shouted, arms raised while she stood atop their marvelous creation.

Out in the pasture the cows look pleased as well. The wind is down, and they turn sideways to the horizon to catch as much sun as they can on their round and heavy flanks. Their babies will start arriving in the next week or two.

So now when we pray for snow, we know it will come at a cost—the time of blithely wishing for a foot is past. "You gotta give a little blood to get a little moisture," the old timers say. If we want the grass to grow, we need more storms, we need more precipitation. But wet snow or cold rain can kill a newborn animal quickly, and damp conditions can cause pneumonia outbreaks even in otherwise healthy older calves. So, what do we hope for when our choices are between bad or worse? What do we hope for when we aren't even sure which is which?

It's hard for those of us laboring in agriculture not to get caught up in "Next Year Country." Next year it won't be so dry. Next year the markets will be better. I've lived here ten years, and so far, next year only came once, and when it did everyone told me, "It will never be this good again."

In other words, next year probably isn't this year either.

Outside, the winter twilight is blooming slowly in rose and gold. The kids are still playing on their mountain, which glows like lavender fire beneath their damp-kneed coveralls and sodden mittens. "Watch this! Watch this!" they shout to me when I stick my head out the sliding glass door to check on them.

There's a roast and potatoes in the crockpot so when they finally come in and throw their wet clothes down to dry by the fire the house will smell rich and delicious. They will still be using their joyful outdoor voices, bringing the earthen chill of old snow and new mud with them, their cheeks as red as the sunset, and I will think, "Maybe it is already next year, after all."

MARCH 28, 2022

LUNA

Sometimes I like to make things hard on myself for reasons that are a mystery even to me. Sometimes it's because the outcome seems worth it, like touring with my kids when they were babies. I didn't want to be away from them, so, even though it was hard, I packed us all up and we hit the road. Sometimes I even played shows with one of them strapped to my back. It was worth the struggles; those are really happy memories now.

Sometimes it's because I forget how hard the hard thing actually is until it's too late, like getting goats. Baby goats are some of the cutest babies of the animal kingdom. Too cute. Cute enough to make me forget over and over again what a terrible hassle it is to have adult goats on a homestead.

Sometimes—perhaps most of the time, actually—it's because my heart is like a homing pigeon, whose navigational coordinates are a mystery. She takes off, and I'm left trailing behind her, over hills and across snow-swelled streams, trying hopelessly to keep up. When we arrive, I am always as thankful for the journey as I am for the arrival at our destination. I have come to trust that pigeon, even if I feel a little nervous every time she starts to stretch her wings.

After we lost our beloved English shepherd, Zuzu, last fall, I thought it would be a while before we got another dog. The loss was too tender. My kids and our older dog felt differently. They were bereft, and waiting a year or two in dog- or kid-time is the same as an eternity, so by Christmas we had a new puppy, a corgi/Aussie mix named Jovi.

Jovi is a delight. He's funny and friendly, in constant motion, and nothing like Zuzu. Having him made me miss her more, even as I fell totally in love with his antics. Then, about a month after we brought him home, I found out Zuzu's mother had had a litter of puppies. The little pigeon began to stir.

Well, that was eight weeks ago, and you can probably guess what I am going to say next: we now have a second puppy, a mostly black English shepherd named Luna.

Having two puppies at the same time is the kind of treachery reserved for the truly brave or the slightly unhinged, or for those of us with homing pigeons for hearts (which might entail being a combination of both). Luna, like her half-sister Zuzu, is a significantly more chill puppy than Jovi, but she's still a puppy, which might as well be a synonym for mayhem. Meanwhile, Luna arrived just in time for Jovi to be well potty trained and sleeping through the night, which means, if not for that darn homing pigeon, I could have finally started sleeping more, too.

In the weeks leading up to Luna's homecoming, I kept writing and rewriting lists of pros and cons, the evidence constantly shifting, the best outcome unclear. But every time I stopped thinking and let myself drop down into the narrow cavern of my chest, I could hear the pigeon cooing, preening her pearly flight feathers. If I decided to open the doors of her little cage, for once I knew exactly the direction she would fly.

I've written before that if you let yourself love what you love, you will not be led astray. Waking up this morning, long before dawn, to the cold, wet nose of a puppy who needed to go pee, I was doubtful this was, in fact, good advice. But then dawn did come, heralded by a rainbow banner on the horizon. I looked down at the two little ones by my feet, their noses upturned, ready to follow me wherever I went, ready to follow me out into that halo of brightness, and I heard that little pigeon cooing again, this time with contentment. "All right, you two," I said. "Let's go." And so we did.

APRIL 4, 2022

HOPE

This morning I woke to a flickering tapping sound. My eyes creaked open to see the pearl-gray of first light seeping beneath the curtains. Everything looked as it should, but my ears still felt confused. Was that sound the scattering flight of birds? No, too rhythmic. Was it the settling sighs of our old house's wooden joists? No, it was too consistent. Perhaps the clattering brush of branches brushing against the glass? Almost right, but there are no trees that close to the house.

I stretched and turned to check the time. Whoa, almost seven? "That's strange," I thought. "That's way after dawn. Why is it still so dark?" And then it hit me. It was raining.

After a lifetime spent in places where rainfall is plentiful, I was totally unprepared for the realities of living in an ecosystem where drought is common. Similarly, as a suburbanite and then an urbanite, the rain was something I thought about only when dashing down city blocks, soaking wet because I had forgotten an umbrella.

The first few years I lived in the western Dakotas, rain was plentiful. Or rather, it was plentiful for this region, west of the Missouri River, where average precipitation is less than thirteen inches annually. To me, having just migrated from Minnesota, it still seemed pretty dry, and I didn't realize I was actually experiencing extraordinarily "wet" years.

I liked it, though. People living in the desert brag about their "dry heat," which isn't nearly as hot as "wet heat." I would argue the same is true of "dry cold." Even when the temperature plummets to double-digit negative numbers here, I swear it doesn't feel as cold as every single winter day in Minnesota. And the endless sunshine offsets the short winter days. The first few summers were also glorious, with just enough precipitation to keep the grasses green through July, at which point they ripened to gold, gleaming and brilliant against the bright blue of the rolling horizon.

When we hit our first drought year since my arrival, I was a little surprised, but I had been warned and took it in stride. When that year bled into a second, when our neighbors started selling off their breeding stock, when my normally unflappable husband became glued to the weather app on his smartphone, compulsively checking and rechecking to see if there was a rain cloud anywhere on the radar, I realized I didn't know the first thing about living through drought.

In the almost twelve years since I arrived here, I've now experienced several cycles of drought, but this past year has been the driest yet. Pastures we let rest all last summer still look overgrazed because nothing's grown in so long. Business at the local sale barns was steady all winter, usually a slower time, as folks ran out of hay. Now that spring is upon us and we've had barely more than a few inches of snow, sales are bigger than ever. A lot of people, us included, know they won't be able to have anything out on grass until we get some substantial precipitation, because there won't be any grass. My husband has already sorted off the cows he will have to sell if the weather doesn't change soon.

The morning rain on the window won't necessarily reverse any of that. A few steady drops, enough to turn the top layer of dust back into dirt, isn't going to give us a summer's worth of growth. But it's a start.

Lying in bed, listening to the soft patter, I realized that living through drought—and the end of drought—has given me a stoic optimism that city life never could have provided. Today might be the day this round of severe drought ends. Or maybe it won't end for another year. Either way, this rain means tomorrow there will be new green grasses where before there was only gray. I think of that now, imagining the roots drinking in the softness and awakening, just a little, to the world and all her possibilities. As long as there is green grass, there is hope.

APRIL 11, 2022

FRESH MILK

When we introduce our bulls to the herd in June, we always make sure our milk cow, Pumpkin, has a few days' head start. Like all good Jersey cows, Pumpkin produces far more milk and cream than one calf could ever dream of drinking. More milk and cream than one calf and one family of four could dream of drinking, in fact, so we like her to calve early, in case there's another baby who can help drink the extra milk.

This year, we had just such a situation arise: a twin born out in the pasture whose mama decided she wasn't interested in raising an extra baby. This poor little one was born too soon, however, and Pumpkin hadn't had her own calf yet. I took over bottle-feeding "Little Jones" for the interim, thinking we probably wouldn't even make it through half the bag of milk replacer. (Sidenote: "Why Little Jones?" I asked my daughter, the main animal namer. "Because it's unique!" she replied with a flick of her wrist.)

A few days turned into a week, and Pumpkin still wasn't "bagging up." For the uninitiated, when one is checking cows or ewes, one of the signs that someone is going to have their baby soon is the size of her "bag," a.k.a. her udder. "Bagging up," or the udder expanding as it fills with milk, is a sure sign that labor is imminent. As you might expect, this is even more obvious on a milk cow. By the time they give birth, I often wonder how they are able to walk, given that their udders look so uncomfortably full!

Five more days passed. Then, last Thursday, I noticed Pumpkin acting a little funny. She had a faraway look in her eye, as though concentrating on something just out of sight, and she was standing off from the rest of her friends. "Hmmm . . ." I thought, but when I walked around to check, her bag still looked relatively small. "Not yet," I said aloud and headed back to the house.

When I returned a few hours later, I spotted her lying flat out in the dirt of the corral. "Oh no!" I shouted and broke into a run, kicking myself because the faraway look had clearly been a sign of illness, not labor. But, as I came up beside her, I realized there was a sticky, wet blob lying there too. She'd apparently just given birth to a little red-and-white calf, and both were resting peacefully.

All's well that ends well, which is to say we have now entered the happiest time of year for a hand-milker. Dawn is heralded every day by a chorus of birds; the dew on the ground may have the sheen of frost, but it doesn't last. Evening is much the same. The air is fresh, scented with the misted green of the first grass. Most importantly, there's not a fly in sight. Morning and evening milkings, therefore, are a treat, not a chore.

Oh, and those cups of good, sweet milk after a whole winter of going without! I could write an entire column about the pleasure of those first sips, not to mention the yogurt, butter, and my favorite—fresh cream in your coffee. The abundance is a daily blessing.

Little Jones agrees. Reconstituted milk replacer is really not a very nice replacement for the thick, rich milk that flows out of a real-life Jersey mom. Little Jones's expanding flanks prove this point, as does the sudden cessation of the mournful "mooooooooos" emanating from the orphan pen.

For everything there is a season. In a few months, I will be singing an entirely different tune, as I milk in the dust and heat, getting swatted by Pumpkin's strong, wiry tail while she tries to shoo away biting flies. And that is also as it should be. Spring milking is a dream within a dream, summer milking a bit of a burden. By autumn we are sick of fresh milk and thankful to let Pumpkin dry up, thus allowing the long cold of winter to transform the burden back into a blessing once again.

JUNE 6, 2022

ON THE ROAD

I wrote this eleven years ago, when I was making my living touring and teaching music:

> Today I was at the Minnesota State Fair playing a show on a big stage, to a big crowd. It was a beautiful day, the crowd was full of happy kids, and from the stage I could see the throngs of families and friends enjoying the festivities, but I felt lost and very alone. Why can't I shake off the feeling that I am living trapped inside the walls of my own life?

Back then, I knew I wanted a family and some stability, but I couldn't see how to create that in the context of my livelihood as a working musician. So, I tore down the walls I had built and started over. I left urban life for one of the most remote places in the contiguous United States: Perkins County, South Dakota.

For those of you who are regular readers of this column, you already know what happened next. I taught school for a while and fell in love with a rancher. We got married and had two babies in two years. The challenges and bliss of motherhood, and the day-to-day chores of ranch life, brought me joy beyond measure, but I missed the thrill of playing music under bright lights. I missed the bite of my instruments' strings under my fingertips, and I missed singing most of all. So, I did something a little crazy. I started taking the kiddos on tour.

There have been challenges along the way. Touring often means spending each night in a different bed, and that usually means all of us in one bed together. When the kids were tiny, it meant navigating hotels and guest rooms with a stroller and a guitar case, shouting "Stay with Mama!" while my son barreled ahead. It meant stitching together a quilt of childcare with help from family and trusted friends. Sometimes it even meant wearing one of my kids in a backpack while I played onstage.

There were some upsides. My years hustling made me the performer and parent I am today, and I wouldn't trade it. Trying to pack up gear while weird drunk guys invade your personal space and make incoherent conversation? Not that different from dealing with toddlers. And rehearsing with a child (or two) hanging off my body pretty much ensures my sets are bombproof. It would take a lot to get me flustered. Plus, all those late nights, and a wildly erratic sleep and work schedule, were good preparation for life with small children.

Eleven years ago, I stood onstage with no idea how I would ever weave together all the bright strands of my longing. As I type these words, my kids are playing a raucous game outside on my mom's patio in Minneapolis. I played a show yesterday, and I will play another tonight. So far on this tour we've seen pelicans fishing at the headwaters of the Minnesota River, toured Legoland at the Mall of America, gone swimming in Cedar Lake, and visited with family members we hadn't seen in years. The laughter, the birds in my mom's yard, and the unfamiliar traffic sounds all sound like a serenade to me, a multitasking symphony.

It comes down to this: I never thought I would get to a place where all the many parts of myself could coexist. One of the gifts of middle age has been the discovery that while it is not possible to have it all, all the time, the possibilities for finding one's "truth" are pretty darn expansive. There's a lot more space than I realized.

For now, the unexpected moniker of Mother/Shepherd/Musician/Writer fits me to a tee. Who knows what will be added or subtracted from that title in the years to come. I'm not worried about it anymore. When I look back on the path of my own unfurling, I'm still a little awestruck. So, here's to enjoying the journey, wherever it takes us next.

JUNE 27, 2022

UNEXPECTED GIFTS

The kids and I just got back from spending a week in the beautiful Black Hills of South Dakota. We camped by a mountain lake, visited family and friends, my son got to go to his first-ever summer day camp, and my daughter got a chance to find out what it feels like to be a part-time only child. (She thought it felt great.)

This time of year is our quietest in regard to ranch duties: there's plenty of weeding and watering to do, but the garden has been planted; the baby animals born in the spring are big and healthy, wandering the pastures with their moms; the bum lambs are old enough to wean; and the harvest is still a long way off. Most of the vegetable plants are just flowering, and the few that are already bearing fruit are not in such an abundance that they'd require canning or other labor-intensive preservation. My husband stayed home from the camping trip to fence for a fellow rancher—one of his side jobs—and to do the few remaining daily chores around our place.

He was able to come up and camp for one delightful night, however, then he took the kids home, while I traveled south to play a show in Hot Springs, South Dakota.

Their return journey was uneventful. I played my show, packed my gear, and started my drive home as well. About halfway there I got a call. "Check your text messages, and then call me back," my husband said, but he refused to say more.

And here's where I have to insert a bit of background. Just over 150 days ago, we brought a beautiful but stinky billy goat named Boo to our ranch for a visit. Between his mellifluous odor and his repeated escape attempts, we decided it was best to return him to his owner after just a week, and we brought a mama goat and her baby home instead. We didn't want to be responsible if Boo decided to take off for the open range, and I only wanted a little goat milk to supplement what we get from our milk cow, Pumpkin, so an already freshened goat seemed a better solution.

Boo and my female goat, Honeybee, hadn't shown any interest in each other, and with such a short visit, it was very unlikely she had been bred. But stranger things have happened, so I marked the calendar, figuring I would keep an eye on Honeybee as the window for a delivery date got closer, just in case.

As I'm sure you've already guessed, goat gestation is approximately 145 to 150 days, the window for which occurred just before we were supposed to leave on our trip. I checked Honeybee the morning we left, and she looked neither especially plump, nor like her udders were filling with milk. I was a little disappointed, but not surprised. We headed down the road, and I didn't give it another thought.

Fast-forward to the text message from my husband. There are maybe two days in a whole year when no one is on the ranch for longer than a few hours. Sneaky Honeybee managed to give birth, clean and nurse her baby, and have him up and bouncing around during the less than twenty-four hours we were all gone. The text was, of course, a photo of a tiny black-and-white buckling, almost an identical twin to his sweet mama.

All's well that ends well, thank goodness. My failure as a goat herder aside, I drove the last leg of my journey home in record time, though it was still long past dark when I arrived. Before even stopping at the house, I pulled up alongside the goat pen and climbed in to congratulate Honeybee. Illuminated only with the headlights, her wee baby was even tinier than I expected but also as feisty as could be, telling me in no uncertain terms he did not want snuggles from a stranger. So, I set him down, patted his hard-working mom on the head, and then went inside to snuggle my own sweet babes.

SEPTEMBER 12, 2022

AUTUMN

Autumn is nearly here, its full splendor peeking out from around the edges of the last hot days. I had intended to write a thoughtful, poignant column this week about this gorgeous season, the passage of time, and the bright, bittersweet days that carry us from the warmest time of the year to the coldest. The weather has been perfect, although in the span of time between sunrise and sunset several outfits are required: coats for the first light chores, sweaters for the morning, T-shirts at midday, and then back to sweaters and coats as the day goes on. In other words, it is beautiful, but there is no denying that summer is behind us now.

Yes, I intended to write a very specific column, but instead I pickled beets, stewed tomatoes, took the kids on a spontaneous overnight trip to the mountains, and then repotted my houseplants because I could do it outside in the afternoon sunshine. Every glorious minute spent in the golden glow was worth it. The buttery shade of the trees, the soft scuffle of leaves falling, the brown loam of the wind, we've arrived at my favorite time of year.

The one downside of the arrival of the autumn season—the harvest and preservation portion of the year—is that the house, including the patio, is usually in a state of semi-disaster. This year has been no different. How can one stay inside to clean when one knows the days of warmth are numbered? Not to mention that vegetables covering every surface does not lead to an organized situation. As I continue to putter away at these fall projects, with no noticeable progress, I often begin to feel disordered as well, which is not the proper mindset for enjoying the last, best days of fine weather. Like the harvest, the changes in temperature, and the appearance of the first golden leaves on the cottonwoods, my descent into anxious disarray is a hallmark of the season.

A few years back, on one bright morning in September, the Man of the Ranch suggested we take a family jaunt down to one of the draws, and I balked. "We can wait," he said, "but the colors are pretty bright. It's probably the peak."

Fall colors? Family hike? This is pretty much my love language. And yet I found myself grumbling, "I should be working on the house. And if I am not doing that, I should be writing my column."

But I got myself and the kids packed up and into the pickup. I figured it would end up being one of those things I'd be glad I did once I just got over myself and did it. I was right! As we ducked down into the winding coves and cuts of the narrow canyons that bisect our land, it was as though we had stepped into the wooded hills of some ancient mountain range. Every footfall was crisp with the crunch of leaves, and though the air was warm as bathwater, each inhale carried the dark spice of harvest and harrow.

With age, every once in a while, comes wisdom. I've kept the memory of that hike tucked in the back pocket of my mind, and this year, I don't need my husband to remind me to take a walk. For the first time, I'm completely enjoying myself; the usual anxiety has been kept at bay (for now). Winter will come, as it has every other year. And I'm not worried. Or, not very worried. Which is some impressive progress.

Meanwhile, Dear Reader, my house is still in ruins, but perhaps I wrote the column I had intended to after all. Also, I can tell you with surety that the cup of my heart is full with the beauty of the earth. Of course, you know this already, but it never hurts to hear it again: if you have the chance, take the walk, rustle the leaves, spend a little longer outside than you need to; soak in the sun and the soil. Let everything that can wait, wait, because the weather won't. In the meantime, Happy Fall, everyone!

OCTOBER 2, 2022

KEVIN LOCKE

On the last day of September, South Dakota lost a great artist and human. Kevin Locke, Tȟokéya Inážiŋ (meaning "The First to Arise"), was a preeminent player of the North American Indigenous flute, a traditional Lakota storyteller, a culture bearer, a recording artist, and an educator. He was perhaps best known for his traditional hoop dance, the Hoop of Life. But he was more than an internationally renowned hoop dancer and a leading reviver of the Indigenous flute—Locke's calling was to share a message of unity to the world. As he taught, when brought together in love, the various "hoops" that make up the peoples of the world create a "hoop of many hoops. . . . There are no corners, no dark place . . . no back row. . . . We are all there . . . shoulder to shoulder. . . ."[1]

Kevin was also my friend and collaborator. We'd recently started working together on a project called the "Kithship Collective." Kithship (as opposed to kinship, which implies a genetic component) is a relationship built on a shared knowledge of place, and the collective's origin story commenced when I hosted Kevin last year on my PBS show. I was totally starstruck during filming, so nervous I had to white-knuckle my way through the performance, but afterward he called me on the phone and told me how much he appreciated what I was building. "Keep going," he told me. "You are bringing people together. It is important work."

I decided if Kevin Locke thought I was on the right track, it must be so! Over the next few months, we exchanged emails and texts, and my idea for the collective began to take shape: this would be an organization whose goal was a celebration of our kith here on the grasslands—human and nonhuman family members with whom we share the literal soil we stand on, and whose well-being is inextricably intertwined with our own. I asked Kevin and Chuck Suchy (another musician who lives on, and loves, the prairie) if they would join me as founding members, and we started laying plans together. We scheduled a filming date for a two-episode arc, and we set up our first show at the Matthews Opera House in Spearfish. It felt like a dream come true.

On the way to meet Kevin and Chuck for that day of filming, I found out Kevin had passed away in the night. How was it possible? I had been texting with him just a few hours before. The loss has felt incalculably, almost insurmountably, vast.

At Kevin's funeral, his wife, Ceylan, shared a beautiful thought with us. We all knew Kevin loved this land, but did we know the land loved him back? She had seen it many times: the way the songbirds shared their songs to inspire his flute, the way the wind wrapped around him when he walked through the tall grass as though in an embrace. I knew exactly what she was talking about because the week before his death I had been listening to recordings we had made during a rehearsal and my ears were suddenly awakened to a conversation I hadn't known was happening at the time. When Kevin spoke, birds in nearby trees trilled responses. When he told a story, the wind rose up to set a wind chime ringing in agreement. I've spent almost a decade writing love songs to this place, but never once had I stopped to consider that the relationship could be reciprocal.

Today, I sat at my desk writing, and I could hear two blue jays shouting in the tree break. They felt like emissaries, so I stepped outside to see what they wanted. I only caught a glimpse of their shadows as they flitted away, but as I watched them, a soft breeze brushed across the grass, jingling the wind chime, and on a whim, I glanced up. Above my head, so high it was barely distinct from the bright blue sky, a single eagle circled slowly, rising until where there had been the distinct shadow of a bird, suddenly there was simply more sky, infinite, beautiful, and full of grace.

NOVEMBER 7, 2022

COTTONWOOD

This week, the sandhill cranes passed over our ranch. Their distinct whirling coo and haphazard V formation are easy to recognize, and it always feels bittersweet to watch them ambling south. Unlike the return voyage, the harbinger of warmth and light, this passing heralds the long cold ahead.

The cranes were right on schedule this year. By the time you read these words, our little corner of the prairie is predicted to have experienced its first winter storm and first negative temperatures of the season. It's what we've been preparing for, and yet, can one ever really feel prepared for winter? I know I never feel ready!

In other news, I learned this week that if you break a cottonwood branch at a growth joint, provided the branch is neither too old nor too young, you will see a star shape inside the pith, the channel which transports nutrients from the soil to the leaves. Apparently, this star shape is common to all the relatives of the cottonwood, such as aspen, poplar, and willow. I love all the trees in this family, but cottonwoods hold a special place in my heart, as it is a small grove of cottonwoods that stands sentinel over our ranch, visible for miles in any direction. Without a compass, a map, or roads, we'd still be able to find our way home just by heading toward their silhouettes against the horizon.

Similarly, three other cottonwood trees stand in the deep draws of our north and east pastures. From our ranch house, the surrounding land looks flat except for the tops of those trees, which reveal the hidden depths. For a person raised with street signs, the cottonwoods have taught me how to find my way in a landscape where human-centered construction plays only a small role. There is comfort and a bit of wonder in this relationship.

According to different sources, many Plains tribes have sacred teachings about the cottonwood. (Full disclosure: I have not been gifted with these stories personally, but only read about them.) Some Lakota people call her the "tree of life" due to her stars, and they use the branches in Sun Dance ceremonies. Dakota storytellers share the tale of a little star who wanted to hear the sounds and the songs of humans and hid in the cottonwood tree to hear them as they worked. Cheyenne and Arapaho people might weave a different narrative: if the night sky needs more stars, they call on the wind, who blows the branches and causes the cottonwood twigs to break off, releasing the stars.

The last one resonates. For years, I've been doodling in the margins of notebooks and on scrap paper a solitary tree, branches leaning to the right as though pulled by a strong wind. The branches still hold a few sparse leaves, but most of the leaves have already been carried away. Some of the leaves captured in the wind's embrace are beginning to change shape. They look like birds. But, if you follow the wind's path, the birds begin to change as well. They are becoming stars.

In the evenings when my kids were still babies, I used to walk them past the grove of cottonwoods and tell them stories about the Hush Hush Trees. "They are singing us a lullaby," I would say in reference to the shuffling rasp of the grove's conversations.

Black Elk, the Oglala Lakota holy man, shared a similar sentiment (although far more profoundly): "Perhaps you have noticed that even in the slightest breeze you can hear the voice of the cottonwood tree; this we understand is its prayer to the Great Spirit, for not only men, but all things and all beings pray to Him continually in different ways."[2]

The leaves are gone now, the whispered "hush, hush" quieted for another year. The cottonwoods' prayers swirl in the wind, waiting to be composted into the rich soil that feeds both the trees and the grasses that surround them. But I am thinking of those stars, released with the prayers, sparkling bright against the darkness, lighting a path to the heavens.

DECEMBER 12, 2022

TAKK

For Thanksgiving this year, my good friend and her daughter traveled across the state in their trusty minivan to feast with us. It was one of the most enjoyable celebrations I can remember attending, let alone hosting. We had a wonderful time preparing and eating delicious food, then just hanging out acting like goofballs with our kids.

In addition to being an extraordinarily fun and funny person, my friend is also remarkably resilient and brave. Which is how we came to enjoy not only the gift of her and her daughter's presence, but also a longer-term guest, because that minivan carried not only two humans and a few family dogs, but a gorgeously fleeced Icelandic ram.

Now, I'm no stranger to transporting livestock in what others might consider inappropriate vehicles. Before I had access to a livestock trailer, I regularly ferried bum lambs, chicks, and even some full-grown hens and sheep in the hatchback of my Subaru station wagon. Cleaning straw and . . . ahem . . . other remnants of these passengers became a not-untypical chore. To this day, we often use a large dog cart in the bed of the pickup to move smaller animals for whom a stock trailer would be stressful and excessive, or even the front seat if the animal is very young and vulnerable.

I have not, however, attempted such a thing for a multi-hour trip, especially not with a full-grown sheep who is liable to have strong, vocal opinions about such an adventure. So, when my friend said she would bring the ram in her van, I was filled with trepidation on her behalf. I imagined the worst, and I was surprised when both she and her daughter pulled up and jumped out looking no worse for wear.

As you might imagine, my surprise was far greater when we opened the back of the van and came face-to-face with a handsome gentleman who was the picture of contentment. He sat peacefully even with the open trunk door and the thousand smells of a new barnyard, simply glancing around with a casual look on his face, as if he traveled a few hundred miles to unexpected destinations in a minivan every day of his life.

I was also worried about actually getting him out of the van and into the corral that held the other lambs, but once again my worries were unfounded. We opened the gate, and he marched right through it, jauntily bouncing his voluminous curly fleece. His manners were, in a word, impeccable.

Now, this is where things did get a little complicated. This ram is blessed with far more wool than any of my other sheep. He also is mostly black with white patches. He pranced into the pen ready to make new friends, but the other lambs weren't sure what he was. My friend and I chuckled to each other in dismay as the poor lad did his best to charm his new flock and they responded by either running away from him or chasing him away. Romance was decidedly not in the air.

Everyone eventually got used to each other, but a new problem has since emerged. One of the reasons I wanted an Icelandic ram is that they are on the smaller side; therefore, he could be put in with my short and stocky Shetlands as well as the lean and leggy Targhees. And while our new ram certainly appears to understand the spirit of his role here in the flock, I am a little concerned because the height differential is more than I expected. Will he be tall enough to play his assigned part for our biggest ewes? Only time will tell.

Meanwhile, we've decided to name him Takk, which is Icelandic for "thanks," partly because he arrived on Thanksgiving, and partly because we are very thankful to have such a good-looking youngster in our midst. But mostly this name suits him because I am thankful to my friend for making the long drive, and to Takk for not making her miserable so she might actually come back again next year.

DECEMBER 19, 2022

YULETIDE

Hurrah! It is Yuletide! Otherwise known as the season of light, at first blush this may seem an ironic moniker, as these are the darkest days of the year for those of us living in the northern hemisphere. By the time we enter December, it often seems like the sun barely rises above the horizon before it lowers back down and the darkness returns.

While this can be a bit depressing, it also means December is the perfect time for twinkle lights and candles and gathering around hearths with loved ones. It's a time of festivities, and it also happens to be my favorite time of year. When I was younger, I waited through the high heat of summer for the piney scent of needles and sap, the buttery warmth of sugar cookies, and the sweet tang of peppermint. Oh, and the twinkle lights, of course, dancing around frosted windowpanes and front gardens.

Instead of preparing for this week of festivities, however, we spent last week weathering a four-day blizzard, then digging out just in time to hunker down for a week of intense cold. Tomorrow's prediction calls for temperatures in the negative twenties. That's real temperature, folks. It'll be colder with the windchill.

What better time to get struck down with a virulent illness than when you are already snowed under? When it rains it pours, or in this case, when it snows it blizzards—literally and figuratively. So, we've been trying to deal with the storm and the deep cold, all while battling fevers, coughing fits, and all the other nastiness this particular bug brought with it.

Thankfully, my husband is descended from prairie stock and is as tough as they come. We had a load of cattle delivered the day the storm finally subsided, and as there was no way to get the truck up the road through the drifts, he went out to lead the cattle home on horseback. In ten-degree weather. While coming down with a nasty virus.

The kids are also built tough, and they bounced back quickly. It's only me who is still dragging around the house coughing. To say some things are getting left off the holiday to-do list would be an understatement.

And yet, I am surprised to be overwhelmed with gratitude by the gifts of this season. Yesterday, my first time venturing out to do chores since I became sick, the air was frosty from the low clouds and snow, the light strangely bright. Past the yard and yard fence, in the windbreak, the seed heads on the tall grass lay like a thousand upended pendulums, each encased in a perfect teardrop of ice. They were the golden brown of toasted bread, suspended between the milky swirls of earth and sky. I stopped my work for a moment, suspended as well, caught between the world of my body in motion, still heavy and sleep-deprived from a night spent coughing, and another world that contained bright coins of magic.

When my babies were still babies, I wrote a December column that included the following about my desire to find peace in the holiday season, which can often feel overwhelming: "I know the solution is to stop, take a breath, and pay attention. My son does this now without any effort, but it won't always be easy for him either. Which is why I am going to do my best to give us both the gift of simplicity this Christmas season, and in the seasons to come. I want there to be plenty of room in our lives to cradle wonder in our hands like a small bird, nesting for just a moment before it flies up and away, a feathered speck against the bright blue heavens."

Somehow, I have achieved this, at least for myself. I am awed and humbled by the beauty of the world, by the way darkness gathers and then lifts, by the way stars cut through the night sky like every prayer ever whispered in a time of need. By the tenderness of the prairie sleeping beneath the snow.

I wish this peace for you, too, Dear Reader, and I am thankful to share these words with you every week. Much love to you all.

2023

JANUARY 9, 2023

DEEP MIDWINTER

We've now entered that vast stretch of time post-holidays when the majority of winter still lies ahead and we have only the brief festivities of Valentine's Day to break up the short, cold days. As an antidote to the doldrums, last year I dubbed this period as "Seed Catalog Season": the time of year to pour through seed catalogs while dreaming of summer's riotous colors, tastes, and smells. It's a reminder we won't always have to swathe every inch of our body in multiple layers of fabric simply to stay alive.

Because of the deep cold and the intense blizzards that surrounded the holidays, the last week has actually felt balmy. It is absolutely true that after minus-twenty degrees, plus-twenty degrees seems like a heat wave. Weather that a few months ago would have seen us moaning in protest, is now a cause for rejoicing.

The tall, well-packed drifts of snow that the blizzards left behind have also been a boon, at least as far as the kids are concerned. (The Man of the Ranch, who is still working on digging us out, might disagree.) One drift in particular, which climbs all the way to the top of the stacked round bales and then slopes gently out into the open prairie, has been a favorite spot for using the new Christmas sled.

"The drifts in the windbreak are good, too, but it's a rough landing," my son says, referring to the trees at the foot of the hills, and sounding so much like his dad I have to chuckle.

The snow is not good for building snow sculptures or forts, but nobody seems to mind. All week the kids have been playing outside, bright winter sunshine on their cheeks, happily screaming their way down an epic drift at top speed. In other words, as miserable and difficult as winter seemed two weeks ago, it is equally glorious now.

In his poem "Go to the Limits of Your Longing," the Austrian writer Rainer Maria Rilke espoused, "Let everything happen to you: beauty and terror. / Just keep going. No feeling is final."[1]

I think about those two lines a lot. When my babies were newborns, they never slept more than an hour or two at a time. Many of those nights truly did feel like they would never end. And the same was true during the recent dark nights of December, when I was sicker than I've ever been and wondering if it would ever pass. Now here we are, baptized by the snow, by the sparkling frost, by the sunshine that isn't hot but still warms us, somehow, into new life, just as the darkness was a different kind of baptism, creating the space for dawn to rise up on the western horizon.

Today, the temperature actually rose above freezing. The chickens are camped on the south side of the long tin barn, where they can stand in the muck and warm their feathers with the reflected heat. The sheep in the corral do the same by the tin windbreaks, while nearby the horses nicker and swish their tails.

It will be bitter cold again before too long, no doubt—for weeks that will turn into months, with no end in sight. We will wonder if it will ever get warm. Then one day, just when we are about to give up hope, the sun will return, soothing the stems of the wind-burned grasses and calling to the seeds buried in the soil, "Come out! Come out!" It will call me out as well, out of the house and down the road to where the wild things are running free and everyone is singing their spring song again.

But maybe I won't rush ahead to that just yet. In between perusing the seed catalogs, maybe I will carve out time to watch the frost fall in sunlit patterns across the yard. I'll rejoice in the woolly cocoon of blankets. When it's too cold to spend much time outside, I'll find a patch of morning light on the bed to rest in, for a moment or for an hour. No feeling is final, but they all have their season, and every one is precious.

FEBRUARY 20, 2023

BLESS THE MESS

February is full of cultural holidays that celebrate cleaning and decluttering your house. For several years in a row, I tried to use Imbolc (or Saint Brigid's Day), which is at the beginning of the month, as a good deadline to have everything from Christmas and the closed-in winter months thoroughly eradicated.

Waiting until the last minute to officially finish any project (the days and weeks before a deadline are for puttering, tinkering, and worrying) worked in my twenties and thirties, before I had children. Now I can't stay up all night. Even if I could, I wouldn't; I can't make myself even want to do things like that anymore. Which means instead of making a big push to finish a large-scale cleaning project, I now seem to get stuck in the "it gets worse before it gets better phase."

I've learned so much about how to be me in the forty-four years I've been doing it. Tough love, for example, is not effective. Gentleness and grace go a long way. A little self-induced brainwashing via repetitive internal mantras is also effective. Aspirational gazing at the social media accounts of women who are fantastic housekeepers actually helps me to find the motivation to clean. Set too big of a project with too soon a deadline, and I am doomed to fail, though I usually don't remember that until I'm at least halfway invested.

A few Februarys ago, for example, in a fit of Marie Kondo-ing, I piled every article of clothing I owned on the guest bed and tasked myself with giving most of it away. The pile sat there for months. Eventually I did sort through it and give much of it away, but the result was a minor devastation that still lingers. I gave away the truly ridiculous—narrow-legged pants that neither fit nor had sentimental value, a lovely flowered dress with no zipper that I kept meaning to makeover once I learned to sew. (Will I ever learn to sew? I really want to learn to sew.) So many ideas of who I was and who I still might become were captured in the fabric of those garments.

I wanted to move from being to becoming. I still do. I didn't want my belongings to hold me back. I still don't. It's hard to relax in a house filled with all the things you haven't accomplished.

But I still miss, like really miss, a lot of the stuff I gave away.

Lunar New Year is another holiday that advocates for a thorough de-clutter and deep clean. I tried to do a deep clean for that this year, too, and though the house did get cleaner, it was by no means clean. Cleared of the clutter, the living room appeared temporarily spacious, but there were still piles of dust, pet hair, abandoned hair ties, Legos, and slow-moving box-elder bugs accumulating beneath the propane heater, the couches, the large comfy chair that's too big for our small house. Where does it all come from?

It comes from us—all the larger items, anyway. The dust sifts down from inside the walls. The bugs creep through the cracks. After one hundred winters of expanding and contracting, the wood frame and the plaster of our home no longer sits snugly against the floorboards. In other words, no matter how much I clean, this house will never be clean.

This week is my birthday. After a few weeks of warmer weather, storms and deep cold are expected to roll our way. It will be a good time to tackle indoor jobs, and I'd like to give myself the gift of less clutter and more room to move around. But I also want to give myself the gift of tenderness. Life is messy—always has been, always will be—and while a tidy room is certainly a pleasant thing, so is building pillow forts with kids, making tasty meals, and undertaking crafting projects from a bunch of random stuff you probably should have decluttered years ago, but thankfully did not.

APRIL 3, 2023

APRIL LIKE A LION

Some years March arrives on the northern plains like a lamb and leaves like a lion. Other years it's just the opposite. This year it was a lion from start to finish, with no real break between roars.

Unfortunately, more often than not, April makes March's lion look like a house cat—for whatever reason, April usually features bigger and more brutal storms—so I doubt there were many who thought the end was actually in sight when the month changed over. And that pessimism is about to be validated because this week we are scheduled to have one of the biggest snowstorms yet.

As I write this, the sun is shining, the huge mounds of ice and snow that are piled higher than I am tall are rapidly melting, and the cows and brand new calves out in the pasture are resting in the first heat we've felt in a long time, but the wind is screeching and howling through the trees in the windbreak and around the eaves of the house, just to make sure we haven't forgotten what's on its way. The sense of foreboding is almost worse because the sun is out, the soundtrack of the yowling winds reminiscent of the creepy music played in a horror movie right before things get gory.

Meanwhile, my husband is out enacting the kind of executive decisions that make me glad I'm just a ranch hand. There are so many variables to consider. We've got some ideas about wind direction, temperatures, and relative duration of the storm. There's less information on snowfall amounts, or how the cows and calves will actually react. Older cows with calves by their sides are often better left to their own devices. They know where and how to find shelter in draws or tree belts, depending on the changing conditions. Drifting snow and high winds can shift the equation, though. Even an experienced mother might end up in a place she doesn't want to be in a really bad storm.

New moms, on the other hand, are more likely to make mistakes or lose track of their calves regardless of a storm's severity but keeping them close or putting them in a barn comes with risks, too. Sickness moves fast when you have a herd of animals milling around in close quarters, and new babies are often better able to handle cold and some snow than germs.

Even worse are the moms who must deliver babies during the storm. There's no foolproof solution for that either: close quarters or out in the elements are both risky, and besides, there's really no way to tell for sure who is going to have a baby in a given time frame unless labor has already begun.

All of this is why I've come to believe my husband's unflappable stoicism may very well rival that of a seasoned Zen practitioner. He works hard—harder than anyone else I know. He is also one of the most intelligent people I've ever met. In everything he does, he considers all angles and possibilities, weighing his options. But once he makes his decisions, and puts his plan into action, he stops worrying. If there's no longer anything tangible he can do, he has to save his energy for the time when a solvable problem arises. Tonight, as the storm blows in, he will probably have the best sleep in a week. He can finally rest knowing he did his best, and that the eventual outcome is now beyond his control.

I'm not sure if everyone raised on a farm or ranch has this level of equanimity, but I know I sure don't. Sometimes I worry so much about things I can't control that it leaves me with little time to work on the things I actually do have control over.

This week, Dear Reader, I'd like to offer a blessing of encouragement to myself and to those of you who are like me: may we find peace where it is offered, even in the midst of storms, and may we find the courage to let the storm rage while we rest.

MAY 15, 2023

RAIN, SWEET RAIN

Here on the short-grass prairie our "average" yearly precipitation is thirteen inches. I put the average in quotes because it can be a whole lot less or a whole lot more, and the difference entirely defines the year for those of us laboring on farms and ranches.

All winter long, no matter how treacherous the weather, every time it snows, someone is bound to say, "Well, we need the moisture." Once the snow melts, we immediately start worrying about drought. Elsewhere the saying goes, "April showers bring May flowers." Here, it could be amended to, "May showers bring HAY."

For two years in a row, it didn't snow and it barely rained. The fields were uniformly gray and brown; the prairie lay dormant, and the trees leaned listlessly in the dry wind. I've never wanted to live in the desert, but suddenly that seemed to be where I had arrived. It was a long two years.

Then, in one twenty-four-hour period last May, it rained four inches and the whole prairie changed overnight. We got only a little more rain the rest of the summer, but it didn't matter. The grass grew tall. Our half-corgi pup, Jovi, would get lost in it, jumping up on his hind legs and yipping to try to find his way back to me when we took walks. The greenery in the draws was so dense and riotous they were almost impassable. Wildflowers we had never seen before came into bloom.

"How is this happening?" I asked my husband.

"When it rains is as important as how much it rains," he replied.

It seemed unlikely that we'd receive that kind of abundance two years in a row, but we had plenty of snow this past winter, so we knew we'd get a green spring. Once the moisture soaked in, however, the greening stalled. The prairie waited, thirsty, and we started checking the ten-day forecast every morning, hoping to see the rain cloud symbol.

Precipitation was predicted last week on several different days. In these parts that usually means it will rain one of the predicted days, if we are lucky. The first day of predicted rain came and 0.2 inches fell. "Not bad," my usually stoic husband said with a smile.

The next night it rained again, but only about 0.1 inches. Still, it was better than dry wind. Thursday morning it started to sprinkle again. It was supposed to rain all day, so my husband stayed home from fencing only to have the rain stay south. By evening we were resigned that 0.3 inches might be it for a while, until, just before bed, it started to rain again, this time harder. I read bedtime stories in a near shout as rain beat the roof and windows like a thousand hammers, thunder and lightning crashing right overhead.

Of course, I'm in the middle of lambing out my small flock, so when I got up at 1:00 a.m. to go check on everyone I discovered the rain had slowed to gentle showers but was still steady. After walking through the little pasture and finding that no one was laboring, I stopped by to check the rain gauge. In the dim light from my cell phone's flashlight, I had to squint and rub my eyes over and over to make sure I was reading the gauge correctly. Rising at dawn later that morning, I thought it must have been a dream, but no, I hadn't dreamed it. It had rained three inches!

And it kept raining. All told we got over six inches, almost half the yearly average in just a handful of days.

I'll admit, checking on and worrying about the flock through approximately fifty straight hours of hard rain was not my favorite experience, but this morning the sun came out and it was all worth it. The grass has already doubled its growth, the trees are fully budded out, and the flowering bushes are beginning their sweet-scented blossoming. Best of all, there will be enough for everyone to eat this summer and fall, and that is the sweetest gift of all.

MAY 29, 2023

LETTING GO

I'm almost done with lambing for another year, and this has been my most successful year yet. Ironically, it is also the year I told myself I was going to take a more hands-off approach (which I have said before) and then actually did it (which I have not done before). Turns out, when you let nature take its course, things work out almost as if that's the way nature intended it.

Around here, most folks either lamb in barns during early spring, keeping a close eye on everyone, or out on the pasture later in spring. Lambing in the barn is labor-intensive, but you can control for many variables that way, like ensuring the babies are getting enough milk and are properly bonded with their mothers before they go out on grass. The downside is that it's easier for infections and other bacteria-related problems to manifest.

Lambing in the pasture offers more privacy, better nutrition, and more opportunity for the ewes to get exercise right up until they give birth, which I've found leads to fewer lambs trying to come out in wonky positions. But obviously it also means it's more difficult to intervene in a calculated and timely fashion if someone is having a problem or if the weather isn't ideal, and the lambs are more vulnerable to predation.

We don't have a well-equipped lambing barn, and we don't run enough sheep to justify investing in one. We do have a lovely little pasture close to our house and a hardworking livestock guard dog, which should make the decision about pasture-versus-barn lambing simple. I am impervious to common sense, though, so for the past five years, I have attempted to hedge my bets by trailing ewes into the corral when I thought they were close to giving birth, to keep a closer eye on them. Consequently, instead of being born on soft new grass, lambs usually arrived earthside into the dry dirt of the barnyard—not ideal circumstances. Worse yet, for some of my Shetland ewes, a "primitive" breed that channels its feral ancestors, lambing in confinement was stressful.

I knew this, but I couldn't stop myself. I was constantly checking and rechecking and fretting and over-intervening. Every time something went wrong and I had a bad outcome, I blamed myself, and yet, I somehow simultaneously believed that my constant presence and endless vigilance was the only solution.

Last year, I had two different sets of twins born to mothers who eventually rejected them. One twin in each set ended up dying of scours, the word we use to describe severe diarrhea in livestock, which was likely caused by bacterial infections. I'll never know for sure, but I couldn't shirk the reality that things might have gone differently if I had followed my own advice and left them in the pasture. I knew I had to make a change, for my own sanity, if nothing else.

This year I had one stillborn lamb, and I had to pull one lamb who tried to make her exit with one front leg extended back behind her. The rest of the births were, I assume, seamless. I say "I assume" because I wasn't there for most of them. More often than not, when I came out to walk through the flock, I found moms with happy newborns, their curly fleeces already licked clean and their bellies already full of warm milk, with only the fresh spring wind as witness.

We were also blessed with near-perfect weather for lambing, and most of my ewes are experienced mothers, but also young and very healthy. In other words, these were ideal conditions that may not be repeated in years to come. Still, I can't help comparing this year to years past and thinking there are some pretty epic life lessons here. Namely, Mother Nature really is here to help us if we let her, and I am not as important as I think I am!

JUNE 12, 2023

BRING ME THE BABIES

I think you might learn everything you need to know about my tendency to overextend myself if you know that last week I took my kids camping and brought along a puppy and a week-old kitten who needed to be bottle-fed around the clock. I love camping, but taking a camping trip with two young children when it doesn't get dark until after 9:00 p.m. and starts getting light at 4:30 a.m. is not a recipe for good rest. Add in a wild puppy and a needy kitten and you've just made yourself a giant bowl of sleep-deprivation salad.

Sleep-deprivation salad? Only a severely sleep-deprived person would think of a metaphor that bizarre, but here we are. Apparently, two nights back in my own bed have not brought my brain fully back online. Meanwhile, as I write this, I can hear the tiny kitten in the next room calling for his tiny bottle. Sigh.

It all feels very familiar. Tomorrow is my son's birthday. He will be a whopping eight years old. As predicted by many others, the days with babies and toddlers were long, but the years have been short. I can't believe how big and independent he and his sister have become, especially with this little kitten to remind me what it was like to have tiny children not so very long ago.

It really is a different world now. This is the first summer we've instituted regular chores, and the kids do them with minimal prompting and no adult help at all. I remember worrying in years past that I was not doing a good job introducing order and self-discipline, that my kids wouldn't know how to work hard and take pride in their accomplishments. Now, watching them trot off to the coop together, egg basket in hand, or telling them to weed a garden bed and coming out later to find it done, I comfort my past self for all the fretting. "The kids are okay," I tell that worried younger mother who still sometimes hovers around the edges of my thoughts.

Yes, the feeling of sleep-deprivation and being needed constantly is a familiar one, but save for this kitten, who will outgrow his tiny-ness far faster than my human children did, the days of being that kind of mother are over for me. I could lament this fact, but honestly, thank goodness! I don't know how I did it back then, and I can't imagine doing it again right now. That week of camping felt like it might end me.

And yet, during our week away, I got to have a quick visit with a dear friend who has three-and-a-half-month-old twins (in addition to a not-quite-three-year-old). I expected to find her exhausted and depleted, but instead she was absolutely glowing. Her babies have the delightful, fat dimpled thighs, tiny, delicate fingernails, and the fluffy, angel-soft hair that are as marvelous and awe-inspiring as they are nearly universal in babies that young. It's hard not to feel joyful in their presence—babies really are magical. And my friend has had a lot of help from family, other friends, and neighbors. She was unabashed in celebrating how all that help has allowed her to enjoy her twins in a way she couldn't with her first baby, when she and her husband did most of the heavy lifting alone.

It was a good reminder that childrearing really isn't something we are meant to do without a village. My babies are growing up, which means it's my turn to snuggle someone else's babies so they can take a shower or drink a cup of tea. Bring me your babies, is what I am saying! I am here for the snuggles! And also I need a nap. So maybe bring me your babies next week. I need a little more time to recover, and then I will snuggle them, and you can have your turn to take a rest.

JULY 6, 2023

LITTLE BEA

For those of you who follow me on social media, you may have noticed a little black dog suddenly appearing in random photos and videos about three months ago. A few exceptionally observant followers asked about the new arrival, but mostly her presence went unnoticed, perhaps because there were already so many dogs in my photos that it was hard to keep track. Her arrival was a big deal, but I wasn't ready to tell the whole story until now.

Regular readers may remember that our whole family was sick in December. You also may remember that I was experiencing symptoms for months afterward and was eventually diagnosed with long Covid.

Unfortunately, I am still dealing with many of those symptoms, although much, much less frequently and much less intensely. March, however, was one of the hardest months of my life. I was sick, confused, starting to feel like I was never going to get better, and perhaps worst of all, despite constant trips to clinics, Zoom meetings with professionals, and a mounting stack of medical bills, no one had a clue what was actually wrong with me. Was it psychosomatic PTSD from being so sick and trapped in our house during those terrible winter storms? Was it solely long Covid? Was it something that Covid had unmasked, or was it totally unrelated? I knew I needed to focus on taking it one day at a time, but some days the symptoms were so oppressive I could barely make it one hour at a time.

Right before we'd all gotten sick, a neighbor had posted pictures of a litter of tiny bulldog-mix puppies. Their wee smushed faces, chubby bellies, and short, wobbly legs were endearing and adorable. I showed the pictures to my husband. "Good thing we already have too many dogs," I said with a laugh.

It was true—with two house dogs (a.k.a. full-time pets) and one aging guard dog (a.k.a. part-time pet) we definitely didn't need another dog. But I kept returning to our neighbor's Facebook page to look at pictures and videos of the puppies as they grew, especially after I got sick, simply because their cuteness cheered me up.

By the end of March, I had forgotten all about the puppies. Endless cold, endless illness, and endless fatigue were all I could imagine. And then, after yet another doctor's appointment where they scheduled yet another expensive test that no one actually thought would reveal anything but somehow seemed better than doing nothing, I ran into that very neighbor in the parking lot of a random farm supply store. At that point I only left the ranch for doctor's appointments, so it was weird that I was even there, but when the neighbor waved me over and opened the door to her vehicle, and into my arms jumped a wriggling half-grown bulldog, it felt like fate. "Oh, it's my puppy," I heard my own voice say inside my head.

I quickly recovered my senses, handed the puppy back, then got into my car for the long drive home. I allowed myself a sigh of longing, and once again, clear as a bell I heard my own voice say, "Look, you can get that puppy, or you can keep getting expensive tests. It's up to you."

Long story short, I haven't gotten any expensive tests since that day. And that little bulldog has slept under the covers by my feet or with her head on the pillow like a human nearly every night since. We call her Little Bea, and she is just as full of the sweetness and naughty delights as you'd expect a tiny bulldog puppy to be. If I'm sitting, she's in my lap. If I'm walking, she's by my side. She has a small bed in the passenger seat of my car for long drives. I joke that she's my therapy dog, but I'm actually not joking.

It's hard to understand why the heart wants what it wants, and there's really no satisfying definition for love. But we know it when we feel it, and love truly can heal in magical and unexpected ways.

JULY 10, 2023

THE WOLF YOU FEED

Six weeks ago, a visiting friend found an hours-old kitten in the corral. He brought her inside, and I thought she was a white mouse or a tiny weasel—she looked nothing like a kitten. When he first spotted her wallowing in the dirt beneath the shuffling hooves of the milk cows and their calves, my friend had thought the same thing. Only the kitten's yowling gave her true identity away.

I wasn't excited about trying to raise a kitten that tiny, and neither was he, so we first put her in a box filled with soft, fresh straw, then placed the box in the barn by the corral. Perhaps her mother had been moving her nest, we reasoned, and had dropped the baby by accident on the way from point A to point B. But when we went back later to check, the baby was still crying with an intensity that seemed impossible considering her frail stature. No mama cat in a half-mile vicinity could have missed the poor baby's howls of hunger and fear. It was clear there would be no feline rescuer.

Honestly, if I were any less softhearted, I would have turned and walked away. I had taken in a few bottle kittens before, though never one so young, and it always ended with heartbreak and exhaustion. Neonatal kittens must be fed every two to three hours around the clock, and even with the best care, the prognosis isn't good. But, as I am quite notably much more softhearted than I am sensible, I took the kitten inside.

Never once in the following five weeks did I expect that kitten to make it more than another few days. And never once did she waver in her desire to live. There were some very rough patches, but through them all she yowled her amazingly loud and resonant yowl at regular intervals asking for milk, even when she was too sick to drink much more than a sip at a time. This morning, I went downstairs to feed her and discovered her calmly waiting at the bottom of the steps. She had figured out how to climb out of the playpen we had been keeping her in and knew right where I'd be when breakfast time arrived. "Well, it definitely seems like she is going to live!" I said to myself.

Meanwhile, after writing last week about my little therapy dog Bea and the cessation of a season of intense illness, the worst of my symptoms returned as if on cue at the publication of that column. Although the coincidence was uncanny, the cause was not the column but both kids and my husband getting very sick with a virus that sent me spiraling back to our scary winter of illness. In other words, the thrill of the kitten's triumphs has been vastly overshadowed.

After finding the kitten waiting at the foot of the steps, then feeding her breakfast, I took her outside for a short play session. She gamboled through the weeds by my feet while the dogs jogged around attending to all their morning appointments. It's been unseasonably cool here, but you could feel the weather had turned. The air was damp from the dew, but warm; the early light caught the microscopic beads of moisture in the air, and everything had a little extra shimmer. I had on a sweater and shorts, and the sun peeking up from the eastern horizon felt like medicine on my bare legs. I turned toward it, leaving my back to the cool shadows of the western horizon.

There's an old adage about the two wolves that live inside each of us, locked in an eternal battle. One represents the parts of us that are expansive, joyful, and loving; the other represents all the parts that are cramped, gnawing, and fearful. The story goes on to admonish: the wolf you feed is the one that will win.

I think of that adage all the time and have spent a lot of my adulthood earnestly trying to figure out if I'm feeding the right one. Turning toward the sun this morning, basking in the presence of my little miracle kitten after so many days of fretting, a younger version of myself would be tempted to tell you that I've finally figured out how to feed the right wolf. That would make a wonderful ending to the column, wouldn't it? But the truth is I could feel the shadows at my back as viscerally as I could feel the sun on my front. And now I'm suddenly wondering if the next chapter of my life won't be learning to accept and live with both wolves, because, after all, both of them are me.

OCTOBER 2, 2023

LISTENING TO BIRDS

I'm sitting on the front porch of my tiny writing shack. The wind is blowing hard today, but it still holds so much sweetness. You can tell it's autumn, but summer isn't long past. There are birds and bees (and, less romantic, wasps) buzzing and fluttering through the gold and green leaves overhead. There are robins, wrens, all manner of finches and sparrows, and a pair of brown thrashers that have been summering in the windbreak this year. They seem to be everywhere all at once.

A quick Google search earlier in the season informed me that brown thrashers are "inconspicuous" birds, but that has not been my experience. These ones seem to love my tiny house, and I often hear one or both clattering on the tin roof, or spot one that's landed on a nearby elm peering at me through an open window. Their irises are ringed with yellow, making them appear unusually alert and wide-eyed; I find their stare disconcerting.

They also have extraordinarily loud and varied singing voices. The male brown thrasher may have the largest song repertoire of any North American bird—some sources state that each individual has upwards of three thousand song phrases. Like the endlessly imitative catbird, they often sound like many different birds, and their music floods the tree belt and rivals the wind with its vivacity.

This weekend marked the one-year anniversary of the sudden passing of my friend and collaborator Kevin Locke, which happened the night before we were to perform together in the Black Hills. When he came to the ranch for a rehearsal in early summer, we sat on this same porch listening to the virtuosic performance of a brown thrasher, and Kevin commented, laughing, "I've stolen some of my best songs from birds."

Kevin was an accomplished player of the North American Indigenous flute. (In fact, he was—pun intended—instrumental in getting it declared South Dakota's state instrument.) On that rehearsal day last summer, as Kevin played a love song written hundreds of years ago by folks who hunt-ed and camped in the river breaks by our ranch, we joked that the birds were probably happy to hear the old tune again. It was the first time it occurred to me that if humans were influenced by the music of the birds, why wouldn't the birds be influenced by the music of the humans? I'm always listening to them, so why would I assume they aren't also listening to me?

Kevin traveled relentlessly as a performer and educator. He had played a show in our tiny town on the prairie the day before, and then our mutual friend and fellow musician, Chuck Suchy, came to chat and rehearse. I wasn't sure when we'd all be able to get together next, so I set up my recording equipment on the porch, hoping that would give us something to listen back to and practice with. As it happened, we booked the aforementioned show soon after, so I sent both men clips from the recording as we planned our setlist, of course not realizing that we would never get to play those songs together again.

Sitting on the porch today, listening to the birds, I pulled out my computer and turned the volume up. The speakers are cheap and sound tinny, the recording very obviously rudimentary, but Kevin's flute still sounded beautiful. The birds in the trees grew quiet, even the brown thrashers, as the stark melody swirled up and into the rustling leaves.

Losing him still feels crushing at times, but Kevin's music and spirit live on in the students he taught, in the audience members whose lives he enriched, and, I would like to think, in the birds who circle above the grassy plains he loved so much, letting the wind hold them as they sing.

FAITH

EPILOGUE: 2024

FEBRUARY 1, 2024
IMBOLC

Imbolc, or Saint Brigid's Day, is a traditional Gaelic festival marking the beginning of spring. Traditionally, it was celebrated on February 1. Imbolc translates to "in the belly" and was associated with the pregnancy of livestock, specifically of sheep, and the onset of the lambing season.

Here on the northern plains, we are nowhere near the beginning of spring, and while there are some brave and well-resourced shepherds who begin lambing now, for most of us, lambing won't start for at least another month, or two, or three. Usually, however, this is the time of year I start dreaming of baby animals, and even (foolishly) start trying to find an orphaned bottle baby, or two, or three, that needs a home.

In many cultural traditions across the northern hemisphere, this is also a time for early spring cleaning, a chance to sweep out the dust and soot that's accumulated over the dark, cold winter months.

A few years ago, I wrote about a Zen teaching that goes:

"What does one do before enlightenment?" the novice asks.

"Chop wood. Carry water," replies the master.

The novice asks next, "What does one do after enlightenment?"

"Chop wood. Carry water."

As anyone living and working on a ranch or a farm can attest, the work is never done, and much of it is physically taxing and monotonous. Previously, I always interpreted the story to mean that even after achieving enlightenment, the chicken coop would still need to be cleaned, the herd and the flock moved from pasture to pasture, the cattle worked, the lambs weaned, and, of course, the detritus of these activities would constantly, exhaustingly, annoyingly need to be removed from one's living space. Presumably, one wouldn't mind because one would have achieved enlightenment.

When I originally wrote about the Zen teaching, I finished the column with the following paragraph: "I'm trying to see the never-ending chore of cleaning as a joyous opportunity to engage with the magic of transformation. I'm not there yet, but just as Imbolc heralds the quiet stirring of new growth, I can imagine the seeds of this new way of being stirring within me too. It's not spring, but we are getting there."

My goodness, so much has changed! The kids are older, more helpful, and (slightly) less like human hurricanes. Consequently, cleaning does not feel like the overwhelming, unending burden it once did. Keeping things relatively tidy is now the work of minutes instead of hours, so I no longer feel I need to be a Zen master to survive the chaos of my own household.

I also, against all odds, have not been feeling the bottle-baby fever that usually characterizes this time of year. After a year of near-constant illness, the idea of waking all hours of the night to trudge out with bottles, not to mention fretting when the lambs do poorly (which is almost inevitable with orphaned livestock), sounds exhausting instead of fulfilling. Taking care of myself is enough extra work for now.

Instead, this year I am feeling the threshold of Imbolc internally. We still have one foot in the depths of winter, but the darkest ten weeks of the year are officially over. Meanwhile, beneath our feet the smallest of shifts is taking place. Tiny seeds, germinating in darkness, are beginning to awaken. In ways I can't yet explain, this feels a little like what illness and midlife are offering me as well.

If we let it, this time is when we learn how to straddle the paradox, to dance with complexity, to set down strong and deep roots. It requires rest and dormancy, but also a slow enlivening that can't be rushed. The earth isn't waiting for spring; she's preparing for the magic of rebirth one soft, quiet moment at a time.

FEBRUARY 7, 2024

FOG

This week featured five full days of dense fog. If you are a regular reader, you may remember my column about the fog calendar from a few weeks ago. The fog calendar predicts that eighty-four days after a fog event there will be either 1) significant precipitation or 2) more fog. This has been the foggiest winter I've ever experienced, which, if you believe in the fog calendar, does not bode well for lambing and calving season.

This week I was also scheduled to travel a few hours away to present at a "Women in Ag" conference in eastern Montana. I generally avoid making commitments in the winter because deciding to make plans on the northern plains seems to operate with a similar cadence to the fog calendar. If you have somewhere you need to be, it's guaranteed to start storming.

I had thrown caution to the wind, however, and agreed to present because I've finally started to feel sturdier after over a year of health challenges, which included long Covid, then Lyme disease, and I was excited for a small adventure. As the conference date approached, I kept watching the forecast, and I was surprised to see warmer than usual weather predicted. No precipitation, no wind, and temperatures above zero? Could this really be the forecast in February?

I hadn't thought to worry about fog, though, and the morning I was supposed to leave we could barely see down our driveway to the road. I was sure it wouldn't last (we live in an arid ecosystem for gosh sakes!), and it definitely couldn't be widespread. I got in the car and started driving.

I was an hour from home when I decided I couldn't take any more of the endless white. The highway between where we live and Miles City, where I was headed, is a two-lane country road. It's mostly flat and it's a straight shot west. The road wasn't icy. The chances of something bad happening were slim—even deer seem to shelter in place during fog—but it still felt oppressive and more than a little crazy-making to keep driving while only able to see a short distance ahead.

Just before the Montana border, I pulled over and called my husband. "Can you check the radar," I asked, "and see if you can tell where this fog lifts?"

"I think you might be near the end of it, but I'm not sure," he replied after a few minutes of scrolling.

I got out of the car and walked into the swirling mist. The grass and trees just ahead of me looked like mirages from another time and place, shimmering gray and gold ghosts inhabiting the world of white; the fog was so thick my skin and clothes were immediately damp from the fine droplets of water.

I started to cry. The thought of going back was as horrible as going forward. I had been so sure the fog would lift at any moment that I had driven farther than my nerves were ready to deal with, and if I turned around now I'd have to drive through it all again in reverse. I stood in the fog for a few more minutes, my face wet with tears and the enveloping vapor. Which way should I go when both options felt equally terrifying? I took a deep breath, got back in the car, and kept heading west.

It was barely ten more minutes before I broke through the dome of white, the horizon line suddenly stretching to span the sharp teeth of mountains fifty miles away. I exhaled and realized that the feeling I had driving through the fog was exactly the same feeling I had living through the year of mysterious and difficult-to-treat illnesses—the oppressive fear of not knowing if or when I'd feel better, and the white noise of my body in distress obscuring almost everything else.

Despite the delays, I made it to Miles City right on time, and I had twenty-four delightful hours hanging out with two of the coolest women I've ever met. I was, and am, so glad I didn't turn around. That night, lying in my hotel room before I fell asleep, I thought: This is what hope feels like. It's the little ember of deep knowing that you'll arrive where you are supposed to arrive, even if none of it is visible yet. It's hard to keep that little ember alive sometimes, but I am going to hold the memory of breaking through the fog close, because that first view of the mountains makes the courage it takes to keep driving worth it every time.

NOTES

Foreword

1. Archer B. Gilfillan, *Sheep: Life on the South Dakota Range* (Minneapolis: University of Minnesota Press, 1957), p. 7.

Chapter 2: 2015

1. Kahlil Gibran, *The Prophet* (New York: Alfred A. Knopf, 1923), p. 35.

Chapter 3: 2016

1. Wendell Berry, "The Peace of Wild Things," *The Selected Poems of Wendell Berry* (Berkeley, Calif.: Counterpoint Press, 2009).

Chapter 6: 2019

1. Paula M. Nelson, *After the West Was Won: Homesteaders and Town-Builders in Western South Dakota, 1900–1917* (Iowa City: University of Iowa Press, 1986), p. 127.

Chapter 7: 2020

1. Gibran, *The Prophet*, p. 35.

Chapter 8: 2021

1. Richard Rohr, "When Things Are Unveiled," Center for Action and Contemplation, https://cac.org/daily-meditations/when-things-are-unveiled-2021-01-08/.
2. Robert Macfarlane, "The Lost Words: A Spell Book," The Lost Words, https://www.thelostwords.org/lostwordsbook/.
3. Laura Ingalls Wilder, *Little Town on the Prairie*, 1st Harper Trophy ed. (New York: Harper Trophy, 1971), p. 89.
4. Virginia Driving Hawk Sneve, "Seasons of the Moon," *South Dakota Magazine*, Jan./Feb. 2020, p. 79.

Chapter 9: 2022

1. Kevin Locke shared the full story explaining the Hoop Dance on an episode of South Dakota Public Broadcasting's *Wish You Were Here*, which is now available to watch on SDPB's YouTube channel.

2. John G. Neihardt, *Black Elk Speaks: The Complete Edition* (Lincoln: University of Nebraska Press, 2014).

Chapter 10: 2023

1. Rainer Maria Rilke, *Rilke's Book of Hours: Love Poems to God*, trans. Anita Barrows and Joanna Macy (New York: Riverhead Books, 2005), p. 119.

ACKNOWLEDGMENTS

Deepest Gratitude to:

Dedra Birzer, Taylor Blumer, Slater Sabo, and everyone else at the South Dakota Historical Society Press for bringing this book to fruition. Thank you for taking such good care of these stories.

Heather Benson and Ruth Wiechmann, two of my favorite writers, whose friendship has carried me through many iterations of this work and myself.

Bruce Roseland and Christopher Vondracek for sharing their words here.

Sion Hanson for always being ready to help when we need him—Sion, you are truly the world's best neighbor.

Libraries and librarians everywhere, especially the Siouxland Libraries and our neighbor and Bison's librarian, Kallie Kronberg, you do sacred work!

All the print publications that have supported my writing over the last decade—I appreciate you more than I can say.

Max, Roo, and Wesley Loughlin—you three are my home. I would be nothing without you.

My first lambs, Pearl & Theo, and all the other animals who taught me how and why to be a rancher.